PRAISE FOR
LIFE ISN'T EVERYTHING

A *People* magazine Book of the Week

"[*Life isn't everything*] is manna from heaven, its brilliantly orchestrated polyphony bringing [Nichols], his work, and his world to vivid life . . . It is properly celebratory and deliciously filled with his bons mots, but from its opening pages, it shirks none of the complexity of the man, acknowledging the darkness so close to the shining surface . . . The breadth of the witnesses is remarkable, as are their candor and perceptiveness."　　　　　—Simon Callow, *The New York Review of Books*

"Legendary director Mike Nichols (1931–2014) refused to write his memoirs, but this scintillating oral history fills the gap splendidly, with wry and heartfelt commentary by '150 of his closest friends,' from Richard Burton, Elizabeth Taylor, and Meryl Streep through Candice Bergen and Christine Baranski, all of whom cherished their professional and personal relationships with a man who seemingly impressed everyone he met as being the smartest and most charming person in the room."　　　　　—Bill Ott, *Booklist* (starred review)

"Captivating . . . What stands out in the memories of Nichols's many colleagues is his ability to guide actors."
　　　　　—Douglass K. Daniel, Associated Press

"A fascinating oral history of Nichols's career . . . [Ash Carter and Sam Kashner] have intelligently chosen to concentrate on the career rather than the life, and on Nichols's working methods and artistic

techniques . . . Most of the 150 voices [in *Life isn't everything*] speak eloquently both of the enormous intelligence Nichols brought to almost every project he was involved in and of the deep respect he accorded his collaborators."
—Brooke Allen, *The Wall Street Journal*

"A candid, intimate portrayal of a man they loved and admired . . . A warmhearted, revelatory composite portrait."
—*Kirkus Reviews*

"It turns out an oral history is . . . the best way to tell the fascinating story of Nichols . . . The quotes are carefully arranged to deliver a narrative . . . that makes each successive fact more shocking."
—Joel Stein, *Town & Country* (Best Biography of the Year)

"Marvelous . . . A wonderful biography of a unique and memorable man."
—Peter Thornell, *Library Journal*

"Deep, in-the-pocket theater devotees . . . are going to feast on this brilliant and terrific oral history of the life and times of the singular Mike Nichols."
—Jeff Simon, *Buffalo News*

"The Irish wake of your dreams."
—Michael Giltz, *Broadway Direct*

ASH CARTER AND SAM KASHNER
LIFE ISN'T EVERYTHING

Ash Carter is a writer and editor whose work has appeared in *Esquire*, *Vanity Fair*, *Town & Country*, *Air Mail*, and *The New York Times*. He lives in Brooklyn with his wife and son.

Sam Kashner is an editor-at-large at *Air Mail* and was for many years a contributing editor at *Vanity Fair*. He is the author of *Sinatraland* (a "notable book" of both *The Washington Post* and the *Los Angeles Times*) and the acclaimed memoir *When I Was Cool: My Life at the Jack Kerouac School* and the coauthor of the recent *New York Times* bestsellers *The Fabulous Bouvier Sisters: The Tragic and Glamorous Lives of Jackie and Lee* and *Furious Love: Elizabeth Taylor, Richard Burton, and the Marriage of the Century*.

ALSO BY SAM KASHNER

When I Was Cool: My Life at the Jack Kerouac School

Sinatraland: A Novel

WITH NANCY SCHOENBERGER

The Fabulous Bouvier Sisters: The Tragic and Glamorous Lives of Jackie and Lee

Furious Love: Elizabeth Taylor, Richard Burton, and the Marriage of the Century

A Talent for Genius: The Life and Times of Oscar Levant

Life isn't everything

Life isn't everything

Mike Nichols,

as remembered by 150 of his closest friends

Ash Carter and
Sam Kashner

PICADOR
HENRY HOLT AND COMPANY
NEW YORK

Picador

120 Broadway, New York 10271

Copyright © 2019 by Ash Carter and Sam Kashner
All rights reserved
Printed in the United States of America
Originally published in 2019 by Henry Holt and Company
First Picador paperback edition, 2020

The Library of Congress has cataloged the Henry Holt hardcover edition as follows:

Names: Carter, Ash, author. | Kashner, Sam, author.
Title: Life isn't everything : Mike Nichols, as remembered by 150 of his closest friends / Ash Carter and Sam Kashner.
Other titles: Mike Nichols, as remembered by 150 of his closest friends
Description: First edition. | New York : Henry Holt and Company, 2020. | Includes index.
Identifiers: LCCN 2019031319 (print) | LCCN 2019031320 (ebook) | ISBN 9781250112873 (hardback) | ISBN 9781250112866 (ebook)
Subjects: LCSH: Nichols, Mike—Anecdotes. | Nichols, Mike—Quotations. | Motion picture producers and directors—United States—Biography.
Classification: LCC PN1998.3.N54 C37 2020 (print) | LCC PN1998.3.N54 (ebook) | DDC 791.4302/33092 [B]—dc23
LC record available at https://lccn.loc.gov/2019031319
LC ebook record available at https://lccn.loc.gov/2019031320

Picador Paperback ISBN: 978-1-250-76364-8

Designed by Steven Seighman

Our books may be purchased in bulk for promotional, educational, or business use. Please contact your local bookseller or the Macmillan Corporate and Premium Sales Department at 1-800-221-7945, extension 5442, or by e-mail at MacmillanSpecialMarkets@macmillan.com.

Picador® is a U.S. registered trademark and is used by Macmillan Publishing Group, LLC, under license from Pan Books Limited.

For book club information, please visit facebook.com/picadorbookclub or e-mail marketing@picadorusa.com.

picadorusa.com • instagram.com/picador
twitter.com/picadorusa • facebook.com/picadorusa

1 3 5 7 9 10 8 6 4 2

For Marion, Daniela, and Ellis

My congratulations to the winners. My love to those who have not won tonight. I just want to remind you of my motto: "Cheer up, life isn't everything." It always stands me in good stead.

—Mike Nichols, acceptance speech, 2005 Tony Awards

CONTENTS

AUTHORS' NOTE

This book does not pretend to be the last word on Mike Nichols's life, nor an encyclopedic chronicle of his career. For reasons of length, we have chosen to focus on a handful of films and plays that we hope will illustrate our subject's versatility, and his preoccupations, well enough to stand in for the larger body of work.

Mike and Richard Burton sharing a moment on the set of Nichols's first film, *Who's Afraid of Virginia Woolf?* (© Bob Willoughby/mptvimages.com)

INTRODUCTION

The Burton Stakes

RICHARD BURTON (*actor*)[1]: I decided to examine my reactions to all the men of talent I have ever met and which company would I prefer. After serious thought, lying on that silent bed, with that killing cigarette between my lips, how I love its round cool comfort, I dropped names all over my brain. Churchill? No! A monologist. Picasso? No! An egomaniac. Emlyn Williams? No. A mind like a cut-throat razor and a tongue to match. Dylan Thomas? No! Brilliant but uncomfortable. William Maugham? No! He cared only about playing bridge with losers. Gwyn Thomas? No! An impersonation of a chap who would like to be big strong and tough and who is actually fat weak and febrile. Camus? Possibly. But he had the infernal impertinence to die young. John Osborne? No! No leavening of humour. Gielgud? A strong contender for the Burton stakes, but I have a feeling that he finds *me* uncomfortable. Edward Albee? No! A week with him would be a lifetime, and he'd feel the same about me. Anyway, why go on? I reduced it to two people. Noel Coward and Mike Nichols. They both have the capacity to change the world when they walk into a room.

NICK PILEGGI (*writer*): Men are divided into two groups: there are guys who want to be Babe Ruth, and there are guys who want to be Mike Nichols. That's it.

---

1. Richard Burton, *The Richard Burton Diaries,* ed. Chris Williams (New Haven, Conn.: Yale University Press, 2012), 297.

NATALIE PORTMAN (*actress*): Mike was like a ball of light in a room that everyone would gravitate toward.

RENATA ADLER (*writer*): No matter where he was, no matter who else was in the room, Mike was the source and center of intelligence and energy. This was not just as a performer. He could be bored or silent. It was his *presence*.

J. J. ABRAMS (*director*): He managed to remain the highest-stature person in any room he was in, yet he would simultaneously make everyone feel like they were his equal. It was just a kind of attitude and tone that he had. He simply had the sharpest wit and knew how to grab an audience and keep them in the palm of his hand.

JACK O'BRIEN (*theater director*): Mike had that ability to make you think you were totally on his level, which was almost never true. You weren't being manipulated; it's a peculiar thing he had that made you better than you ordinarily were—wittier, more attractive, more alert.

NICK PILEGGI: Around Mike, everybody got wittier. The anecdotes and stories you thought to tell were better. He just raised the level. He relaxed people and helped them become their best.

JOHN LAHR (*writer*): Mike was a sort of an entrepreneur of aplomb. He was prowess personified.

SAM WASSON (*writer*): Only the people who met him will ever know that as good as *The Graduate* was, Mike was better.

WOODY ALLEN (*director*): I was always in awe of Mike. He moved so effortlessly in any group. Never at a loss for conversation, always comfortable with the most celebrated people, always witty, always charming, always a desirable guest. And I was always such a schlemiel socially, and so awkward. I felt, that would be wonderful to have that kind of social charm and grace.

HANNAH ROTH SORKIN (*former assistant*)**:** Somebody wrote a letter to "Mike Nichols, Famous American Director," and it got to him. I worked in his office, so I actually got to see it—it's all true.

TOM HANKS (*actor*)**:** Mike's imprimatur went on and on and on, from the '50s to well after the year 2000. Who transcends decades like that?

HANK AZARIA (*actor*)**:** Oh my God, perhaps the greatest career ever—arguably, I suppose, but I don't know many who have done what he did for as long as he did it.

MATTHEW BRODERICK (*actor*)**:** Anytime somebody would send me a script and ask, *Who would you like to direct it?*, I'd always say Mike.

JOHN LAHR: There isn't anyone whom I can think of, except, I guess, you'd have to say Woody Allen, who was a sort of triple threat. Mike was a star as a comedian, a star as a stage director, and a star as a film director. If you cover the theatrical scene as long as I have, those kind of people just don't come along very often—once in a generation.

CHER (*performer*)**:** For me, he was more than a director. He was always more than a director.

JOHN CALLEY (*executive*)[2]**:** There are other directors who have a great love affair with the talent until it's over. Mike is loyal, and he's capable of astonishing friendship.

---

2. Courtesy of the John Lahr collection at the Howard Gotlieb Archival Research Center, Boston University.

CHRISTINE BARANSKI (*actress*): He's the one person in show business I felt I never could afford to lose touch with.

JACK O'BRIEN: They say of Noel Coward, his genius was friendship—that it wasn't necessarily his erudition or all the rest, it was the fact that he was such an enthralling friend. He had that genius, which I think Mike had, in retrospect.

CHRISTOPHER WALKEN (*actor*): I absolutely adored him. In one's life, there are certain people who are just examples of how it's done.

HARRISON FORD (*actor*): We formed a friendship that doesn't always happen in the movie business. I think he took his relationships with people and his loyalties to his friends very seriously. In fact, I don't think; I *know* that he did. I'm not a guy who has a lot of friends, and few of them were as important to me as the relationship I had with Mike.

ART GARFUNKEL (*musician*): Didn't he have a great, rich, educated voice? Wasn't the sound of him making sentences the work of a consummate actor who was brilliant? Slightly nasal, resonant, very educated, witty—making you fall in love with him sentence by sentence by sentence. The way he records is just amazing. It's so erudite. It's sophisticated. It's New York at its absolute best.

CANDICE BERGEN (*actress*): Everyone who was in his orbit—and it was like an orbit, because he was the sun—unconsciously or consciously started to sound like him, because he had this great archness that he spoke with. Every now and then I'd meet someone who knew Mike, and I'd think, *You sound like Mike Nichols*.

MIKE HALEY (*assistant director*): To me he had two cores. One core was as blue-collar and common as I was. On another level he was from the court of Louis XVI. There was nothing false about it. Here's a guy who couldn't remove a gas cap from a car, but he was game. I always felt he was born in the wrong century.

JON ROBIN BAITZ (*playwright*): Lee Grant and her husband used to have these great dinners at their Upper West Side apartment. On a typical night, there would be Joan Didion and John Gregory Dunne, Robert Altman, Pete Hamill. Jack Nicholson would occasionally be there. It seemed like a diorama of a past New York. Mike and I were at one of those, and he had just seen my latest play. He leaned over and said, "Well, of course, you and I have to talk," in that Mike, *well, of course, you and I have to talk* voice of his.

JOHN LAHR: I remember seeing him at the opening night of *Elaine Stritch at Liberty*, which I co-wrote. I think [Richard] Avedon was with him. After the show, he just leaned over and said, "A triumph, I believe," and walked off. Who talks that way?

TOM HANKS: You get a call from Mike, it's like, this is going to be an hour of delight on the phone, because eventually we'll get around to the thing we're going to talk about, but before that, there will just be the most scintillating, effervescent conversation about everything in the world.

JULIA ROBERTS (*actress*): I knew very quickly into our relationship together that he was always going to tell me the truth, and I came to really rely on that so completely. Even if he was saying something particularly unflattering, it was said with love and probably incredible cleverness. He was an invaluable human being because that's such a rare commodity. People would say, well, in show business that's very rare, but I think globally.

PETER GALLAGHER (*actor*): Just knowing that the way you saw the world had enough in common with the way Mike saw the world, you were just immensely reassured that you weren't crazy—and if you were, you were in good company, and you were pursuing the right things.

ANJELICA HUSTON (*actress*): He had that incredible capacity for friendship that makes you think you're absolutely unique, that nobody matters to him in the same way that you do. And, of course, he must have had it with over two hundred people.

MARIE BRENNER (*writer*): Mike was the most supremely generous friend, and if you ever wanted to talk to him about something, he would say, "Of course, come over." And then there would be that wonderful Mike pause. "I'll give you cookies." And indeed, there would be cookies.

MATTHEW BRODERICK: He was very generous with his time, but you knew not to drive him crazy. I only made the call when I was really stuck. I remember getting to his house late at night, and his answering machine was flashing, and he said, "And all of them want something."

HARRISON FORD: Diane [Sawyer] called me up and said, "We're going to have a surprise party for Mike," on some birthday, "and it's going to be very relaxed, just a bunch of Mike's friends." I forgot what "a bunch of Mike's friends" meant. The only one who didn't show up was Jesus Christ.

LIZ SMITH (*columnist*): He had this whole phalanx of women whom he referred to as "my wives." I'd say, "Are you going to see this play?" "Yes, I'll take one of my wives."

SUSAN FORRISTAL (*actress*): Diane doesn't like the theater and Mike went to the theater constantly, so I would become his date. And he couldn't be in the theater and not go backstage, because word would pass among the actors, and very often, he knew them. So we'd go backstage and as you're let in, right away, the guys who open the door, who pull the curtains, would go, "Mr. Nichols," "Mr. Nichols." And he'd be stopped all along the line, by the actors heading down the stairs—not because he could give them a job, but because they respected him so much.

DAVID HYDE PIERCE (*actor*): He once said something like, "The art of being charming is giving away a vital part of yourself which you can absolutely part with."

JOHN CALLEY[3]**:** Mike said, "Charm is no mystery to anyone who's ever had a nightclub act." And it's so much more about Mike because it is the quality of the comment, the wisdom to perceive the reality of the comment, to be able to be inside the process to the extent that he can do it, but also be able to be observing what he's doing at the same time. He's incessantly operating on four levels, at least.

JOHN LAHR: Mike could speak in epigrams, and the thing about epigrams is not only are they startling, but they don't want a response. There's no comeback to an epigram. In other words, the wit completely disarms the other, and a lot of what Mike is about is disarming the other. It allows him to be both hidden and seen.

RICHARD AVEDON (*photographer*)[4]**:** I think he goes into every experience in life expecting to be attacked—armed, ready. And then if you've proven yourself a friend to him, you're a friend for life.

He said his dream was, he's on an island that belongs to him, manned on the turrets by men with machine guns. People can only get in with a passport, and then only his friends.

JOHN LAHR: Part of his—I don't want to say masquerade, but part of his performance of self was this sort of perfect equipoise. From an early age he was always braced, he was always powerfully defended, and fortunately he was so smart that he could pull that off, so you didn't mess with him. If you did, you did it at your peril.

CANDICE BERGEN: He knew he intimidated people—I was intimidated for years and years—and part of his job was to relax them. He was the most generous audience. He would laugh the hardest at other people's jokes, even feeble attempts at jokes. He really extended himself to make people feel comfortable. And he paid attention to you,

---

3. Courtesy of the John Lahr collection at the Howard Gotlieb Archival Research Center, Boston University.
4. Ibid.

which people of success and achievement and intellect rarely do. He was very forgiving. Until he wasn't. The fact that there was this RPG missile hidden behind this vibrant façade always kept you on your back foot, at least in the earlier years. It was a brilliantly elaborate defense system.

CHRISTINE BARANSKI: He could in the course of a conversation be so fabulously—I don't want to say superficial, but fabulously worldly. And in a millisecond, he could go to a very deep place.

SHIRLEY MacLAINE (*actress*): You know, I found him, for all of his wonderful humor and tolerance of different brands of talent and eccentricity, frankly, I found him one of the most serious-minded people I've ever met. I just knew that his highest priority was survival. And then when we talked about his background and who he really was, I understood why.

CANDICE BERGEN: He had a kind of triumphal presence that seemed grounded in great confidence, but if you knew him, you knew that he was always trying to keep a grip on his demons. He masked his struggles so much more artistically than most, but he was a cauldron.

MAUREEN DOWD (*columnist*): It's so counter to his image as a bon vivant—you realized how many layers were underneath that effortless wit. He was a Noel Coward figure with a Jerzy Kosinski past.

CHRISTINE BARANSKI: My God, can you imagine the memoir he could have written? Ninety-nine percent of people in his position would have written not just one, but volumes three and four.

WALLACE SHAWN (*playwright*): I thought a hundred times of proposing to Mike, "Let's write your autobiography." But I didn't, because I knew that he would never sit down.

MARIE BRENNER: He said, "I would hide! I would pretend I wasn't there. In would walk the biographer, a perfectly wonderful person, and someone would have to tell them, 'Mr. Nichols has gone out.'"

TOM FONTANA (*screenwriter*): That book came out, *My Lunches with Orson.* I was on fire about that, because Mike wouldn't do an auto-biography. I kept saying, "When are you going to write all this down?"

SHELLEY WANGER (*book editor*): When I came to Knopf in 1991, I thought it would be great to do a book about his career. Nothing about his personal life, just about directing plays and movies. He could put a bit about being an actor in too, of course, but I was thinking of those Mamet books about film and theater. He was so busy, though. So then we thought maybe we could get someone whom he liked to debrief him.

JOHN LAHR: I was going to do a book with him. It was meant to be about not just directing, but on dealing with actors, on directing for the stage, on all sorts of theatrical and artistic issues. It was an indirect autobiography in the sense that the examples he would use would be from his own work, and he'd worked with everybody. The idea was to scrupulously avoid his private life, which was okay by me, because I was only interested in him as an artist.

SIGOURNEY WEAVER (*actress*): I always wished he'd written a book, not so much about his life, though his life was fascinating, but just about his approach to things—finding the events. It was never really about the jokes.

SHELLEY WANGER: He really didn't want a contract; if it got done, there could be a contract at the end. I did announce it at one point, but he never took an advance.

He told me, "I'm thinking about calling the book *Another Fucking Beautiful Day,* and making it about the experience of first going out [to Los Angeles] as Nichols and May to do *The Dinah Shore Show,* and being stunned and frightened by how constantly nice everyone was after our bohemian lives of sarcasm and snottyism in Chicago and New York, and then when I returned to LA as a man of the moment with all those hits in New York, directing the Burtons and so on."

We went back and forth for a while. I don't know how he could have done it—he was just always going in so many directions, and he was always flying off to Los Angeles or wherever. I'm sorry I never got him.

SUSAN FORRISTAL: He told me he didn't want to do it because he didn't want to have to do the book tour. I said, "I'm sure you wouldn't have to go on the book tour." He said, "Yes, you have to go on the book tour." Shelley kept talking to him about it over the years, but he just wouldn't do it.

TONY KUSHNER (*playwright*)[5]: A lot of people, me included, kept begging him to sit down and write a memoir. And he just said it was the last thing on earth he would ever want to do. I'm not entirely sure why. He was not, I think, a person who particularly wanted to be locked up in a room with only his brain for company. It's such a great brain, it would have been anybody else's choice. But he was such a completely social being. He loved being in the company of people. It was always a little bit of a mystery, when he found the time to do the amount of reading he was clearly doing. But being in conversation, being in dialogue, working on something with somebody was where he lived.

DAVID GEFFEN (*executive*): He absolutely considered it, but he decided he would never do it. I talked to him about it many times. He didn't want a biography. He didn't want an *American Masters*, which Susan Lacy was begging him to do, and I did everything I could to make that happen. I said, "Do it for your kids." He was sure there were all these people who would have these terrible stories about him, which is not true at all, but that's one of the things he worried about, because he could not forgive himself for so many things.

---

5. "Mike Nichols," *American Masters*, directed by Elaine May, produced by Julian Schlossberg, season 30, episode 1, aired January 29, 2016, on PBS.

JULIET TAYLOR (*casting director*)**:** When I closed up my office, I had these notebooks for all the movies that I had done, and the Academy archives wanted them. I mentioned it to Mike, and he said, "Fine, send them. I have no archives. My past is just going to go to the wind. Let it all blow away . . ."

JOHN LAHR: Before he died, he said he felt that nobody would be interested in what he had to say. He actually said that to me. I was surprised, because, of course, I venerated him. Because his persona was so strong and vivid, his front, it's hard to gauge the insecurity of the man. He was a strange guy—very complicated, psychologically. But without shadow, no brilliance.

Life isn't everything

Igor Mikhail Peschkowsky—soon to become Mike Nichols—and his mother, Brigitte, in Berlin. After the passage of the Nuremberg Laws, they would join Mike's father, Dr. Pavel Peschkowsky, in New York.

CHAPTER 1

Dybbuks and Golems

DAVID HARE (*playwright*): Mike liked being Mike Nichols: very, very good at his job and known to be very, very good at his job. He got this tremendous sensual pleasure from being in America. He liked being king in his town. But underneath it, there was that sense that he'd come out of the midcentury catastrophe—that he'd managed to get out, and very few people had.

EMANUEL AZENBERG (*producer*): It would be presumptuous to try to figure out Mike's life, but you can't get away from the fact that he escaped the Nazis.

JEREMY IRONS (*actor*): In a way he was carrying the flag for those dead brethren, not wasting his life, because his had been given to him while it hadn't to many others.

ROBERT NICHOLS (*brother*): My mother always emphasized how extraordinarily intelligent our father was. And yet: Hitler became chancellor in 1933. It was obvious—the dislike and humiliation of Jews was out there—but my father didn't leave for five years. Why the hell did he stay around? German Jews often feel more German than Jewish, and I'm afraid my father, who was a Russian Jew but had gone to medical school in Germany and practiced medicine in Berlin for many years, may have shared that attitude.

By the time of some of the Nuremberg Laws, Jewish doctors couldn't see Aryan patients, and then with the later Nuremberg edicts, Jewish doctors couldn't see patients, period. At that point he left, in August of 1938. My mother was in a convalescent hospital. She had had, possibly as a complication of pregnancy with me, deep-vein thrombosis in the leg, so she was not able to come with Mike and me, and didn't get out until 1940, so she got out very late.

Mike and I left in May of 1939, less than four months before the war started. I was three, and he was seven. We traveled on the *Bremen*, one of the biggest ships in the world at that time. Mike erroneously believed it was the Nazi-Soviet non-aggression pact that allowed us to leave. That pact came later, though it may well have helped that we were regarded as Soviet citizens, not German. I didn't know it until about two years ago, but Mike and I were never German citizens. We were born there, but in those days citizenship was exclusively through the father. Then, even if you were born in the country, you were not a citizen unless your father was. On the ship's manifest, we are listed as Hebrew-USSR.

I remember that we were obstreperous at dinner, and we were sent to our stateroom. Mike had much more coherent memories of the trip. He told me that we had a great time. We weren't just two little boys on the loose—somebody he referred to as a stewardess had been assigned to keep an eye on us—but we did travel as unaccompanied minors. We just roamed around the ship, looking at the engines, whatever we could do. People, especially women, regarded as heartrending the idea of these two little boys alone on the ship, but to me it sounded more like a great adventure—at least in Mike's telling of it.

EMANUEL AZENBERG: His brother tells the story about when they first came—they traveled by boat, just the two brothers, and when they got to America they saw a store with Hebrew letters on the window, and Mike evidently said to his brother, "Do they allow that here?"

HANNAH ROTH SORKIN: He would never ever, ever touch anything vaguely Holocaust-related. He had tremendous survivor guilt.

PETER LAWRENCE (*stage manager*): At the opening of *Death and the Maiden*, I was standing in front of the theater talking to Fred

Zollo, the producer, when Mike drove up in a huge, top-of-the-line Mercedes that he had just bought. When Mike got out of the car, Fred said, "It's the Mengele 500." The next day, Mike sold the car.

PAUL SIMON (*musician*): We were once at dinner with Lorne Michaels and Tina Fey, and Tina said that she speaks German. I think Mike was surprised. They started talking about how people who speak German don't tell you that their second language is German.

RENATA ADLER: Mike and I came from similar backgrounds. We were both refugees. Our first language was German. Every once in a while, he would use a little phrase from our childhood, "*Riech mal dran,*" if there was a question whether something was spoiled or not. Meaning literally, "Smell at it." Quotations, jokes, rhymes. When he bought the rights to Brecht's *Threepenny Opera*, he thought we could translate it right. Then, he would remember a few lines from Brecht, so perfect and simple that there was no way to translate them. Not if you had the original in your head.

PETER LAWRENCE: When I first met Mike, I thought he was from Wisconsin or something. I didn't know that his name was Igor Peschkowsky.

CANDICE BERGEN: At what age did he become "Mike"? Because it couldn't have been easy being Igor in New York at that time. I don't think any child was ever put through more.

ART GARFUNKEL: Let's face it: "Mike Nichols" is a construction of a human being. He is busy leaving this guy who left Germany behind and becoming a very appealing American guy named Mike Nichols. What a choice: Mike Nichols.

ROBERT NICHOLS: Mike's name was not Mikhail Igor Peschkowsky, it was Igor Mikhail Peschkowsky. I have documents with seals on them showing that. Buck Henry famously gave Mike a director's chair that says "M. I. Peschkowsky" on it; it should say "I. M. Peschkowsky," though it doesn't make any difference now. Of course, Mike couldn't bear the name Michael Nichols. I don't think it's so terrible, the lack of poesy in Michael Nichols, but Mike did. He just didn't want it as a professional name. He was never Michael Nichols—always Mike.

JEFFREY SWEET (*writer*): The McCarthy era to a large degree was cloaked, not terribly well, in anti-Semitism. Look at the questions they're asking: they say to Joe Papp, "Your real name is Papirofsky." Or to Judy Holliday, "Well, your name is Holliday, but your real name was what, Tuvim?"

I think that a lot of the satire boom—Lenny Bruce, Mort Sahl, Carl Reiner, Mel Brooks, Tom Lehrer, Philip Roth, Saul Bellow, all these people who had a satiric tinge to their work—came out of Eastern European Jews, whose parents and grandparents had fled the pogroms, taking a look at people like Joe McCarthy and Karl Mundt and these other horror shows and saying, "Oh, they're Cossacks. They may not have horses, and they may not have sabers, but they're Cossacks. They can't kill us, so let's mock them." I think that's why you had this explosion of satire in the '50s. It wasn't exclusively Jewish, but it was 95 percent Jewish. Interestingly, Jonathan Miller disagrees with me entirely. He said, "No, it's just that everybody was educated and was ready for smarter comedy." To which I said, "Then why were they all Jews?"

ROBERT NICHOLS: My father's name was Pavel Nikolaevich Peschkowsky. His father's name was Nikolai, so he took Pavel Nikolaevich, and that became Paul Nichols—he didn't just pull it out of the air. But I've always wondered, and no one will ever know, whether my father realized when he changed his name that he was changing ethnicity too, because Nichols is certainly not a Jewish name.

EMANUEL AZENBERG: Mike always knew he was Jewish, and like almost all of the Jews of that generation—not all, but many—was conflicted about that identity. It competed with being an American. You see it with Neil [Simon]. You certainly see it with Woody Allen,

Mel Brooks—all of them. The essence of their cultural roots comes from that identity, and they run away from it as much as they run to it. Mike had that too.

ROBERT NICHOLS: It was not a secret that we were Jewish. All of our friends were Jewish. A lot of my boyhood friends were Jewish. It was just an entirely Jewish milieu. At that time, New York was by far the largest Jewish city in the world, and there were more Jews in New York than there were Protestants or Catholics. It was the largest single religion. Practically everybody I knew was Jewish. They were all trooping off for Hebrew lessons and had bar mitzvahs; we had none of that. We were totally secular. I would go to school on Jewish holidays. And we always had Christmas trees, Christmas presents—no menorah, nothing Jewish. Not atypical for German Jews. Very different from Eastern European Jews, with hostile feelings on both sides.

PETER LAWRENCE: There was a *New Yorker* cartoon, or maybe a Feiffer, in which there was the outline of a man in a suit holding a briefcase, and inside him was a tiny angry little boy jumping around trying to get out. There was always Igor Peschkowsky in Mike. There was always that German Jewish boy who arrives in America looking like a boiled egg. He said the only two things he knew in English were "I do not speak English" and "Please do not kiss me." I'm sure that's apocryphal, but he claimed it was true.

ROBERT NICHOLS: Mike loves that story. My memory is the words were not "Please don't kiss me" but "Please don't touch me," and it was I who said it, not Mike. I could be wrong, but I'm 83 percent sure.

DOUGLAS McGRATH (*screenwriter*): Mike didn't speak a word of English. He spoke German, which was one of the least popular foreign languages in 1939 in America. He's away from the physical danger of Hitler's Germany, and the new crisis for him, because he's seven, is: *How do I fit in?* But to fit in, you have to figure out what in *is*. I think that's where he developed what I think is the defining characteristic of his talent, which is his acute and very precise understanding of human nature.

RENATA ADLER: Mike said that if you are a refugee, you begin to read people's minds. Which is true in a way. It's from learning a style of comprehension. In order to assimilate, to become one of them.

TONY KUSHNER[1]: Mike's grandfather was Gustav Landauer, a major figure in European anarchism. And Mike's grandmother wrote the libretto for Richard Strauss's *Salome*. So they weren't coming from some shtetl in Russia. They were the royalty of European Jewry. And Mike brought with him that sense of the importance of culture and the importance of the intellect, the effortless marriage of high art and low entertainment and serious intellectual and emotional engagement. He really drew from a deep well, a very old and polished notion of cultural production, and I think you see it in his films. It's one of the things that makes them feel so shocking in the context of their times. They're not exactly of the American tradition. There's a slightly European feeling in them.

MAUREEN DOWD: I asked him once why triangles are so potent. He said, "We're born in a triangle about parents and a newborn. That's the most important one, the triangle that determines who we are, the one that affects the other triangles that you get into in your life. It's about that first triangle, what it gives you and what it takes away from you."

ROBERT NICHOLS: We lived at 155 West Seventy-First. I remembered this huge entryway and a big, imposing front door. Some years back I took Paul, my son, to walk by it, and here's this tiny little building. We lived on the fifth floor, and my father's practice was on the first floor. He commuted by elevator. The apartment had one bed-

---

1. "Mike Nichols," *American Masters*, season 30, episode 1, aired January 29, 2016, on PBS.

room. Mike and I were in the bedroom, and my parents slept in a hide-a-bed in the living room.

MARIANNE MOSBACH (*former babysitter*): When my mother and I came [from Germany] in '38, my father didn't have his medical license yet, unlike Dr. Nichols. We had very hard times, because money that we thought was in Switzerland wasn't there, and so I had to babysit, which I didn't like at all. I was sixteen, and I was interested in dancing and in boys—dancing first, boys next. It was a very active German-Jewish community, especially in Washington Heights. There was a little cluster of more prosperous people around Seventy-Second Street, and that's where they lived. It was a nice apartment, better than most refugees had. There was a famous restaurant on Seventy-Second Street called Eclair that was run by German refugees. All the refugees would meet there for coffee and cake.

ROBERT NICHOLS: Our mother used to say there are eight people in the world who understood Einstein's theory of relativity, and my father was one of them, which is nonsense. But we are related. That actually was not a legend, but a fact, that we are related to Albert Einstein. A distant cousin. Henry Louis Gates, the Harvard professor who does the genealogy program [*Finding Your Roots*] on PBS, did one on Mike; somewhere in there is a link to Einstein.

Our father had this showbiz-music practice. I think Vladimir Horowitz was a patient of his. Sol Hurok definitely was. My father was charismatic. He held his own at gatherings. I think Mike must have inherited quite a bit of the brain, the humor, and the charisma from him.

MAUREEN DOWD: Mike said, "When I became a comic, I used to see Sol Hurok, the impresario who had been my father's patient, in the Russian Tea Room. He always said the same thing. 'You're very funny, but your father was funnier.' So it was announced to me that I had already lost the competition with my father."

ROBERT NICHOLS: My mother [Brigitte] was known to be a beautiful woman. Many men adored her, apparently. But she was also what used to be called neurotic. She had many fears, including something resembling agoraphobia. She was afraid to go out in the world. What she was afraid of mostly, and this is probably true for most agoraphobics, was not that something bad would happen in the elevator or at the movie theater, but that she would panic. She was afraid of fear. She was very clingy about us—with good reason, given her background—and Mike bore the brunt of her emotional strain. She and Mike had a difficult relationship at times. I was kind of a good little boy, so I didn't really suffer, but Mike did. I give her a pass to a greater degree than Mike, because of the difficulties she had had in life, but, then again, I didn't have the troubles that he had with her.

My mother was orphaned before she was twelve years old. Her father, Gustav Landauer, was a member of the provisional leftist government that was set up in Bavaria after World War I. He was murdered by what my mother always referred to as pre-Nazis. The previous year, her mother had died in the influenza pandemic that killed 50 million people around the world, at least, so she was orphaned. I believe she was raised by an uncle in Karlsruhe. She had two sisters: Gudula, and a half sister, Charlotte, known as Lotte, from her father's first wife, Margarethe Leuschner. His second wife, Hedwig [Lachmann,] was a known poet and translated Oscar Wilde's *Salomé* into German. The San Diego Opera gave a performance of *Salome* two, three years ago, and it said in the blurb for it in the paper, "Libretto: Hedwig Lachmann," my grandmother. Gudula was a lovely, cultivated woman, a musician who came to live with us in our small apartment. She was hit by a bus on Central Park West and killed two weeks after she got here. I still get choked up when I talk about it. She was hidden away outside of Berlin by a social worker, survived the entire war, came over in 1945 or early '46, and two weeks later was hit by a bus and killed. So that's our family.

ART GARFUNKEL: I once asked Buck [Henry], "Do you remember Mike from the Dalton School?" "Yeah, he was the kid with the hat."

JAMIE BERNSTEIN (*writer*): We were all hanging out in the living room of the house in Fairfield, Connecticut, and I was going around giving people scalp massages. That was my thing that day, I don't know why. I couldn't have been more than nine, tops. So I'm going around giving these head massages, and when I get to Mike, he demurs. "No, thanks. No head massage today." I said, "Oh, you'll love it. I'm really good at it." "No, no, it's okay." For whatever reason, I insisted, until my father had to bark at me, "Jamie! He says he doesn't want a scalp massage!" Our father never barked. My brother and I went running up the stairs and went into our shared bedroom to cry.

After a few minutes, our dad came upstairs, and he sat down on my brother's bed. And he said, "I'm sorry I yelled. I didn't mean to upset you, but you have to know that Mike, when he was a little boy, a terrible thing happened to him. He had this terrible fever, and when he woke up in the morning, all his hair had fallen out." We were just horrified, and then, of course, we had to go back down eventually to confront Mike, and that was the most embarrassing thing in the whole wide world, but Mike was so nice about it. I will bet that he gave our dad permission to go upstairs and tell us the truth. "It's okay, you can tell them." Otherwise, I don't think my father would have done it.

ROBERT NICHOLS: Mike had what's known as alopecia totalis universalis, which means total baldness everywhere. That's exactly what those words mean, and that means eyebrows and eyelashes and everything, so you couldn't miss it, until he was able to cover it. I remember lying in bed crying, because I was so sorry about what Mike had to go through.

The cause of what he had is not clear. It was probably an immunologic reaction of some sort, but whether to a childhood illness or to a vaccination, I don't think anyone will ever know. He was around four, maybe five. He usually wore a baseball cap. Nowadays being bald is kind of a symbol of masculinity, thanks to Michael Jordan and others—half the guys are walking around with shiny heads now—but not in those days. Our father, for some reason, did not want him to have a hairpiece, and so only after my father's death did he finally get one. I don't understand it. It wasn't money. It was expensive even then, but we had money while he was earning. We were not poor. Our father had strong opinions.

MARIANNE MOSBACH: Mike was seven or eight. He already was bald, as my parents had warned me, which made him quite angry. He didn't want me to fix him anything. If I wanted to make him a sandwich or get something out of the fridge, he'd say, "I can do that"—indicating that he really didn't want me there. He would come home with a baseball cap on, but he took it off at home. For some reason, his father wouldn't let him wear a wig, which I think would have helped a lot. He didn't like to go outside. He was old enough to go, and the park was very safe then, but he liked to stay inside and read.

Becoming a comedian makes sense. People, when their life is difficult, they have two ways: they can either keep feeling sorry for themselves, or they can look for humor. A lot of Jews turned to humor.

JOHN LAHR: Mike had this powerful affinity for animals, I think because animals don't judge. The eyes of others were humiliating. I think he felt humiliated by his physical circumstances and humiliated by not speaking English initially very well. When you get down to great comics, it's all about vindictive triumph. It's all about revenge over childhood humiliations.

JON ROBIN BAITZ: These Ashkenazi terrors—all the dybbuks and golems and shtetl monster mothers, all that endless fleeing—Mike was so steeped in it, not that you would ever know it to look at him, with his Italian tweeds and perfect wigs. I think Mike felt that life was very terrifying and that you had to have very good clothes and very good jokes in order to just get through the day. I think that's his "Rosebud," in a way.

SUSAN SONTAG (*writer*)[2]: It was absolutely unmentionable. This says something about me maybe. Never could be mentioned, and wouldn't be mentioned.

I can't tell you exactly when—it was the later '70s, early '80s, and

---

2. Courtesy of the John Lahr collection at the Howard Gotlieb Archival Research Center, Boston University.

I had breast cancer. We'd had dinner, gone back to his place. Talking, talking, talking. And I said to him: "I just cannot accept the mastectomy. Every time I take a bath I'm horrified." And he said, "Susan, now you know how I felt all my life." And that was the first time—I was in my forties and so was he—that he ever mentioned it.

I would happily have become his girlfriend physically, except I felt that he was—I was intimidated by the hair problem. It's not as if Mike had a modest sexual life or anything, but at the time he felt untouchable to me.

SUSAN FORRISTAL: After Mike and Annabel [Davis-Goff] separated, Mike and Lorne [Michaels] and I went on a continental tour of Europe, first to Paris, and then to the South of France to see Candy [Bergen] and Louis [Malle], and then to London. In London, we shared a suite. Mike had his room, and we had ours, with the living room in the middle.

One morning I was walking by, getting ready to go out, and I suddenly said, "What is that *smell*?" Mike was in his bathroom and he said, "It's my glue." I said, "Are you kidding?" And he goes, "No. I have to do this every day. Doesn't it stink?" He was very frank about the things he had to deal with in life, no matter what they were.

CANDICE BERGEN: Having to go through that every morning—I mean, I can't imagine what that was like for him, just to get ready to start your day.

PETER LAWRENCE: We were standing outside the Goodman Theatre in bright sunlight, and I suddenly noticed the lace front on his eyebrows, and my eyes flicked for a second—a millisecond—and he said, "Oh, you saw them." He was always aware that he had to put himself together.

He had those wigs shipped to him from Paul Huntley all the time. They would be sent back, redressed, and sent to him again. He put on a fresh wig virtually every day, and they were all the same wig, and they all went back to Paul Huntley to be redone—the eyebrows too.

JEREMY IRONS: The wigs would change every day. They'd get slightly longer, and then he'd have a "haircut," and he'd go back to the shorter wig. It was seamlessly done. I suppose we're all created people in a way, but Mike had done a fantastic job creating himself.

ROBERT NICHOLS: I had one or two friends, but Mike was social. He had lots of friends. He went out with girls and, as far as I know, did stuff with girls I could only dream of. Even with the handicap that he had, he was far more social and successful socially than I was. His hair loss didn't define him. It stopped being an issue, of course, later, when he was an adult and the quality of what he was wearing was so high, but I can only imagine the impact.

Our father died in June of 1944, when he was forty-four. Mike was twelve. I only have a handful of memories of my father, and one of them is of him announcing his illness, standing on the top of the two steps down from the dining area into the living room, his hand on his throat, saying, "I have a terrible sore throat." He looked at a smear of his own blood under the microscope in the lab with my mother standing right next to him, and the way my mother told the story, he said, "You poor child, I have only two weeks to live." What he saw were very young white blood cells—so-called blasts. Even one or two is not normal, but he had sheets of them, which meant acute leukemia, and in those days, acute leukemia meant death. There was no treatment. You died from bleeding and from infections, and the infection was his sore throat. I don't know whether it was literally two weeks or ten days or fifteen days, but in about two weeks he was dead. I was off at summer camp and some poor counselor had the difficult task of telling me that my father had died.

My mother told me that one of my father's girlfriends, Frieda, came up to her at his funeral and said, "I am the true widow." Kind of a world record for tactlessness. They had a difficult marriage. Their troubles go back to Germany, apparently. Mike knew more than I did. Nevertheless, she loved telling stories about my father after his death. When people die, they become sanctified in memory. My mother went on and on with stories about how brilliant he was.

MARIANNE MOSBACH: He was well-established here, which was quite unusual. He was a union doctor, so that gave him a steady income. All that was gone when he died. I remember my parents and other friends saying they were very concerned about the death of the father. People collected money.

ROBERT NICHOLS: I think he was very poorly insured, either poorly or not at all. At any rate, it was inadequate, and our mother was left with two little boys, ages eight and twelve, and no clear source of income. The great struggles our mother had with loss—before she was forty, she lost both parents, both sisters, and her husband—was her own personal, private holocaust. I don't know how stable her mental health was before, but she had her problems. She was physically ailing too. She had asthma and was troubled greatly by migraines.

After my father died, we had so little money. We were truly poor, not genteel poor—no money. My mother rented out the one bedroom. I slept on a couch in the living room and she slept in the hide-a-bed for a couple of years. She sold goods out of the apartment during the day, leather goods and things like that, to try to make money. She typed up manuscripts for PhD and master's students. She borrowed from Household Finance so often that I remember she got a wall plaque honoring her for paying back so much. We also had the kindness of friends who gave us baskets of food and helped her out, because she struggled mightily. Our next apartment was terribly dirty, overrun with roaches. I remember going into the kitchenette we had and turning on the light, and there would be roaches everywhere, disappearing at high speed. My mother forgot something in the hallway closet when I was eight or nine and asked me to go get it. I rang the doorbell and the woman who lived there said, "Dirty people," with contempt. She was right. I was embarrassed. I didn't want my friends to ever come to my house, because most of them were wealthy. They lived on West End Avenue in these seven-, eight-room apartments, and we had this little tiny place, and it was disheveled and slovenly for some years. I guess my mother just couldn't cope.

Mike was at Cherry Lawn School, a private school that I also went to my senior year of high school, in Darien, Connecticut. I think he had a scholarship. Mike wasn't very emotionally accessible. It troubled my mother, because he was independent. She said, "He doesn't really need me." Of course he did.

MAUREEN DOWD: Mike thought that the father-son relationship was the most important relationship in drama and literature. He told me, "The following or not following in the footsteps of the father is a tricky and anxiety-producing discussion between fathers and sons." He said, "I've had conversations with him"—meaning his father—"about what I've accomplished and what I didn't. I've had to be him and me, him proud of me. He was proud once when I won a horse show in boarding school, and he was proud once when I broke my arm, and, man, I've hauled those out innumerable times." A psychiatrist once told him, even after he was a success, that he was holding himself back because he was frightened that he would harm his father. "I was told that my problems were partly not wanting to symbolically kill my already dead father, or to surpass him."

ROBERT NICHOLS: My father was a doctor. His father was a doctor. Most of the men in our close family, friends—everybody was a doctor. I liked science. I just kind of assumed I would be a doctor. I don't recall considering anything else. Mike thought he might like to be a psychiatrist. He had read a book about Freud and some of Freud's writing. I think when Mike found out you've got to take chemistry and physics and zoology and physical chemistry and things like that, he left that behind.

His interest in theater was evident very early. He used to hang out on Broadway and mingle with intermission crowds and go in and see the second and/or third acts of plays when he didn't have the money to buy tickets. Tickets were cheap in those days, $2.40, $4.80 tops, but even then, it was hard to come up with $3.00 sometimes. *A Streetcar Named Desire* and *Death of a Salesman* are the two plays that had the biggest impact on him. His life was just transfigured by having seen them.

JAMES GRISSOM (*writer*): *Streetcar* completely changed his world. What was he, seventeen, eighteen? He said he became embarrassed with the girl he went with, and I went, "Why? Did you get a hard-on or something? Did you wet yourself?" He goes, "No. It was the humanity, the brutality of it. The thing I could compare it to is if I went to a cockfight with someone, or when Travis Bickle takes Cybill Shepherd to a porno.

"I was really taken with the character of Blanche. *Who's going to take care of her?* And then ten minutes later, *Oh, she's so annoying, I want to punch her. I've got to take care of her. Oh, my gosh, she's such a phony. How can Stella do this?* And then the next, *How can Stella not do this? She has to move on.*" That's what he meant by "I was embarrassed": that we are like this, and we all have done this. He said, "Even at that young age I had betrayed people."

Tennessee [Williams] talked about how you walked down streets and you'd hear a snatch of a song and it takes you back to a certain year. He called them "emotional strings." Mike told me, "Every time I work, there are strings that go back to when I saw *Streetcar.*"

Mike and Elaine May performing what became known as their "Teenagers" sketch onstage at the Compass Theater in Chicago. "They fucked up a lot," the company pianist, Allaudin Mathieu, says of their early improvisations. "However, there were some scenes that just happened. The teenagers scene was one of them." *(© William A. Mathieu)*

CHAPTER 2

To Sell Another Drink

SUSAN SONTAG[1]**:** Chicago either made or confirmed a very crazy idealism in its best students, in its most devoted students, of whom I'm one and Mike is another. Somewhere you're always measuring yourself against that idealism you felt then.

CANDICE BERGEN: He was talking the year before he died about being at the University of Chicago, because it was so idyllic for him there, meeting Susan Sontag in line, registering for classes. Finally he had a home.

JEFFREY SWEET: A lot of U of C faculty was made up of Jews who had fled oppression in Europe, whether it had been in Germany or Russia.

JOY CARLIN: Robert Hutchins was the youngest president the University of Chicago ever had. He designed the curriculum, and basically, it was the Great Books. You didn't have textbooks; you had the real thing.

JANET COLEMAN (*writer*): There was no applied anything there. Some of these kids were overwhelmed by the amount of studying that

1. Courtesy of the John Lahr collection at the Howard Gotlieb Archival Research Center, Boston University.

was required. A lot of them dropped out, including Mike. Including my friend Severn Darden. I don't think Barbara Harris was ever enrolled.

JEFFREY SWEET: Nobody took attendance, which is how Elaine [May] managed to get a University of Chicago education without actually enrolling.

JOY CARLIN (*actress*): Really smart kids came from all over the country. There was no football team. There was no drama department. It was all serious education.

JANET COLEMAN: Hutchins was famous for saying, "When I feel like exercising, I lie down until the feeling goes away."

JEFFREY SWEET: Hutchins's whole idea was, if you could pass the entrance exam, you could get into the U of C even if you didn't have a high school diploma. And that meant that a lot of very young, very bright people were there. And because it was after World War II and guys were going to the U of C on the GI Bill, you had freshmen who were sixteen years old and thirty years old in the same class.

JOYCE PIVEN (*actress*): If you passed the test, you could come. Unfortunately, a lot of people were casualties of that, jumping out of windows, depressed. Young people who were intellectually brilliant but not mature.

HEYWARD ERLICH (*actor*): The student body was a collection of oddballs and misfits, compared to Northwestern, which was very straight.

ALLAUDIN MATHIEU (*composer*): You couldn't get in unless you were weird.

SAM WASSON: Out of that intellectually progressive environment comes improvisation. It makes perfect sense. You can't imagine improvisers coming from an intellectually conservative East Coast Ivy League university.

JOYCE PIVEN: There was a synergy that was unbelievable. And that's what I feel started all of Chicago theater.

ALLAUDIN MATHIEU: Mike had six years on me, but he was still unfound as far as the public was concerned—and even as far as he was concerned. I was then living with a woman who was to become my first wife, and we would feed him. He still owes me thirty dollars!

HEYWARD ERLICH: Mike was impoverished. He had to live by his wits. But I've had the feeling he knew how to exploit his exploitation. He always owed people twenty-five cents, seventy-five cents. He was bedraggled—ill-fitting clothing. It was embarrassing. He didn't have a good wig, which was occasionally the subject of commentary. But he made up for it in his presence. He was always interesting, always lively, always fun.

The pain and suffering of those years became a dynamic element in his comedy. It had to come from something. He wasn't living a life of privilege and comfort; he was living a life of insecurity. There was a sense that things shouldn't be this way.

JANET COLEMAN: One University of Chicago wag described him to me as "a man who would go into a White Castle and send back the hamburger."

JOYCE PIVEN: He carved out his looks in a beautiful way, but when I first saw him, he was wearing a red fright wig. What an evolution. His personality was very strong, though, and he was scary, because he was so smart, so verbal. Everybody at the university was verbal, but he was especially so, and you didn't get into an argument with him.

ANDREW DUNCAN: When you were in a scene with him, particularly if you were standing eye to eye arguing with him or something, you couldn't help staring, looking at that white skin with the wig and fake eyebrows. It was sort of like you were looking at a mannequin, and yet from this mannequin were coming these brilliant statements.

HEYWARD ERLICH[2]: There was something about Mike that was like the abused child who turns the abuse on others. He always seemed to be vying with others for power and authority. I liked him in those days, but you had to endure him. He was a pain in the ass.

SAM WASSON: He had descended from the cultural aristocracy in Europe, but now in America, having found himself pretty much like everyone else, he was trying to peacock his way back to prominence in the intellectual circles of Chicago. He worked as a deejay to make money, and that was a great job for him, because Mike, not only is he a classical-music lover, but as any comedian does, he had an incredible ear. You cannot do comedy if you do not have an ear. It's even more important, I think, than having a mind, and Mike, of course, had both.

JOYCE PIVEN: He created *The Midnight Special*, which is still running every Saturday night on WFMT. He was very conscientious about being self-sufficient and had a sense of responsibility and struck me as being very cautious.

When I was feeling down, I would just call the station to talk to Mike, and he would have me on the floor, crying tears of laughter.

DEBORAH EISENBERG (*writer*): I was a child in the Chicago suburbs, and his voice was an absolute lifeline for me on the radio. There I was, in the middle of the country, in the middle of the century, in a very repressive time, in the suburbs, which were scrubbed clean of any complexities, and just longing, longing, longing for something that seemed like reality to me. Once a week this voice would come through the air: it was the voice of freedom, possibility, joy, expansion, and sheer intelligence.

---

2. Janet Coleman, *The Compass: The Improvisational Theatre That Revolutionized American Comedy* (Chicago: University of Chicago Press, 1991), 18.

ALLAUDIN MATHIEU: Mike had a light around his body is all I can tell you. There was something about his intelligence and his power of observation which was so keen that he seemed almost luminescent. Later on, when he got famous, I was not surprised.

JEFFREY SWEET: Chicago still had that sense of being a second-rate place. There's that famous article that A. J. Liebling did called "The Second City." (Liebling subsequently said that the only thing anybody would remember him for was having inadvertently named a nightclub. It was a theater, but never mind.)

There was very little indigenous Chicago theater, and the stuff that we saw was mostly plays from Broadway three years ago, with actors who had been on TV three years ago. And it was not taken terribly seriously.

JOY CARLIN: One day I saw a flyer on a tree that said, *Do you want to join a theater? Come to Mandel Hall at 6:00.* I had a secret desire to be an actress, so I went. There was a group of people, and Paul Sills was the leader. Mike was there, Ed Asner, Elaine [May], Fritz Weaver, Omar Shapli. When it started out, it was called the Tonight at 8:30 Players.

HEYWARD ERLICH: There was a university theater, which did mostly classical repertory—Greek plays, Shakespeare, Restoration. And there was a renegade group, calling itself Tonight at 8:30, and it did other stuff, stuff the university theater wouldn't do, working with borrowed chairs and borrowed space and borrowed lights.

ANDREW DUNCAN: I played Hjalmar in a two-week run of Ibsen's *The Wild Duck*, and I got great reviews. At the end of the performance, the University of Chicago had this—it was kind of a pretentious thing with wine and cheese where the bourgeoisie of the campus came up on the stage to rub elbows with the actors. I see there's this huge lumbering guy coming up these steps up to the stage, and all the way I hear around me, "Paul Sills . . . ," "Paul Sills . . ." I said, "Who's Paul Sills?" and I swear somebody said, "Who's Paul Sills?" like I was a dumb rube from the country.

Paul came and leaned over me and in a mumbled tone said, "I liked your performance very much," and then took off. Everybody looked at me, like: *Paul liked your performance!* Then he came back down and he said, "Hey, I'm doing a little thing. Do you want to run some scenes?" I said, "Where?" He said, "Here, a week from tonight." I said, "Yeah, sure. What time?" "Seven thirty."

So that night I appear. I'm going up the stairs, and there's a big line of students and these hangers-on, and Paul comes by with his mother, Viola Spolin, and Barbara Harris, who was going with him at the time.

About an hour later, Viola turns to me, and she said, "I want you to do a scene with her," and she pointed at Elaine May, who I didn't know. She's very striking and dynamic. So we went backstage, and Elaine said, "What do you want to do?" and I said, "Well, I don't know." She said, "Let's do an office scene. They're fun." I said, "Okay." She said, "What's your action?" I said, "You mean motivation?" She said, "No, no, *action.* You're going out to act. What's your action? Are you going to seduce me, to impress me, to find something out?"

Elaine did a very funny telephone operator, and of course the scene worked. She made me look good, but I didn't know that. I just thought, *Hey, I can do this.*

SAM WASSON: Paul Sills was working at the cafeteria, and Mike, who didn't have any money, was stealing food. Sills, being a good Jewish lefty, saw that this was his type of guy, and then from there they found they shared this obsession with the theater. Although their approaches were significantly different, their passions for it were equally intense. Sills was a radical, avant-garde, looking for new forms. Mike wasn't so interested in new forms, just great traditional theater, the great works of Broadway and the world.

JOYCE PIVEN: Paul was at the University of Chicago on the GI Bill. He was a bit older than us and had been in the army.

ALLAUDIN MATHIEU: He was a great director and a passionate director of people, though he was pretty volatile. I saw him get quite violent a few times.

JANET COLEMAN: Paul was extremely bossy and tyrannical in his own crazy way. When he got into a conflicted situation, he was known to throw a chair and run away and let the actors work it out.

JOYCE PIVEN: Paul was not articulate by choice. He felt the minute you spoke about it, you killed it. Somehow he communicated to us what the truth of things was. He was very demanding and sometimes not too kind. It never seemed quite enough for Paul. But we all responded to his vision, whatever it was.

JOY CARLIN: Paul was very influenced by his mother and would carry around her book, *Improvisation for the Theater*, which is still in print today and used by drama teachers.

ALLAUDIN MATHIEU: Viola said a lot of things that were deliberately mystical. One of her mantras was, *Let the space support you.* The first time I heard that, I thought, *This woman is crazy.* But that, like a lot of what she said that seemed impenetrable to many of us at the time, turned out to be quite profound.

JEFFREY SWEET: One of the things she told me was that she and her father and the family friends used to play these games in the living room, with Paul lying on the bed, and he just absorbed them from an early age. Viola worked with Neva Boyd for a while at Hull House. Boyd had gone around Europe collecting storytelling games, and she believed that playing games was an expression of equality. Not competitive games, but structures of play by which one could create narrative. This was part of the whole ideal of creating the melting pot of America. Have people from different cultures able to play games together, and this will bring peace, and so forth.

SAM WASSON: Viola, the child of Russian immigrants, grew up in Chicago at a time when there was no radio, no TV. What did children do? They played in the streets. So she grew up playing games, but it was only when she studied with Neva Boyd that Viola started to become interested in how play can socialize children. The games were a way to create a common language and achieve a democratic ideal. It would then be Paul Sills who took those games and made a theater out of them.

JOY CARLIN: The games help actors to open up and learn and be spontaneous and listen to one another and say *yes* instead of *no*.

JOYCE PIVEN: I was in a play with Mike called *The Typewriter* by Jean Cocteau, and Paul did it in the round, which was revolutionary. It put Paul on the map.

We spent six months doing this play, and going to Jimmy's Pub, drinking beer and talking about the theater. *Is the theater really dead?* We were very idealistic. From there, Paul and David Shepherd opened Playwrights [Theatre Club].

JANET COLEMAN: David Shepherd was a Vanderbilt. Related to the Gwynne family through his aunt Alice. An only child, living among the WASP wealthy. His mother was in an institution, and he was raised by nannies. All he knew was servants, and he became interested in the way they lived. He was sort of a Johnny Appleseed who came to start a workers' theater.

JEFFREY SWEET: David Shepherd was the Marxist son of a millionaire. He gave early expression to this ideal by mounting a production of Molière, which toured through the Catskills in the 1950s, and was shocked when nobody turned up. A member of that company told me he actually remembered a couple of occasions when the cast outnumbered the audience.

So Shepherd just cast his fate to the wind and hitched a ride with a truck driver, and the truck driver took him to Chicago. Shepherd said, "Where's the action at here, man?" to the truck driver, and the truck driver, having gotten an earful of Shepherd's Marxism, said, "I think you might not get killed at the University of Chicago." This is Mayor Daley's Chicago. The school's nickname, which was not much embraced by the trustees, was "Red U." Shepherd sees Sills's production of *Caucasian Chalk Circle*, and he asks to meet with Sills. In creating the Playwrights Theatre Club, Shepherd was essentially moving the Sills gang from the academic environment of the University of Chicago to a professional arena.

SAM WASSON: Shepherd is the odd man out, because he's the WASP in a sea of Jews. He's more political, where Sills is more mystical. Sills wants to create theaters *for* communities, and Shepherd is really interested in creating theaters *of* the people. There's some overlap there, but they didn't always see eye to eye.

JOY CARLIN: For David, theater was not high school stuff. He believed that you could say something that would really make a difference in the way people think about politics, about life, about progress, about fairness; we can't just show cocktail parties and marital problems. He was very influenced by Brecht, as Paul was, as we all were. Brecht's famous alienation effect, it doesn't mean you make enemies of the audience; it means just that you keep them on their toes. You break the spell. Remind them that we have to think as well as cry.

HEYWARD ERLICH: I was complimented by someone who said I was the most Brechtian actor in the company, which really meant I was the lousiest.

ALLAUDIN MATHIEU: I never thought of David as a theater person, even though he was inventive theatrically. I always thought of him as an intellectual who wanted to see his ideas manifested.

ANDREW DUNCAN: David kind of mused when he'd talk, and we'd all be rolling our eyes at the meetings. He didn't try to direct much. He would just say things like, "Let's try to be a little more sober and not fool around so much."

Paul could be really demanding. He used to say things like, "I don't want that Carol Burnett shit in here, actors breaking up like they're having fun." Or, "I see anybody drop their pants, they'd better make sure their ass is painted blue," meaning you'd better have a reason.

JEFFREY SWEET: Playwrights Theatre Club is the first storefront theater in Chicago. It was the beginning of the whole renaissance of the Chicago theater movement.

JANET COLEMAN: Most of these people, they had no theater at all. Omar Shapli was an Egyptologist. Roger Bowen was an English major. Barbara Harris was a high school girl, practically, from the West Side of Chicago.

JOYCE PIVEN: At Playwrights, for almost two years, we did everything in the theater canon that could be done by young actors. We did *The Dybbuk; Red Gloves* by Sartre; *Henry IV, Part I; Midsummer Night's Dream;* Chekhov's *The Seagull; Murder in the Cathedral; The Overcoat.*

All the people who came out of Playwrights also became famous: Barbara Harris, Mike, Eugene Troobnick, Ed Asner. All those theaters in Chicago now—Steppenwolf, Lookingglass, Goodman—Paul started all that.

ALLAUDIN MATHIEU: Everybody was so into what they were doing. There was such a belief. There was such a conviction.

SAM WASSON: They're theater addicts. They're acting in each other's plays, and they're directing each other's plays. Incredibly, they start to get local critical attention. Who knows why? Were those shows good? Were they pretentious? We'll never know. We know by Mike's admission that he was pretty shitty as Jean the valet [in *Miss Julie*], but who knows?

What is obvious is the ambition. These are twenty-year-olds doing Brecht, Cocteau, and Ibsen. That sets the intellectual stage for Mike and Elaine's parodies later on. Their frame of reference was as highbrow as it gets, very young.

JEFFREY SWEET: Sills is having a pretty good time. But Shepherd is getting angrier and angrier, because it's all about kings and people sipping cocktails. He thought that theater should reflect the lives of the people in the audience and help reveal to them how oppressed they were.

He decided to come up with a modern version of the commedia dell'arte. These troupes would travel around with a batch of outlines in their repertoire, and they would hang the outline of the story they were going to play that day backstage. And you would check your outline: *Oh, I'm supposed to cheat the lecherous old doctor out of some money, okay.* And you'd go out and you'd improvise cheating the lecherous old doctor out of money. The big difference is that what Shepherd wanted was stories of contemporary Chicago. So the Compass Theatre was started partly out of David's disgust with Playwrights. But because nobody was actually writing plays about life in Chicago at the time, they had to improvise them—that was the only way they could generate them fast enough.

The guy who was running the bar, in whose back room they were playing, said, "Can you make this show a little bit longer, maybe a half hour longer so I can sell another round of drinks?" They said, "We worked all week to come up with this hour, and you want another half hour?" And somebody, I don't know who, said, "Well, why don't we take suggestions from the audience?"

And from that imperative—to sell another drink—the whole tradition of taking suggestions from the audience arose. And that took off. The audience was more interested in that than in the long pieces.

JANET COLEMAN: What really captured the audience wasn't the date rape or the Marxism or the [improvised scenario] "The Minister's Daughter"—these stories of class and of class investigation—but middle-class life, Jewish mothers.

SAM WASSON: Improv was definitely a part of this cultural exploration of spontaneity in music and art and writing that were a reaction to the strictures and conventions that we like to think of as the '50s. It's also about the post-bomb world of chaos, and how do we integrate chaos into our work? Once America tasted the possibility of annihilation, people understood the importance of the life force and the moment and being in the now. Around the same time, psychoanalysis is getting real hip in New York. There's all this post-nuclear, postwar anxiety, and all of the European intellectuals have come over to practice—really a flood of psychoanalysis hit New York—so that interest in the unconscious is right next door to that interest in spontaneity. When Mike entered the University of Chicago, he was studying to be an analyst.

HEYWARD ERLICH[3]**:** In those days, [being in psychoanalysis] was not something one advertised. If the secret came out, you'd say, "Excuse me, I'm late for my therapist," and that was the end of it. Not for Mike. He was very outspoken about it. Mike's therapy was at the top of his conversation. He publicized his handicap. He shook his tin cup.

JOY CARLIN: We rented a cottage in Cape Cod in August, because that's what my husband, Jerry, had off, and Mike would come and visit us in hopes of seeing his analyst on the beach. A lot of analysts were there in August, and he wasn't the only one wandering around Ballston Beach. I could do a great scene with people scanning the blankets.

SAM WASSON: Mike was playing Jean the valet in a production of *Miss Julie*, one of the many *Miss Julie*s produced by this group at University of Chicago—they were obsessed with *Miss Julie*—and Mike was declaiming at the foot of the stage, overacting, and there in the third row was this beautiful girl staring at him with contempt. He immediately respected her for hating him. A day later he picked up the review in the newspaper, and to his incredible shock, he got a rave. Sills, who directed the show, came up to him, and said, "Mike, I want you to meet the only other person on campus who's as hostile as you are: Elaine May." She looked over Mike's shoulder at the rave and went, "Ha!" and walked off. It's the beginning of a romantic comedy.

Then, of course, Mike was coming back from the radio station one day, and he sees Elaine on a bench in a train station reading a magazine. He goes up to her and says, "May I *seet* down?" He starts improvising as a spy, and she's immediately there with him, and starts

---

3. Coleman, *The Compass*, 20.

improvising back: "If you *veesh*." They improvised all the way back to Elaine's apartment.

JANET COLEMAN: She served him a cream-cheese-and-olive sandwich—you can imagine what kind of cook she must have been. I heard they did sleep together. They did it one time, and that was it. But he might have been madly in love with her. Everyone was.

ANDREW DUNCAN: I think it was Eugene Troobnick who said to me, "Don't fall for her. Don't ask her out and try to go to bed with her, because she's a killer. She's a ball-cutter, a castrater." I figured from the way he talked she had done some damage to him.

ALLAUDIN MATHIEU: I was both sexually attracted to Elaine and afraid of her. She was over the top, but with great conviction. The only thing to say about everything she did was, *That's Elaine.* I knew her when she was young and there was no stopping her. Turns out there was.

HEYWARD ERLICH: The theater was on the second floor of a former Chinese restaurant. It was a six- or seven-night-a-week show, unlike community theater now, which is Thursday, Friday, Saturday afternoon—there's nobody there on Monday, Tuesday, Wednesday.

ANDREW DUNCAN: It was a long, narrow building, tin ceiling, paint peeling. Paul Sills and I were the only ones who had any carpenter experience, so we built the stage. It was about six or eight feet by ten or twelve feet. For the background, we had these huge doorlike louvers that spun on these steel cylinders. There were panels in between, and up above were openings that you could use as windows or a balcony or whatever for *Romeo and Juliet*-type scenes. It was very versatile. I painted each panel a different color, and I remember Mike Nichols, onstage one night during rehearsal, he stopped and he said, "Tell me, Paul, how in the fuck am I going to do this scene in this riot of color?"

Everybody pantomimed, which is unusual at first, but you get used to it. The word was "accept": accept what was said, accept what was done. We didn't wear makeup. We didn't wear costumes. You wore shorts if it was hot. You had sneakers on, and you took your shirt off onstage. Mike never did that. He was always more aware of costume. Elaine was raw and raunchy. I never saw it, but I heard that she used to go onstage without underwear—she would literally flash the audience. You could hear gasps every once in a while.

ALLAUDIN MATHIEU: I was the intermission pianist. Sometimes the crowds were pretty thin. But on the weekends, there were times when the joint was jumping. The intelligentsia of the University of Chicago came, including my professors. It was an underground hit. The bar was just a bar for working-class people, so you've also got people wandering in, wondering what the heck this was.

ANDREW DUNCAN: We did a scene called "Football Comes to the University of Chicago." The whole idea of the University of Chicago having a football team was funny in itself. Mike was in it, Shelley [Berman], and Mark Gordon. I played the coach. I'd say, "There's a two-hundred-fifty-pound lineman coming across the line, and he's just going to smear you," and Mike would say, "Couldn't we *discuss* this?"

David [Shepherd] didn't like scenes like that. He wanted a workers' theater, and one night he got them. Steelworkers with helmets. These guys started heckling from the audience. They almost started a fight. Mike was ready to run out the back door.

JOYCE PIVEN: Mike and I went to the theater together one night. And Byrne Piven came and we started talking and he said, "Come on, let's leave." I said, "No, I'm here with Mike." But one thing led to another, and I left with him. My son, Jeremy, would make jokes with Diane and Mike, saying, "You could've been my father."

Mike used to follow Byrne around, because Byrne was the only Method-trained actor in the company. So Mike would go home with Byrne on the El and ask, "How do you do that?"

JOY CARLIN: After I'd graduated from the university, I went to Yale School of Drama for two years. At the end of the second year, I got a call from Paul to come back, because he'd started the Playwrights Theatre at the Chinese restaurant.

Mike and I looked at each other and said, "Do you know how to act?" I didn't. I'd spent two years at Yale, but I came out of there not really feeling secure. Of course, now I know, with many years of experience, it takes a long time whether someone's teaching you or not. So I went to New York, and then he went. We both got into Lee Strasberg's class. I was living with some girlfriends from the university, in a terrific apartment on Eighty-Seventh Street. Mike was across the street in a brownstone, in a terrible little room with a shared toilet on the floor. We saw a lot of each other. He was working at Howard Johnson's or something, and he was so poor. He told me he was eating the mustard and ketchup off the tables.

We were all sort of scared to death of Strasberg. Gene Hackman and George Morrison were in the class; Inger Stevens; Marilyn Monroe was in the back row. Mike was, of course, interested in the girls. The first day was exercises. You had to pick something to do that you would ordinarily do in private. People chose what Lee called tasteless things. We saw Marilyn take a shower.

MAUREEN DOWD: Mike told me that he called Marilyn Monroe to work on a scene. I said, "Are you sure you weren't hitting on her?" and he said, "I wouldn't have dared dream of it." He said, "A woman with a famous breathy voice answered, and somebody said, 'Hello,' and I said, 'Hi, is Marilyn there?' and she said, 'No, she's not,' and I said, 'Well, this is Mike. I'm in a class with her. Could you take a message?' and she said, 'Well, it's a holiday,' because it was the Fourth of July weekend. That to her was an excuse for not taking a message for herself."

SAM WASSON: That was a lonely, depressing period. Mike didn't have any money. And his face is not very distinctive. It's not even a strange face. It's certainly not a beautiful face. I don't think Mike *has* a face. He doesn't look like anything. Mike recognized that, and took stock of himself, and said, I'm not going to be an actor looking like this. Plus, he missed Elaine.

JOY CARLIN: I moved into his apartment eventually. That room was just a horrific mess. It had crap all over the floor and it smelled of acetone. Mike went back to Chicago, and then that led to Mike and Elaine.

JANET COLEMAN: Mike came in the sort of second wave of the Compass Theatre. They were beginning to professionalize a little bit. They were importing actors from New York. I don't think all of them had that sophistication that he had. If you were from Chicago, you hadn't seen *A Streetcar Named Desire*.

ANDREW DUNCAN: Shepherd called a meeting and said, "We've got two actors coming out that Sills has hired in New York: Severn Darden and a guy named Michael Nichols."

JEFFREY SWEET: Mike carried a piece of paper in his wallet of a joke that Severn came up with. Severn was improvising, playing a marine biologist, and at one point he says, "Of motion, the oyster has but a dim racial memory." Mike said whenever he was depressed, he would take that out and say, "I know somebody who could spontaneously make a joke like that."

When Shelley Berman joined the Compass, he discovered that these people actually had read all these Great Books, and was permanently mortified. Shelley did not get along terribly well with the others. They recognized that he had talent, but his ambition was too naked and his desperation was too naked. And he was also a little bit older than the others. He felt, *Here I am at this age, and I failed.* But he knew there was an opportunity here.

JANET COLEMAN: Of all of them, Mike Nichols and Shelley Berman had the least involvement in the political ambitions of Shepherd and Sills.

SAM WASSON: Shelley would always negate onstage to get a laugh. Someone would say, "Do you want to pet the bunny?" and Shelley would say, "That's not a bunny." He was the unintentional instigator of "Yes, and."

ANDREW DUNCAN: Mike hated working with him. They, of course, were fighting over Elaine. Shelley did funny stuff, but I didn't like working with him either, because every scene I ever did with him—we'd improvise one night, and the next night when we tried to repeat it, he would steal lines that I had come up with.

Once a month on your night off, you did a few shows for community kids. "Little Red Riding Hood" or "Rip Van Winkle," something like that. Mike did that too, but he would always insist on working with Elaine. I remember going onstage after Elaine had just finished a scene. There was always a chair that Mike sat in, and then surrounding it were these stamped-out butts of Kent Micronite filters.

He didn't really go out of his way to come up with scenes with anybody else. When we'd get suggestions form the audience, Mike would sit there very glum and say, "There's nothing that appeals to me."

JEFFREY SWEET: Mike is playing somebody who's going to be called in front of the House Un-American Activities Committee. Severn, who's playing his lawyer, comes in and says, "Great news: You don't have to testify!" Beat. Severn says, "Mike, you're not giving me any reaction. I've just given you this great news!" And Mike, under the influence of Strasberg, says, "I didn't believe you." Severn goes out and comes back in doing somersaults, shouting, "Hooray!" And Mike turns to him and says, "I still don't believe you."

JOYCE PIVEN: Mike was good, though he didn't excel as an actor. But he was a comic genius.

HEYWARD ERLICH: He was much more interesting in person than he was on the stage. I think his big discovery was that his genius was not in being a serious actor but in doing a form of comedy that was revolutionary at the time. It was breakthrough stuff.

When I later heard some of Mike and Elaine's stuff on a record, I was blown away by it. Because it was not only marvelous in itself, it was doubly marvelous coming from someone who I never imagined would achieve this. I mean, Mike did not seem destined for fame and achievement. How he turned it around, I have no idea.

JANET COLEMAN: Mike said himself, "Elaine could improvise with anybody. I could only improvise with Elaine."

LAURA PIERCE (*actress*): Mike said, "That was the secret of Elaine and me, that we knew all about each other—all about each other. We had an absolutely mutual frame of reference. Even if you're not that good in the beginning—and I wasn't very good in the beginning—once you have someone who knows you that completely, you can do some very nice things onstage." Finding your people—people you're drawn to, that you want to work with, that you connect with on some level—that was very important to him.

SAM WASSON: Their first great comedy sketch was "Teenagers." These are two teenagers nervous about making out. You don't see a lot of comedy around young people's sexuality in 1955. Even grown-ups aren't making out. Sex is something that married people do, and they do it somehow in separate beds. No one knows what to do with sex, and here Mike and Elaine are doing it as teenagers, and they're doing it with anxiety, which means they're doing it with a degree of psychological reality that had never been seen before. It's a breakthrough in sexuality. It's a breakthrough in psychological naturalism. And it's a breakthrough in form.

JANET COLEMAN: The other actors would run back from wherever they were smoking to see Nichols and May when they took the stage. They wanted to see what they would do next.

HEYWARD ERLICH[4]: His new characters were the Mike of a previous period. The Nebbish, The Schlemiel, The Snobby Sophisticate—all the types he played with such perfection—were Mike himself.

ALLAUDIN MATHIEU: I got to sit there and watch Elaine and Mike go through their early stuff, and it was amazing, absolutely

---

4. Coleman, *The Compass*, 129.

amazing. Subsequently, through Second City, I met a lot of bright people, but I never, never saw improvisation so crisp, so sparkling, and so important. It was as though I was seeing something that had never been created before created in front of my eyes, and, indeed, that's what was happening. Mike and Elaine had such extraordinary insight into and investment in each other's psyche. When they did scenes together, it was like you never saw people so naked in your life.

Incidentally, they fucked up a lot. We forget that when you're around a new sensibility or new art form being built—you forget about all the failures. However, there were some scenes that just happened. The "Teenagers" scene was one of them. From time to time, I was there when they did happen, and there was an ebullience. This is the last thing they would have ever said, but it was just like a divine ray had come through. Some energy had come through them, and at times like that artists experience two things. They experience mania, but they also experience total ego loss, because it's not them—something's happened. Me and my college friends were too young to drink, but we would go to just watch, and we'd go back to the dorm room and pretend to be them and improvise scenes.

JEFFREY SWEET: A turning point happened when somebody before a show said to Mike, "Hey, I hear you guys did this great scene about two teenagers in a car last week. Are you going to do it this week?" And Elaine said, "We don't repeat scenes." And Mike said, "Why not? Why don't we repeat them? Why don't we polish them, and make them really good?"

SAM WASSON: Del Close would say there's only spot improvisation. Mike would say that what they did was as improvisational as a jazz musician riffing off a melody; you know the melody, but you don't know from moment to moment necessarily what's going to happen.

JANET COLEMAN: They would develop them through improvisation, then freeze them, more or less.

DAVID SHEPHERD (*producer*)[5]: Mike had the capacity to remember everything he said the night before, and block it, and redo it, and go for the same point. Elaine was interested in playing to the drunken sailor in the audience. Or nun. She always knew that last night is not tonight.

MARK GORDON (*actor*)[6]: Michael's role was the commentator. He always stayed outside. He was keenly aware of the audience. Elaine thought of what the audience *should* want. She didn't give a damn.

ANDREW DUNCAN: He was always directing the scene while he was doing it. Elaine would never do that. Her bursts were spontaneous. I always felt that in their act, she was really the driving force.

SHELLEY BERMAN (*comedian*)[7]: Elaine May was also a true improvisationist. Pure. It was a cause of friction many times between her and Mike when she would deviate from that which had already been set. Mike knew a good thing when he came upon it and he wanted to stay with it. Mike as a director now does not insist on these results and does not insist on going for a laugh moment. His idea is that you be true to the action. It seems to be a contradiction of what I had noticed in him much earlier when he worked with Elaine. If there was a laugh to be gotten and she didn't set up the feed line, he would work with her until she did. He did everything but lasso her.

EUGENE TROOBNICK (*actor*)[8]: [People] think improvisation is getting up and saying funny lines. When you practice it, you learn that funny lines aren't it. The rule is to be truthful to the moment, and the funny stuff will flow from that. With Mike and Elaine, those rules did not apply. They could get up and say one funny line after another.

---

5. Coleman, *The Compass*, 167.

6. Coleman, *The Compass*, 146–47.

7. Jeffrey Sweet, *Something Wonderful Right Away: An Oral History of the Second City and the Compass Players* (1978; New York: Limelight Editions, 2004), 127.

8. Coleman, *The Compass*, 130.

Verbally, Mike Nichols was the fastest person I've ever known. He was a consummate wit.

ANDREW DUNCAN[9]: He was developing an approach that was anti-Viola. (He always rebelled against the Viola stuff.) In Viola's thing, you stay within the reality of the character. Mike would always step outside it. He was always for the wisecrack, the brilliant remark.

SAM WASSON: No one intended this theater to be funny. But when Mike and Elaine took off, there was nothing you could do. Sills's dream of a community theater and Shepherd's dream of a political theater were now compromised by these highly verbal, highly analytical Jews who became the stars.

One day, Mike's mother called him and said, "Mike, it's your mother. Do you remember me?" and Mike was like, *Thank you, Mom, for that little Jewish nightmare,* and calls Elaine immediately to say, "Let's do this tonight."

We look at it as a cliché now, but a mother in the 1950s was God on Earth; so was a father, by the way. The family unit was as unassailable as America. Bob Hope could always make a mother-in-law joke, that was safe, but to criticize the woman who gave you life? And the way they did it was merciless. By the end of the piece, you see that the son, far from being the victim, is actually colluding in his own infantilization. It's devastating.

ANDREW DUNCAN: Mike had a wonderful satirical tone, and he did accents—he was probably the most versatile in that department. But I always got the feeling he really wanted to be a director. I always felt that. When they left the Compass, I was amazed to find out that he and Elaine were going to do an act.

SHELLEY BERMAN[10]: Mike and Elaine and I did try to become a trio. This was while we were still at Compass, but we knew that

---

9. Coleman, *The Compass*, 179.
10. Sweet, *Something Wonderful Right Away*, 129–30.

Compass was going to break up soon. The problem was Mike didn't want to do things with me. He admired my work, as far as I knew. I think he did admire my work. But our personalities were so involved. Occasionally there would be a quarrel . . .

The interesting thing was how much I wanted to work with him. *God*, I loved working with him! When we did work together, it worked out fine, but there was resistance. Eventually, when we tried to become an act together, I was asking them to please think up some things with me included because they had too many things they were doing together. I did do two things with Elaine. One was "The Driving Lesson," in which I taught her how to drive. It was very funny . . .

I also did a thing with Elaine we created one night at Compass, an improvisation called "The Lost Dime." . . . Eventually that routine became Mike and Elaine's. I made a single out of it called "Franz Kafka on the Telephone," but it was never really a dynamite routine. But the duet version was a dynamite routine.

Anyway, we weren't doing things as a threesome, which made it difficult for us as a trio. We had no three-person scenes. I did do one thing with them in "Pirandello." I was a stage manager who originally began it by describing it and then came on later. But "Pirandello" was essentially a two-person scene. It didn't absolutely require the other character. So we had no real three-person scenes and we abandoned the idea of doing the act together.

JEFFREY SWEET: They were kicking around doing a trio, largely because Elaine didn't want to lose the telephone sketch. But Mike really didn't want to work with Shelley, and there was not a lot of competition. Shelley and Elaine once did a scene where they're a couple in the Catskills, and Shelley knocks at the door. "Who is it?" Shelley says, "Baby, I've got something for you!" And Elaine says, "Shove it under the door." That was sort of a metaphor for the relationship. Shelley invents his solo act because nobody else would work with him. Nichols and May continued to develop their work at the Crystal Palace in St. Louis.

SAM WASSON: They're away from the political and metaphysical preoccupations of Shepherd and Sills, and under the directorship of Ted Flicker, who was very much into entertainment. The group said, "Okay, we've got to find a way to make these improvs work. It's not enough to just be political and to improvise. We want to satisfy an audience here. How are we going to do that? What are the rules for this thing?" That's when they developed the "Westminster Place Kitchen Rules." They lived at Westminster Place, and Elaine and Ted Flicker came up with a list of these rules, all of which are negotiable, with the exception of one, which I think at first they called "Don't negate," but it's the same thing as "Yes, and."

JOY CARLIN: I studied with Lee Strasberg and went to Yale School of Drama, but when I teach or when I'm acting, my technique definitely involves improv, because it makes you spontaneous, makes you aware when you're being phony. For Paul, it led to Story Theatre, which became a big phenomenon.

JANET COLEMAN: Unbeknown to any of their fellow players, Mike, Elaine, Del Close, and Nancy Ponder had talked about forming an improv group and going to New York. And according to Del and Nancy, they took actors' photos on a flatbed truck. They were all set to leave St. Louis and form their own company. Mike and Elaine said, "Pool your money and send us to New York. We have an appointment with this manager, Jack Rollins." They audition for Rollins, and lo and behold, they get the job. And that was the last Del and Nancy ever heard from them.

There was a book written about Del Close, and Mike told the author that the story wasn't true, Del was a chronic liar, and he made this up. Except I had it corroborated by a number of people who were there—Nancy Ponder, Del Close, Severn Darden, Ted Flicker, David Shepherd. Nancy Ponder showed me the pictures they had taken as a foursome on the flatbed truck. I think Mike didn't want to be known as treacherous. They left all these people behind, and those people began to struggle. The Compass was failing.

ANDREW DUNCAN: There was a kind of reluctance to be part of a group with Mike. It's just something I sensed. I don't think he ever felt at home in Compass. I hope it wasn't us, because everybody opened up to him.

ALLAUDIN MATHIEU: When Mike came here, he wasn't anybody. He was literally an alien, and he had to construct a self. He had to construct a way to be in the world, and I think he tried everything out through improvisation. He was the lost kid. He was the sexual supplicant. He was the snob. He was the know-it-all. He knew exactly who each guy was, and that's why it was funny. He was really searching, and he found aspects of himself.

SAM WASSON: Elaine liberated Mike's unconscious. Those improvisations could not have happened without Elaine, just like a patient-therapist, and this analogy was not lost on them, by the way. Look at how many patient-therapists they played. She was Dr. May for Mike, and a lot of the time you will see in these pieces Mike being not the person in power, but the scared, nervous one, and that was not Mike's outward persona. He came to grips with that shadow side of himself.

JANET COLEMAN: He stopped improvising. Elaine really never did. She would go to these workshops, always experimenting.

ALLAUDIN MATHIEU: Years later, I hear that Paul and Mike are at lunch, and Paul asks Mike, "What are you up to?" and Mike says, "Well, I directed this, and I'm going to be directing that, and then I have two shows on Broadway"—one incredible success after another. Then he says, "What are you up to?" And Paul says, "Well, I started up a little theater, it's called Story Theatre. We just take these scripts that I develop, and work them out, and then we give shows for the community." And Mike said, "Well, you're still active, and I'm still passive." Mike always felt that he was responding.

JANET COLEMAN: It is amazing how disparate their paths were, Sills's and Nichols's.

JEFFREY SWEET: After Paul Sills died [in 2008], Mike felt that he was now the daddy of the community, and he really assumed those responsibilities. Some of it was, quietly, financial. I know this was the case with Barbara Harris. Now that Barbara's dead, I can say this. He wanted to get some money to Barbara but he didn't want her to know it was coming from him, because he didn't want to deal with her gratitude or her sense of indebtedness. He said, "Do you have any ideas?" I said, "Well, she's in Chicago, maybe you could fund a teaching gig at the Northlight Theatre." And sure enough, Northlight got in touch with Barbara and hired her to do some teaching, and she never knew that Mike funded it.

PETER GALLAGHER: I once asked Mike, "What do you think is important about raising kids?" He said, "Well, just as long as they know that things that start out poorly don't always end poorly, and things that start out well don't always end well. That, and study improv." He felt sure that it was his experience with Elaine, and his background in improv, which gave him the facility and the confidence and the words to deal with the studios. It allowed him to think on his feet and not crumble in the face of opposition. Both my kids have now studied improv.

SAM WASSON: Mike is not going to become a career improviser, so, in retrospect, he's going to regard this Compass work as a stepping stone on the way to this other thing. That reduces, in his mind, a little bit of what was going on in the Compass, because it's not polished, and, finally, that's who Mike is. His view of it was, *Isn't it wonderful that as kids we got to do this? What an incredible learning tool.* But it wasn't the full story of who he was.

A hit on the nightclub circuit, Nichols and May became overnight stars after appearing on *Omnibus,* a Sunday variety show hosted by Alistair Cooke. For a period, they were frequent guests on the national radio show *Monitor,* where they would improvise live in the studio, as seen here. *(© Paul Fusco/Magnum Photos)*

CHAPTER 3

Premise Envy

JACK ROLLINS (*manager*)[1]: I was [Nichols and May's] personal manager for about eight years. I had a small office up on the roof of the Plaza Hotel, and in this little office they began to do what they do, which is improvisational comedy. I had never seen this technique up to that point, and I almost couldn't believe what I was seeing.

They asked for an opening line and a closing line, which was their usual request when they started a sketch. Suddenly comedy was being formed right in front of my eyes, and I mean comedy that was side-splitting and irresistible. I was howling! They were writing hilarious comedy—not on a typewriter, or with a pencil in hand, but on their feet. I was awed by it. I fell in love with these two people immediately.

JAMES GAVIN (*writer*)[2]: Starting in the late 1940s right after the war, New York City became this remarkable melting pot of talent. The Broadway musical was at its height, television was just being born and introduced to millions of households, the long-playing record came into being, and New York gave birth to seemingly a little intimate nightclub on every other corner. These clubs became places for young, unknown kids to try out their acts and break into Broadway or television, which at that time was centered in New York. It really was a kind

---

1. "Nichols & May—Take Two," *American Masters*, directed by Phillip Schopper, produced by Julian Schlossberg, season 10, episode 5, aired May 22, 1996, on PBS.

2. Courtesy of Julian Schlossberg.

of fairy-tale time in show business that has never been repeated, and I don't think ever will be.

TOM LEHRER (*comedian*): These days, cabaret just means some middle-age lady singing old songs, but then, it was several acts. And the Blue Angel was really one of the best. Four people did twenty, twenty-five minutes; then there'd be a second show. It was a small place—150, 200 seats, maybe even smaller. And it was expensive for those days because there was a cover charge *and* they charged you for drinks. But it was the place to be in New York for somebody like me.

They always had a straight singer who would start—when I played, the singer was Johnny Mathis—then a comic, then another singer, and then some other comedy act. You'd go in, and there was a small room with a piano and a bar—Bobby Short used to play there occasionally—and then the main room where the so-called entertainment was. Upstairs were the dressing rooms.

The crowd was mostly New Yorkers, maybe some tourists staying in hotels. They dressed nice, they were with-it people, read the newspapers. A friend of mine used the term "self-congratulatory humor": you laugh because you get the reference. If I said "Schopenhauer," it didn't matter what the sentence was, that would get a laugh.

So you'd go to the Blue Angel the way you'd watch Jay Leno, to see these acts that you'd never heard of. But once you had Johnny Carson on TV, there's no point in going to a nightclub, so these places all folded—the Crystal Palace in St. Louis, Mister Kelly's in Chicago, the hungry i and the Purple Onion in San Francisco.

JACK ROLLINS[3]: Max Gordon, who owned the Village Vanguard, owned the Blue Angel with Herbert Jacoby. I took Mike and Elaine down for an audition, and they were hired. We booked them for two weeks, which was extended to ten, as the excitement about them built.

---

3. "Nichols & May—Take Two," *American Masters*, PBS.

MILTON BERLE (*comedian*)[4]: My late wife and I went into a place called the Blue Angel. We used to make all the clubs. It was in the '50s—not the year, though it was that too—but the '50s, in Manhattan. I'd heard of Nichols and May, but I didn't know they were playing there because this cheap guy who owned the club didn't spend any money on publicity. I even bawled him out about that after I saw them. Their billing was so small, dogs could pee on it.

I was so surprised at their talent and their manner and their style. I said to the people at my table, "Boy, this is something. I've never seen anything like it in my life." I knew they had it. They had the knack. They didn't act; it was real, and it was honest. After a few weeks, they were jammed. I had nothing to do with that. It got great notices.

TOM LEHRER: We shared a bill at the Blue Angel. We chatted, and we certainly knew each other, but you know Leonard Bernstein's father's famous remark: "How did I know he'd grow up to be Leonard Bernstein?" How did I know that this guy Mike Nichols was going to become what he became? If I had known he was going to be this great director, I would've asked him for advice. But of course, since I was the star, he probably wouldn't have dared to make suggestions. He knew about me because he had been a disc jockey at WFMT in Chicago, and he played my songs occasionally.

On the nights when it wasn't full, the help would sit in the front room and kill time talking showbiz. But I don't think Mike and Elaine did that much. They probably were rehearsing. I would either come in early and see their first show, or I would stay and see their last. So I got to know a number of their routines by heart.

They asked the audience for the first line, the last line, and a style. The last line was a great idea, because then the light man knew that it was over. Otherwise you could just go on and on. I remember seeing The Committee in San Francisco, and the people would huddle together for a moment and decide what they were going to do. But Mike and Elaine didn't do that. Part of the fun was they didn't know

---

4. Courtesy of Julian Schlossberg.

who they were, who the other one was. My favorite example was, the first line was something very romantic, flowery, suggestive even—a declaration of love. And so Mike said this line, and Elaine said, "What the hell kind of thing is that to say to your mother?"

STANLEY DONEN (*director*)[5]: I saw them do an improvised sketch, and you knew they were doing it on the spur of the moment because they asked members of the audience to shout out an opening line, which could be, "I'd like some tomato soup," and then someone else would shout out the closing line, which seemed as far away as possible from that—I don't know, "The atom bomb just exploded." And then a third person would shout out, "Do it in the form of William Shakespeare," or Molière, or a Japanese Noh play. They had those three pieces of information and they were off. That really was a trick the audience had never seen.

TOM LEHRER: The trouble was that they'd always get Shakespeare or Tennessee Williams for the style. But one night I wasn't there—I cursed my luck that I missed it—I heard that somebody suggested Edgar Rice Burroughs, the author of *Tarzan*. And they were thrilled, because, at last: a challenge!

JULES FEIFFER (*cartoonist*)[6]: You won't find people picking literary classics in improvisational comedy today. Nobody in the audience is going to say Henry James or Tolstoy. They're not part of the grammar anymore. You're much more likely to get showbiz references.

BUCK HENRY (*screenwriter*): Mike once told me that he was very well read, but Elaine, not necessarily. She simply intuited what great writers sounded like from knowing about them.

JAMES GAVIN[7]: The old cliché about lines forming around the block really was the case with them, literally within weeks. That's why

---

5. Courtesy of Julian Schlossberg.

6. "Nichols & May—Take Two," *American Masters*, PBS.

7. Courtesy of Julian Schlossberg.

they were picked up so quickly for *Omnibus*. Within months they were appearing regularly on all the top variety shows, having sprung out of a little nightclub on East Fifty-Fifth Street.

Television was, I think, the key to making a lot of these people stars, and that was certainly true of Nichols and May. TV was still an infant medium throughout the '50s. There were variety shows galore, and all these hours of programming which needed to be filled, and one obvious way was to go into these nightclubs and pick young people out. If you made a hit at the Blue Angel, which was the hottest club of its kind, then chances were good that within about two months you would be on Ed Sullivan or Steve Allen or Dave Garroway or *Omnibus*.

JACK ROLLINS[8]: In no time at all, the whole city was talking about them. It was like a white phosphorescent flash. The press kept coming in, and were just completely, totally knocked out, and suddenly Mike and Elaine were overnight stars—but only in New York City. In order to become true stars, they needed television. And that was very difficult to get, because they do not do jokes, they do situations, which take time, and time is the enemy of television. It's all a sound bite of twenty seconds. They needed eight, ten solid minutes, but that's half a show, and who's going to sit for that in television?

The staff for Jack Paar came down to the Blue Angel and were completely awestruck. They asked Mike and Elaine to come up to their office, and I accompanied them, to perform for the rest of the staff. And of course the same thing happened: everybody thought they were just utterly wonderful and wanted them on the show.

So they set the booking and told Mike and Elaine, just do what you did in the office. Both Elaine and Mike said, "We can't do it, we have to do it fresh." They were full of trepidation because they never had the situation of having just done an improvisation and then being asked to repeat it. Now, this was not accepted by the staff. They thought, *Of course it worked, we saw it work.* I had no formed feelings about it at all because it was all so new to me. Mike and Elaine decided they would take a chance and do it.

---

8. "Nichols & May—Take Two," *American Masters*, PBS.

And they went on, and Jack introduced them in that hesitant manner of his: "I haven't seen these people, but my staff tells me they're wonderful." He was not going out on a limb for something he hadn't seen. On the show, he had a couple of regulars, Jonathan Winters and Dody Goodman. Mike and Elaine began to do the improvisation that they had done in the office, and it didn't work. They should have done what they always did and have somebody in the audience give them an opening and a closing line. It wasn't terrible, but it didn't work as it should. At which point, Jack pushed Jonathan and Dody into improvising something. The whole thing was pretty disastrous. So that was their first television experience.

ROBIN WILLIAMS (*actor*)[9]: I vaguely remember seeing them when I was a kid because my father used to watch the old *Tonight Show* with Jack Paar. It hit me later—through therapy, I realized that Nichols and May is deeply embedded in my psyche. I have premise envy. I remember being three and going, *God, they're amazing. Who are those topical people, Mother? I have to stop breastfeeding for a moment and listen.*

RICHARD LEWIS (*comedian*)[10]: You'd be watching the Cleavers on television and switch to Paar introducing Mike and Elaine and go, *Whoa—where did this sensibility come from?*

STEVE ALLEN (*TV host*)[11]: Having heard how wonderfully funny they were, we booked them. It was that simple. I had not seen them perform before they appeared on our show. We were opposite Ed Sullivan for a good part of that prime-time stretch, but his show was pure variety. Ours was 90 percent comedy and 10 percent variety. They wouldn't have made nearly as much sense with Ed, because we were already doing a good deal of satire and cleverer material than one might have found in the typical East Coast nightclub. They were right at home with us and we provided a warm, loving embrace to

9. "Nichols & May—Take Two," *American Masters*, PBS.
10. "Nichols & May—Take Two," *American Masters*, PBS.
11. "Nichols & May—Take Two," *American Masters*, PBS.

them. Had they been interested, they could easily have become permanent members of our cast.

JAMES GAVIN[12]: If you think of network television comedy today and then go back in time to the late '50s, when Nichols and May could go on Steve Allen and make a splash in a sketch that talked about Bernard Baruch and Albert Schweitzer, you can see how far we've come from a period that was a lot more accepting of sophisticated humor. It was aimed at the highest possible common denominator while still winning the hearts of millions. They came up with sketches that rang a bell in everyone, even if they'd never heard of Bertrand Russell.

As intellectual as the humor was, and as highbrow and filled with references to classical music, scientists, authors, and playwrights, and so forth, they were enacting scenes that everybody had lived through: a man sparring with a telephone operator, a man trying to buy a sixty-five-dollar funeral and finding out that that got him nothing more than a body dumped in a hole, basically. These were scenes that anyone could relate to, but their flair for picking up on the pretentious aspects of these individuals really struck a chord. They were truly intellectuals and yet their humor was not limited to an intellectual audience. This was not surface humor. They didn't go for the obvious, ever.

JACK ROLLINS[13]: There was a show called *Omnibus* on Sunday afternoons. For some reason they had a prime-time special, and they had two hours to fill. They asked Mike and Elaine to come on, and I asked for two spots. Now, on this show, they had *time*. And the whole nation saw what we would see in a little cabaret. And that was the beginning of Nichols and May. The reaction was monumental.

TONY WALTON (*set designer*): I think that Elaine was the one who was kind of uneasy with this new fan following, whereas Mike was kind of taking it in stride, possibly even giving the impression: *Well, of course!*

---

12. Courtesy of Julian Schlossberg.
13. "Nichols & May—Take Two," *American Masters*, PBS.

JULES FEIFFER: I was working at a schlock cartoon studio called Terrytoons. I came home one night—I was living alone—and had my usual dinner, tuna noodle casserole, and I had *Omnibus* on, and Alistair Cooke, the emcee, introduced this new young couple, Mike Nichols and Elaine May.

I mean, it was as if I had thought this up, except it was funnier and better. I didn't know there was anybody working this vein except me. They had reached the end of the road before I had even gotten halfway there. At the end of it, I said, I have to meet these guys. I later discovered that they had been following me in the [*Village*] *Voice*.

Within a month or so, they were opening at the Village Vanguard, and I raced to see them and became a groupie. I must have seen their nightclub act a dozen times or more. They didn't seem to be professionals playing off each other by script. It all seemed real. The frustration seemed legitimate. And the electricity between them was very, very real and quite exciting to see. What you saw was not just a comedy act. It was a piece of drama, of theater, because that's what they came out of—not vaudeville, like the old comics.

If you're young and educated, or semi-educated, as I was, there was nothing out there in print or any kind of media that represented you. There was still Bob Hope and Red Skelton and Burns and Allen, but however wonderful they were, they had nothing to do with the people I knew. Suddenly out of nowhere, this generation begins to form.

TONY WALTON: Mike was very interested in who else was doing anything in their vein, which was nobody, but the Beyond the Fringe people in England got closest, and they were all folks I knew well. Mike would ask me to bring any recordings of these guys back from London, which I did, and the Beyond the Fringe guys were desperate to get anything of Mike and Elaine, whom they'd heard about but weren't able to see much of in England.

ARTHUR PENN (*director*)[14]: I had spent the previous few years working on *The Colgate Comedy Hour*, and those comedians did a kind

---

14. "Nichols & May—Take Two," *American Masters*, PBS.

of orthodox comedy, stuff they'd developed in nightclubs. Martin and Lewis, and Bob Hope, and Eddie Cantor—all those people. When I got to New York, it was clear that that kind of comedy had exhausted itself. There was a desperate desire for a new voice. A new voice that took on the institutions of America with a kind of irreverence. This was the beginning of saying, *I'm not afraid of the government, I'm not afraid of the institutions.* Perhaps historically, one can even, from a fairly grand view, say that it's from these kinds of artists that genuine social change takes place.

STEVE ALLEN[15]: In the '50s we were coming out of a simpler, sweeter period—the Eisenhower period, the Ozzie and Harriet period, whatever you want to call it—into a comedy form which on the one hand was gentle and refined in its style, but was often saying something quite meaningful, something philosophically heavy. The times were both hip and square, but then mankind is both hip and square.

There were many of us—a statistical minority, but arithmetically, many of us—who were doing clever material, satire, takeoffs on popular forms: Mort Sahl, Shelley Berman, our own show, and the Sid Caesar show gang. It wasn't old-fashioned vaudeville comedy. That was great in its way, but it was old-fashioned.

BOB NEWHART (*comedian*): Nichols and May were really the start of this new shift in comedy. It was a new direction. There weren't jokes. It wasn't the Buddy Hacketts and Alan Kings. I was an enormous fan of theirs, in addition to Shelley [Berman] and Lenny [Bruce], of course, and George Gobel, though George never really got the recognition he deserved.

RICHARD LEWIS[16]: Lenny Bruce, Shelley Berman, Nichols and May, Bob Newhart, Mort Sahl: these are Mount Rushmore types. They had an intellectual bent to stand-up. A sensibility that up until that time really wasn't around. And it gave people more courage to be in touch with their feelings onstage.

---

15. "Nichols & May—Take Two," *American Masters*, PBS.
16. Ibid.

MARTIN SHORT (*actor*): What's fascinating about the Nichols and May stuff, if you play it right now, is that it could have been done yesterday, because it's not tied to references, it's tied to human behavior.

SAM WASSON: I asked Mike: "All the theater that you're seeing in the '50s, what's exciting about it is that it's Kazan and it's Method. What comedic performances did you see that brought that kind of naturalism?" He talked about seeing Ruth Gordon in *The Matchmaker*. He remembered that as a comedic performance that did not sell reality short to get a laugh, which a lot of the comedy of the '50s does. You have to suspend your disbelief for a lot of '50s comedy. You have to go with a certain amount of schtick, burlesquery, and buffoonery. Jerry Lewis, Frank Tashlin, George Abbott: these guys are not really dealing with psychological reality. That's Mike and Elaine's breakthrough: they were the Kazans of comedy.

ROBIN WILLIAMS[17]: Mike said they used to go watch Lenny Bruce, because they'd be playing back-to-back some places, and he would watch Lenny, every night, just go on and play. It was an amazing time for them to be doing comedy, after the war, all this repressed intellectual energy just went *BOOM*.

JAMES GAVIN[18]: Prior to 1957, nightclub humor was more sophisticated than your usual Catskills or Borscht Belt brand of humor, but it still dealt with gentle topics in a gentle manner. It didn't stray too much farther than the home, the community, making fun of Hollywood stars or television personalities. In 1957, 1958, 1959, that started to change in a big way, and Nichols and May were at the center of that. Lenny Bruce, Mort Sahl, Shelley Berman, Dick Gregory, they weren't content to let things be in that '50s manner and just pretend that everything was all right, because obviously it wasn't. One article that I recall in *The Christian Science Monitor* in the early '60s summed

---

17. "Nichols & May—Take Two," *American Masters*, PBS.
18. Courtesy of Julian Schlossberg.

up the whole problem. It said, "Who can laugh in the shadow of nuclear stockpiles?"

TOM BROKAW (*news anchor*)[19]: Until Nichols and May came along, we were all hostage to our parents' brand of humor. Nothing wrong with that stuff, but we needed our own. I was at the University of South Dakota, which I've often described as well outside the beltway of hip and cool. I would sit in my apartment, on my own late at night, doing what passed for a South Dakota beatnik thing: burning some crayons into a Coke bottle and trying to make a candle out of it, dimming the lights, and listening to Nichols and May. It was like a voice from another planet. It said to me, *There's intelligent life out there, beyond this barren cultural landscape*. It allowed me, in my mind at least, to go down the steps of some smoky cabaret in Chicago, or to the Village in New York, without leaving my tiny basement apartment in Vermillion, South Dakota. You felt kind of like a sophisticate, even though you didn't deserve the title. I think there were a lot of us like that, across the country, in college rooms or in darkened apartments, listening to *Monitor* on the radio on Saturday afternoons. Mike and Elaine connected these people—intellectually, emotionally, culturally—in ways that I'm not sure even they could have appreciated. Radio's a magical instrument, it really is.

STEVE MARTIN (*comedian*)[20]: When I was seventeen or eighteen, a friend of mine gave me some comedy records, and among them were Nichols and May. I'm trying to remember who it was now—I wish I could thank him. I used to listen to their records over and over, like music. I would play them at night and go to sleep to them. It was my first introduction to comedy that had an edge to it. It was the first time I ever heard irony in someone's voice. I had read it, but I had never heard someone deliver irony just in the tone of their voice.

LORNE MICHAELS (*producer*): I was in high school in Canada. When Beyond the Fringe arrived, then Nichols and May, and later

---

19. "Nichols & May—Take Two," *American Masters*, PBS.
20. Ibid.

[Monty] Python, we went, *Oh, these are writer-performers.* The same thing was happening in music, Neil Young and Joni Mitchell and Gordon Lightfoot. Something turned in the culture, and it's never been the same since.

These were really smart people with some level of sophistication and education. It was intoxicating. And then, I think because of the collapse of the studios in the late '60s, it started to spill over into movies. And in '75, we were finally able to spill it over a little bit into network television.

Mike and Buck and a few other people were the parent generation to what this became. I remember Mike and I had dinner one night, and he came back to the office with me. The writers and cast members just kept dropping in to ask something—Bill Murray and Dan Aykroyd and Gilda [Radner]. It was just an enormous level of excitement that he was actually here.

STEVE ALLEN[21]: Those of us in the new school were doing things in a fresh way. And we occasionally ran into objections from sponsors. Mike and Elaine displeased the funeral industry with their hysterically funny sketch about a poor slob whose father has just passed away. Almost every week we would get a few letters from people who'd say, *Well, if you think it's so funny to do a joke about a fireman, maybe nobody will come to your house if it burns down.* Sweet sentiments like that.

BOB NEWHART: I had just made a comedy record, it was just starting to get some notice, and I got a call do the Emmy Awards for that year. I was on it, and Mike and Elaine were on it. Their routine was a send-up of shampoo commercials. The producer went to Mike and Elaine and said, "Do you have another routine? Because our sponsor has a problem with that." I guess one of the sponsors was a shampoo manufacturer. And they said, "No. This is the one we want to do, and if we can't do it, then we don't want to be on the show." So they left.

---

21. "Nichols & May—Take Two," *American Masters*, PBS.

JULES FEIFFER[22]: I know that when I started my strip in the *Voice*, what I got less of was, "My, you're funny" or "My, you're original"— mostly what I got was people stopping me and saying, "How did you get away with that? How did you get that into print?" That's what one saw when Nichols and May were on television. It was the first time a man and a woman—or a boy and a girl in a car—actually talked about having sex. It had never been done before. It was as groundbreaking as, say, *The Graduate* was some years later.

TOM BROKAW[23]: You must remember that in the 1950s and early 1960s, America took itself very seriously. And then along come Nichols and May. It's like having a stuffed-shirt uncle walk into the room and Nichols and May stand up and undress him right there in front of you.

JACK ROLLINS[24]: They were shocking in their day, without question. They did things that were taboo. The famous sketch of two teenagers in a car, necking. This was not the kind of thing that you did. The funeral parlor sketch. The famous adultery sketch. People did not do comedy based on death in those days, or touch a subject like adultery. They were totally adventurous and totally innocent in a certain sense.

STANLEY DONEN[25]: I love the rocket scientist and the Jewish mother just browbeating her son until he's a bloody pulp. At the end, he says to her, "I feel awful." And she says, "Oh, honey, if I could believe that, I'd be the happiest mother in the world." That sums up everything about Jewish mothers in one joke—it encapsulates the nightmare.

JOHN LAHR: "I don't want my mouth to be full when my son calls me." I loved that sketch. It was all so smart and different. It was educated. It was psychological. It wasn't the kind of sketches that my father did, which were low comic.

---

22. "Nichols & May—Take Two," *American Masters*, PBS.
23. Ibid.
24. Ibid.
25. Courtesy of Julian Schlossberg.

JACK ROLLINS[26]: When they talked about mothers, they talked about your mother as well as theirs. They would uncover little dark niches that you felt but had never expressed—they expressed it for you.

JULES FEIFFER[27]: Everybody, of whatever background, had a Jewish mother. But nobody criticized or made fun of Mom before that, because we had just come out of a period when Mom was sacred, Mom was holy. Hard to believe now, but that's the way it was.

JEFFREY SWEET: I said, "Did your mothers ever recognize themselves in that?" And Mike said, "No, they would've said, 'I know a woman exactly like that.'"

RICHARD AVEDON[28]: We went to see Lenny Bruce at the Oak Room, Evelyn [Franklin], me, Mike, and whatever girl he was seeing. And I said, "My God, he's wonderful. I mean, he's really reinvented the language." I was raving about Lenny Bruce. Mike snapped at the waiter in a way that was so cruel, and I realized right away it was about my talking about Lenny Bruce. He must have recognized that Lenny Bruce was the real thing.

I once said something about the courage that he and Elaine had to tackle these issues of mortuaries, mothers, whatever it was. And he said, "We do it whenever it's part of the mainstream. There's no courage in what we do." He was saying, *Lenny Bruce goes into the unknown, and we know just how far to go.*

STEVE ALLEN[29]: Mike and Elaine, they could never have gotten into the kind of trouble and the degree of trouble that Lenny did. He was really hitting things very hard, whereas they worked with a more delicate, genteel approach. They were a little bit like a certain kind

---

26. "Nichols & May—Take Two," *American Masters*, PBS.
27. Ibid.
28. Courtesy of the John Lahr collection at the Howard Gotlieb Archival Research Center, Boston University.
29. "Nichols & May—Take Two," *American Masters*, PBS.

of cartoon character. I don't mean the Sunday-morning comic strip. I mean *The New Yorker* or Jules Feiffer sort of cartoon. In fact, some of their routines could have been written down with balloon captions and perceived as equally funny in that form.

ARTHUR PENN[30]: We were on the edge of a new movement forward, politically and socially: civil rights, concern about the nuclear bomb. There was a meeting at my apartment, the beginning of an anti-nuclear movement, that Mike and Elaine attended. And yet the country was simply not dealing with it.

This was a period, too, when psychoanalysis was very lively in this age group. New York was the place where many of the European analysts had taken up practice—it was a social phenomenon. The audience for Mike and Elaine—as well as probably Mike and Elaine themselves—was part of that psychoanalytic audience.

JULES FEIFFER[31]: Everybody was beginning to talk about analysis, and dropping Freudian terms. There was a strange mix of social conformity and the need to release intimate details of your life. I remember years ago at a *Village Voice* lunch, the staff was being photographed by a big magazine photographer. After the shoot, he sat down and started talking about his impotence. Twenty years ago somebody would have committed suicide before he talked about this, even in private. And now it's out there.

RICHARD LEWIS[32]: Not only do I remember when I first saw them—I remember when I first brought their albums in to my shrink! *Go listen to them! It's not just me—I'm not alone! Listen to Nichols and May, for crying out loud!* So I consider them one of those unconscious seeds which gave me the courage to ultimately find what I wanted to do, which is basically talk about my own anxiety. They dealt with anxiety and with stress, and with how hard it is for people to communicate directly, and

30. "Nichols & May—Take Two," *American Masters*, PBS.
31. Ibid.
32. Ibid.

they could slip in sexual tension through the thinnest line of dialogue. Their brains are fertile with anxiety, and I mean that in the most affectionate way. I listened to about an hour of their stuff last night, and it got me so jazzed to see my shrink tomorrow, you have no idea.

MILTON BERLE[33]: I'd like to take part of the credit for bringing them to California. When I got back to the coast, in '57 or something, I called up my very close friend Charlie Morrison, who owned a place in Beverly Hills called the Mocambo. About a week later, I got a call from Charlie, who said, "You know those two people you were taking about? Mike something and Elaine something?" I said, "Yeah." He said, "I spoke to their manager and I got them booked in here."

I don't want to tell tales out of school, but let's tell the truth: they were kind of nervous, and I would be too if I was about to debut someplace that I'd never been to before. We went to dinner at the Mocambo and I sat down with them and said, "Just cool it, they're going to love you. They have never seen anything like this out here."

STANLEY DONEN[34]: I first saw them at the Mocambo in Los Angeles. My reaction was so enormous that I kept wanting more. I thought of myself at that moment as their biggest fan, which is probably something a lot of people were trying to claim. They were hysterically funny if you got it, and a lot of people got it. Those moments where people explode on the scene come so rarely in life. I saw Marlon Brando, and that was a moment. I saw Barbra Streisand, and that was a moment. No other two people arrived together like that. You knew no one else could have written that material but the people who were speaking it.

WOODY ALLEN: I first saw them on one of those Sunday-night shows. They did the routine in which he interviews a vacuous movie star, and she talks about dating Albert Schweitzer. It was just flabbergasting. They captivated not just me but the whole country.

33. Courtesy of Julian Schlossberg.
34. Ibid.

I saw them live at a place called the Den of the Duane, which was in a downstairs room in the Hotel Duane on Madison Avenue. They did that thing where they asked the audience to give them the first and last lines.

Elaine wasn't anything like the kind of female comedians around at that time who stood up and hit too hard with self-deprecating one-liners. She was a lovely creature who was just amazingly, inexplicably hilarious, everything she said. I offered her a part in the first movie I directed, *Take the Money and Run*. She said, "No, you wouldn't want me, I have a neck brace."

STANLEY DONEN[35]: Mike didn't appear to be as good an actor as Elaine. Equally funny, but not as believable. When I made a movie called *Two for the Road*, I sent her the script, and pleaded with her to take the part of the American who travels with Albert Finney, because she's just an incredible actress. I don't think she'd ever been in a movie at that point. She refused, of course.

WOODY ALLEN: Everything she does is funny, everything she says. It's in the voice. I'd seen it before with Groucho Marx. And Mike had a version of that. He would say things that were not, in themselves, jokes. But they would sound funny because of his delivery. Mike just had a great thing in his voice. I don't know what it was—the contempt, the arrogance. But it was earned contempt, earned arrogance.

I just found them hilariously funny, these two geniuses. They came along with that wave of comedians—Mort Sahl, Jonathan Winters, Shelley Berman, and Lenny Bruce. The three greatest to me were Mort Sahl, Nichols and May, and Jonathan Winters. They helped create the atmosphere in the country of receptivity to literate comedy.

There was an audience for them, and I felt, without thinking of it in those words, it's the same audience for me. An audience of people where you don't have to come out and do the same mother-in-law or Eisenhower golf jokes. You could talk about the things that you talked about in your social life, and everyone would be tuned in to them.

---

35. Courtesy of Julian Schlossberg.

JACK ROLLINS[36]: I'm three times blessed with having had the privilege of working with genius: Woody Allen, Nichols and May, and Robin Williams. I got to meet Woody because of Nichols and May. He came up to my office, and he opens the door, and a shy, thin, bony-faced little fellow looks in and says, "May I come in?" He introduced himself and said he's seen Nichols and May and thought he could write for them. I said, "Well, I'm afraid you can't because they don't use writers. They write for themselves." He was somewhat disappointed.

WOODY ALLEN: Before I became a comic, I asked their manager Jack Rollins if I could write for them. And he said he would talk to them, but that they basically wrote their own material. I did the same thing with Mort Sahl.

These new comedians were so personal, they weren't like the last generation who would buy material from comedy writers. They were expressing their own lives and their own sense of things, so they all wrote for themselves.

I was a reclusive writer. By definition, you're alone in the room—it's a very introverted kind of life. But I thought, if I ever had the nerve, this is what I'd like to be doing. And so when I said that to Jack Rollins, he would not get off the topic from me making the switch from a writer to a stand-up comedian.

JACK ROLLINS[37]: Woody came back about a month later, and said, well, would Rollins and Joffe be interested in managing him? I told him that we didn't manage writers, we did actors. And he said, "Well, would you consider starting with me?" So we said, "Bring us some samples of your work." He came back and read us two or three of his sketches. He read them perfectly straight-faced. He didn't perform, he just read them. And it was hilariously, hilariously funny. We said, "Listen, we think this could work. Let's take a six-month shot and see what we can do for you as a writer."

---

36. "Nichols & May—Take Two," *American Masters*, PBS.
37. "Nichols & May—Take Two," *American Masters*, PBS.

During the six months, we felt there was something about Woody as a performer that was wonderful. If you ask me what it was, I can't tell you. It was a mysterious thing. Charlie and I said he ought to try performing. He gave it some thought and wrote a little act. In a way, you might say it was because of Nichols and May that Woody found himself in the field of performers. He had only ever thought of himself as a writer.

JANET COLEMAN: Jack was an amazing fellow—something out of Damon Runyon, with the New York accent and the cigar and the good taste. He wasn't interested in show business. He really wanted to cultivate the artistry of his people. They called him "the poet of managers."

WOODY ALLEN: I didn't speak at Jack's funeral, but I gave a statement: "Jack lived up to the hype." He had a gift of being able to discern talent before anyone else. He saw it with [Harry] Belafonte, Nichols and May, Robin Williams, Dick Cavett, David Letterman. He saw it with me before I thought that I had any chance of being a stand-up comic. His instincts for what would move an audience were sensational.

He was a guy who was not in it for the money. He advised me, as he advised all his clients, "Don't think about money and you'll make money." He took a lesser percentage than many managers took. He was always encouraging us to take risks, to take the jobs that were not necessarily the best-paying jobs, but the ones that had the most potential for development. He wouldn't just take an act like Nichols and May, two literate kids from Chicago, and stick them in the Copacabana, where the audiences come expecting Frank Sinatra and Alan King. He knew they needed the quieter, smaller, more attentive, more offbeat, literate rooms, like the hungry i and the Crystal Palace and the Blue Angel. I mean, if he had just stuck me at Caesars Palace, I'd have been lost. But at the Blue Angel, or the Bitter End in the Village, it was a different dynamic. These people wanted new acts, wanted different things, wanted the literacy. The people in the more commercial rooms were used to a much brassier kind of approach.

And he loved that after-hours life. I would go on at twelve thirty or one o'clock in the morning. We would retire to the Stage Delicatessen, his favorite haunt, and he'd sit there until three or four, saying, "This was great, but if you could be a little warmer here, and change this . . ."

I used to think, if the jokes are great, the people will love it. He taught me, it's the person. If they buy your personality, they'll buy everything. If they like *you*, the material is secondary. In a strange, after-hours, nightclubby way, he was sort of a genius.

JAMES GAVIN[38]: In the late '50s and early '60s, Nichols and May were regulars on two major radio shows, *Nightline* and *Monitor*, where their real improvisational prowess came through. They came up with a quick idea on the spot and they really went with it. Listening to these sketches, what's remarkable about them is how quick they were, how they were able to instantly click into a characterization or an accent and develop it into something that as often as not really did have a decent payoff and was funny. Even if the jokes failed, you could see how their minds worked on the spot. Nichols and May did hundreds of these, a remarkably high number of which are very successful, and nearly totally extemporaneous. There were virtually no other comedians of that era who could do it.

They simply sat down at a table and said, "All right, what if I play the flaky host of a women's morning radio show based on cooking? Let's call it 'Culture and Cooking.' You play a German scientist who's written a book called *Theory of the Universe*. Roll it." That sketch was heard once on the radio and never again.

What is not widely known is that one of their three albums on Mercury, *Mike Nichols & Elaine May Examine Doctors*, is taken from that series, and on that album, you can hear how quick-witted they were.

RICHARD LEWIS[39]: The pain of working out the material can sometimes be funnier than the final product, or more interesting to watch. I would have loved to have seen Mike and Elaine onstage when

38. Courtesy of Julian Schlossberg.
39. "Nichols & May—Take Two," *American Masters*, PBS.

they were working this stuff out. The people who had the luxury of seeing that are very fortunate.

TOM BROKAW[40]: It was so intelligent, their use of language, their appearance, their style. But they did speak for the common man. Think about the funeral scene, or the frustrations of dealing with the telephone company. Letting the air out of institutions like the Emmy Awards. They come along and say, *Wait a minute. There's another part of this, and we're going to speak for the viewers who are putting up with that part of it.* These are two wonderful minds at work. Maybe some of it, in some small way, will rub off on you, and even if it doesn't, you can claim that it did.

JULES FEIFFER[41]: Just as the Mafia began to act like [Francis Ford] Coppola's creation after they saw *The Godfather*, people, myself included, began to act like Nichols and May's characters after we saw them onstage.

STEVE ALLEN[42]: Anyone who couldn't appreciate the sheer simple funniness of Mike and Elaine would be too square to waste time on. It wasn't just "Who's on first?" or a joke-joke. There was a perception that was so inherently funny that you didn't need jokes of the traditional sort.

MILTON BERLE[43]: A joke is a one-liner: "That's a lovely suit. Who shines it for you?" Joke over. Laugh or no laugh. Mike and Elaine were not what we call on-the-nose, on-the-button joke tellers. Everything was situational. Everything was slice-of-life. A comic is a guy who says funny things and a comedian is a guy who says things funny. A comedian is one who is not afraid of silence, of taking that pause.

40. "Nichols & May—Take Two," *American Masters*, PBS.
41. Ibid.
42. Ibid.
43. Courtesy of Julian Schlossberg.

I always thought that Nichols and May were originals. They were maybe imitated but they were never duplicated. They were two of the greatest improv performers I ever saw. Nothing that they ever did together ever sounded rehearsed. Make it new. Make it sound new the first time you play it, the second time, the tenth time you play it. That was their great forte.

ROBIN WILLIAMS[44]: It's like great jazz: you're playing and you're building, and here comes your moment, and you go for it, and you take it, and then you back off, and then they take theirs. They have almost psychic timing. It's like their comedy has a half-life. There's a reaction and then there's a secondary reaction that builds, and there's a resonating between the two. Like in the funeral sketch, they're getting a laugh in just a pause. To me, it's the closest thing to music. If it's not improvised, it sure has the feeling of it.

JAMES GAVIN[45]: Most of the famous Nichols and May sketches were not, contrary to popular belief, true improvisations. They would start by working out a routine and then hone it from night to night, settle it into a pattern.

JACK ROLLINS[46]: The way they achieved a set piece was by doing it on their feet first. And then like a sculptor chipping away at a piece of marble, they would then build on what they had done. But it always originated on the floor. People didn't know what their technique was. Nor did I. Nor, in fact, did they.

RICHARD LEWIS[47]: Springsteen was born to run, they were born to improv. Seriously, that's how I look at it. Sometimes you can get hoodwinked by how brilliant their performance is and forget that the writing is near perfect, and vice versa. Because their words are so

---

44. "Nichols & May—Take Two," *American Masters*, PBS.
45. Courtesy of Julian Schlossberg.
46. "Nichols & May—Take Two," *American Masters*, PBS.
47. Ibid.

magnificent, you can get mesmerized by the material. How much of it was done through improvisation and how much was just written, it doesn't matter to me. They just did what they did best, and what they did best, few people could ever do as good.

Years later, I saw Mike Nichols scurry into this restaurant with Diane Sawyer. I followed him in, went over to him, and told him how much he meant to me. I've done the same thing to Groucho, bless his soul, and Bob Dylan.

STEVE ALLEN[48]: Another thing I've always loved about Mike and Elaine is that they worked calmly. I am daily angered by the popular misuse of the word "cool." I don't mean it always has to be applied to the weather or a block of ice, but originally it simply meant somebody who was calm and composed and not easily excited, didn't fly around the cage if something went wrong. They were truly, properly cool in their attitudes. Groucho Marx was not a loudmouth in his performing style. George Burns was cool. Fred Allen was somewhere in between. Robert Benchley. And Mike and Elaine, certainly.

STEVE MARTIN[49]: One thing that really distinguished them from what had come before especially in terms of comedy teams is that they were *still*. Comedy teams prior to them were manic and very physical. But they were just still onstage. That was new, and made it visually different and contributed to that intellectual image.

ROBIN WILLIAMS[50]: It was kind of a highbrow-lowbrow thing. "Huguenot-Walloon Drive" is an obscure reference, to say the least. But they've also got "Teenagers." They always kept a certain level of elegance. I don't know if I've ever heard of a routine where they said "fuck."

---

48. "Nichols & May—Take Two," *American Masters*, PBS.
49. Ibid.
50. Ibid.

STEVE ALLEN[51]: Many of their references were to things that for the most part only intellectuals or at least university students had even heard of. There was definitely a high-minded element, a sophisticated wit to their comedy. But you didn't have to be an intellectual yourself to perceive the funniness of it. I hate comedy where it's for our little in-group, and the square human race doesn't understand it. There actually is very little of that in their work. George S. Kaufman once said, "Satire is what closes on Saturday night." But the kind of satire Mike and Elaine did was not of that obscure and too utterly refined sort. It was just plain funny.

MILTON BERLE[52]: They don't do things that are too "in." They're not playing down to the audience; they play intelligent people, but the subject matter and the situations can relate to anybody. They played up to the audience, and when you play up to the audience, you make them feel good.

STEVE MARTIN[53]: However smart it got, it always stayed funny. It never got smug. You could approach it from a smart place but you could also approach it from a dumb place, which I think you have to be able to do in comedy, 'cause otherwise you'll outsmart yourself.

ARTHUR PENN[54]: Alex Cohen had the idea to do an evening of Mike Nichols and Elaine May on Broadway. Mike had seen some of my work on *Playhouse 90*. At that point, I was on my way to becoming a very successful Broadway director. I think I had three or four shows running at the same time: *Toys in the Attic*, *Two for the Seesaw*, *The Miracle Worker*, and *All the Way Home*. With the exception of *Two for the Seesaw*, the others were very hard drama. The opportunity to do some comedy was delicious, and I couldn't resist it.

51. "Nichols & May—Take Two," *American Masters*, PBS.
52. Courtesy of Julian Schlossberg.
53. "Nichols & May—Take Two," *American Masters*, PBS.
54. Ibid.

JACK ROLLINS[55]: Arthur said he did not do that much directing. Nobody had to do very much with them. The only thing I had to do was to warn them that in a cabaret situation, as opposed to a theater situation, brevity is commendable. Otherwise, they were completely self-fulfilled.

ARTHUR PENN[56]: We took it on the road that summer and developed all these bits. They had been done on television—extremely well, mind you—but for the theater, a kind of vividness had to be introduced to the work. I can't claim real credit for it. I just sat there most of the time and laughed my head off. That was the extent of the rehearsals. We recorded a lot of these improvisations and somehow those recordings got left in a taxi. It just breaks my heart to think about what was on those tapes, which were never recovered.

In the conventional sense, I wasn't directing them. I was really providing the third eye. I would just sit there responding, laughing, making notes, and then we would discuss it—the shape of it, whether it had gone beyond its ability to sustain itself. Quite often I was wrong. We would argue. I'd say, "You've got to finish the goddamn skit, it's gotta have an end to it." And Mike would say, "No, it's gotta just go on and just end—like that." He kept saying, "You come out of the punchline tradition." And I'd say, "You guys won't finish your skits." That sort of thing went on all the time. But it was an exquisitely delightful and original time, and I'd give a lot to have another experience like that.

JULES FEIFFER[57]: Mike told me that in all the years he worked with Elaine, she never ended a scene.

JACK ROLLINS[58]: Mike was very conscious of the practical problems that all of us face, and he was very good at solving them. Elaine found living in this world a chore. She was in the clouds. She was the

---

55. "Nichols & May—Take Two," *American Masters*, PBS.
56. Ibid.
57. Ibid.
58. Ibid.

consummate artist, without any thought to the day-to-day requirements of living in this imperfect world. The creative process was all-consuming with Elaine. Whereas Michael was as creative as could be, but if you did a cabaret act, he would know that it should be five minutes long. As far as Elaine was concerned, it could go on for twenty-two minutes. In that regard, they were perfect as a team. They were ham and eggs.

ARTHUR PENN[59]: Elaine is absolutely fearless. She has the bravery, the impetuosity to catch a comic line and go with it as far as it'll go. Sometimes Mike would look at her with a kind of bewilderment and then have to bring it back into the circumstances of the skit, because that was a part of his organizational mind. One part of his brain is clearly concerned about, *What is the shape of the piece?* and *How is it holding?* I don't mean to suggest in any way that Mike wasn't exquisitely funny, but there was this future director in his personality. Elaine's brilliance is that she doesn't concern herself with those limits, the limits of the rest of us mortals. She pursues an idea to its illogical end.

BOB NEWHART: In order to do it on Broadway, they had to program cues for the light grid, so their routines were written out. Elaine came to Mike and said, "We can't do that," and he said, "But it's worked. It's one of our strongest routines." She said, "It's not funny. I just read it on a piece of paper."

JULES FEIFFER: They were going to do a show on Broadway at the Golden Theatre, but first they tried it out on Town Hall, with Arthur Penn directing. I found myself waiting in line for my tickets, standing behind Kenneth Tynan, who was just about to take over as drama critic for *The New Yorker*. He had just written the introduction to the British edition of my first book, *Sick, Sick, Sick*, so I introduced myself. After the show, he invited me to dinner with George Plimpton and Peter Matthiessen and Bill Styron—all these people who would become my friends and acquaintances for the rest of my life. And all because I was in line to pick up tickets for Mike and Elaine.

---

59. "Nichols & May—Take Two," *American Masters*, PBS.

ARTHUR PENN[60]: It was an extraordinary show in that it took risks. And there's nothing more invigorating for an audience than the sense of danger in the room. Among the very funny bits they did— of the rocket scientist or the man going to the funeral home, very solid bits that we knew would play—they closed their act by doing an improvisation in which they asked the audience, "Give us a first line and a last line." And then they said, "In what style would you like it done?" And on the spot, they improvised a skit. The ability to do that, and the sense of, *Are they ever going to get there? How can they do it? How can they possibly be this funny and on this subject without having had any preparation and arrive, finally?* Almost inevitably it would be Elaine who would come in with this crashing closing line in a circumstance that was totally inappropriate for it and absolutely devastate the audience and me night after night. The audience was totally participating in it, and totally available to the moment. I'd be in the back of the theater, laughing my head off. It was a muted time, as I say, but in the theater, the edge of change was coming, and it was coming fast and hard.

ANDREW DUNCAN: All the stuff they did, they did it at Compass [Theatre], and they never mentioned David Shepherd or Compass, and that's why there was enmity between Mike and David. The scene they borrowed of mine was one I saw in the *Chicago Daily News* of a seventy-nine-dollar funeral. I played the guy, Elaine played the funeral director. She might have felt that she was entitled.

JANET COLEMAN: There was a kind of tension between Nichols and May and Shepherd until the very end. Whose material was it, anyway? David's point of view was that he produced it, he paid the rent, he gave them the salary, such as it was, and he owned the thing. I don't think that would really hold up in court. You need a contract.

JEFFREY SWEET: David once said to me, "I should have sued Mike and Elaine." I said, "Why?" David, notwithstanding that he was a committed—he thought—socialist, said, "They created all that stuff

---

60. "Nichols & May—Take Two," *American Masters*, PBS.

as work for hire for me, and I think I have a right of ownership." I said, "David, the smartest thing you ever did was *not* suing Mike and Elaine!" Was he really going to ask other actors to do Mike and Elaine's material? I later heard that Mike, somewhere along the line, got in touch with David, and although it wasn't a flowery communication, said, "You were very important to my career, and I thank you for that."

JACK ROLLINS[61]: "Pirandello" was the single most startling phenomenon that I personally experienced in working with them. They start off as two children who are left at home, and they say, "Let's play Mommy and Daddy." And they start acting out the things they heard Mommy and Daddy do. And in a totally subtle way, they suddenly become the parents. It's all subtle and seamless, and you never notice where the hinge is.

The first time my wife and I saw it on a stage, we were absolutely positive that this was the breakup of Nichols and May. We had the compulsion to get up and say to them, *Take it easy, what are you doing?* And we did! We actually moved toward the side of the stage, and at that point, they froze and they said, "And that is Pirandello." They brought you to the literal brink of disaster and stopped right at the cliff's edge. There was a remarkable technique of acting.

ARTHUR PENN[62]: Something apparently went wrong in the skit, and they began to drop out of the characters they had been playing and became Mike and Elaine having an argument. It was clearly frightening to the audience in a titillating way. You could feel the audience sort of shifting in their seats uncomfortably. *Oh my God, they're really attacking each other. This is no longer the skit.* The coda was Mike saying to Elaine, "Elaine, what are you doing?!" And she turns to the audience and says, "Pirandello." Blackout. And that was how we closed the first act of the show.

It was a genuine theater piece. It was not nightclub work. You needed a sizable length of time. And you had to have a sophisticated audience to

61. "Nichols & May—Take Two," *American Masters*, PBS.
62. Ibid.

understand it. I remember on opening night—I've never done this before or since—standing at the back of the Golden Theatre, and a couple who obviously didn't like it got up and started to walk up the aisle and out of the theater. I said to them, "You can't leave." And I physically held them there. And just as Elaine was saying "Pirandello," the woman swung her pocketbook at me and said, "We have to get out of here!"

RICHARD LEWIS[63]: They're great actors, period. The types of films that Mike went on to direct, it just made sense. It made sense that he did *The Graduate*, and it makes sense that Elaine May worked with [John] Cassavetes. It's naturalistic, and that's what they are. You're eavesdropping on people's anxiety.

JULES FEIFFER[64]: It's interesting that when talent like this occurs and it's unusual, and the subject matter is unusual, the first thing you get from critics is, "I like them, but they're too smart to go very far. It's too hip to go national." The experts will always know and they're always wrong.

PAUL SIMON: I think the records really hold up. Surprisingly for me, Lenny Bruce doesn't hold up, and he was my idol. Artie was a big fan of his, too. We used to do Nichols and May lines all the time right before we went on.

ARTHUR PENN[65]: I remember one night at Lillian Hellman's house, Edmund Wilson said to Mike, "You should direct the full canon of American plays, beginning with"—I can't remember now, a play about the American Revolution—and Mike looking at him with a rather startled expression, thinking, *What the hell are you taking about?* But it was a genuine appreciation by people like Edmund Wilson and Noel Coward. They knew they were witnessing the new voice in social satire.

63. "Nichols & May—Take Two," *American Masters*, PBS.

64. Ibid.

65. Ibid.

RICHARD AVEDON[66]: [A friend] said to him, "We're going to the Bernsteins' Saturday night, why don't you come with us?" And he said, "*That* crowd." And then he dominated the whole crowd. He became necessary to all of them. He was an outsider and he became an insider.

SUSAN FORRISTAL: Mike used to say Dick Avedon taught him how to be rich.

EMANUEL AZENBERG: Think about what it is for Kazan, Nichols, Neil Simon, Woody, to grow up in the teenage years and you're not the most beautiful, and you don't get all the girls—in fact you don't get anybody—and then at age thirty you're a star because you write or you're funny or you're Mike or you're Neil or you're Woody, and then people take their clothes off because you walk into the room. They did it for Paul Newman and [Robert] Redford, you understood *that* . . .

MAUREEN DOWD: When Marilyn [Monroe] sang "Happy Birthday" to Jack Kennedy in the famous dress she had to be sewn into, the sequined Jean Louis gown, Mike was there that night. He and Elaine May were performing in Madison Square Garden. He told me, "I was standing right behind Marilyn, completely invisible, when she sang 'Happy birthday, Mr. President,' and, indeed, the corny thing happened. Her dress split for my benefit, and there was Marilyn, and, yes, indeed, she didn't wear any underwear."

RENATA ADLER: When he was rowing a boat in Central Park with Jackie [Kennedy], people would shout, again and again, "I'm sorry for your bereavement!" Well meaning, presumably.

MILTON BERLE[67]: I've been often asked who are my favorite funny people. And people are amazed when I say I like this type of comedy. They say it's so far from your style, jokes with one-liners—*ba da boom*

---

66. Courtesy of the John Lahr collection at the Howard Gotlieb Archival Research Center, Boston University.

67. Courtesy of Julian Schlossberg.

with a rim shot—and pratfalls and seltzer and pies in the face. But my preference, I go the other way. I prefer situational stuff. You would never think that was how my mind works, but I go in the direction of Nichols and May. I like their easy style, which is the antithesis of me, because I know too much about how my laughs work. They never did anything for a laugh. They were very selective. If the audience don't get it: fuck 'em.

JACK ROLLINS[68]: There were definite signs, in my view, that each would eventually have to go their own way, because staying as Mike and Elaine forever was too confining for hugely gifted people like this. They simply had too much talent in every direction.

JULES FEIFFER[69]: When you've done what you've done and you haven't found a way to go further with it, or investigate more with it, or to dig deeper with it, there's no place to go but repeating yourself, which clearly they were too brilliant to do.

Those of us who were die-hard fans were terribly upset about it. But looking back, it seemed the only thing to do, because otherwise they would have become as tired and clichéd as all the things they were making fun of.

RICHARD AVEDON[70]: Elaine said that she didn't want to end up as Comden and Green, doing their improvisations until they're seventy years old.

STEVE MARTIN[71]: That initial spark, which is so exciting, eventually dissipates, and either it becomes a nice routine, like a marriage, or you can move on to something that keeps the spark going. I experienced it when I broke up with myself doing stand-up comedy. It just came to a natural end and I knew I was done with it.

---

68. "Nichols & May—Take Two," *American Masters*, PBS.

69. Ibid.

70. Courtesy of the John Lahr collection at the Howard Gotlieb Archival Research Center, Boston University.

71. "Nichols & May—Take Two," *American Masters*, PBS.

STEVE ALLEN[72]: I think sometimes partners have some perception that audiences or critics might think that they really needed each other. A needs B, or B needs A. And that A without B, or B without A . . . I'm getting too algebraic here, but in the case of two people so talented as these, it would be a very annoying public perception if indeed there ever was such. There might have been a sense in which unconsciously they were saying to themselves, *I can make it on my own.*

To me, the fact that they stopped working together always seemed an unmitigated misfortune for the rest of us. It's a pity that along with all the other things they did—all the films and the scripts and the marvelous solo performances—they did not also continue to, from time to time, work together. Thank God we have it on film and tape, so that a thousand years from now they can be appreciated, if language has not deteriorated too much.

JOHN CALLEY[73]: I think what happened is that they came from the Compass, and because they had that amazingly collaborative structure, they sort of thought that's the way it is. They didn't value the symbiosis. Not to say they didn't know how good they were, or that they didn't show great respect to the interaction that produced what they produced, but I think they thought that if it's not working, we'll split up and find somebody else. But there wasn't anybody else.

RICHARD AVEDON[74]: They were offered the biggest television show. She walked right out of the meeting, said, "I'm not going to do this anymore." So Mike was cut off from what he thought would continue forever. And he went into complete decline. Right then, he thought he couldn't do anything. I remember he wrote this little piece about something, either for *The New Yorker* or *The New York Times*, and it was like, *Will they publish me?*

---

72. "Nichols & May—Take Two," *American Masters*, PBS.
73. Courtesy of the John Lahr collection at the Howard Gotlieb Archival Research Center, Boston University.
74. Ibid.

JOHN CALLEY[75]: Mike was to some extent lost. I'm sure that Elaine suffered separation from it too, but she had a dream and a life and stuff, and Mike didn't. And then Mike directed and it changed him intensely.

STANLEY DONEN[76]: What they had was unique. I've never seen anything like it, and I never expect to see anything like it again.

I knew that Mike was going to direct a movie. I think I had the temerity to say to him, "Mike, you know, it's difficult for me to say this, but I think you're making a terrible mistake. I mean, what you and Elaine have, it's more than an act—they're *plays*. What you have is far beyond what anyone else has ever done, it's truly unique, for God's sake, don't stop doing that just to direct *movies*!" So you can see how prescient I was.

75. Courtesy of the John Lahr collection at the Howard Gotlieb Archival Research Center, Boston University.
76. Courtesy of Julian Schlossberg.

Mike with Neil Simon in Washington, D.C., during a rehearsal for *The Odd Couple*, the second of five plays they did together. The show was a hit in previews, but they continued to make changes, some of them significant, before taking it to Broadway. *(© Burt Glinn/Magnum Photos)*

CHAPTER 4

Don't Act It Funny

JOHN LAHR: In October 1962, Mike took the lead in Elaine's play *A Matter of Position*. The play was sort of about Mike, which Elaine never quite admitted.

RICHARD AVEDON[1]: I said, tell me about the play. "Well, this guy won't get out of bed." And I remember saying, "Mike, don't do it. You will kill the play. You'll get in bed and you'll stay there." As I predicted, he got in bed and didn't help the play at all.

JOHN LAHR: For the first time, they weren't standing shoulder to shoulder as equals. Now Mike was onstage taking direction from Elaine. Their relationship, the power dynamic, had irrevocably shifted, and this made Mike terribly self-conscious. He said to me, "It was horrendous." There was this pall of fiasco that hung over the entire production. Elaine was looking for a replacement for Mike, and Mike was saying to other people, "Get her to cut the play or I'm leaving." The *Philadelphia Sunday Bulletin* critic wrote that "those members of the audience who had not already beat a hasty retreat before the final curtain, as many did, were left with the sensation of numbness that was too far down to be attributed to heartburn"—in other words, it was ass-aching. As they say in vaudeville, they laid a cake: twelve

---

1. Courtesy of the John Lahr collection at the Howard Gotlieb Archival Research Center, Boston University.

eggs. So the play died, and so, for a long time, did their relationship. Mike told me it was cataclysmic. I don't know how long the *froideur* lasted. I can't imagine Mike could stand too much time away from Elaine, though maybe he could.

TONY WALTON: I remember how heartbreakingly divorced Mike seemed to be from Elaine. He seemed to be presuming that it was his own fault, whereas in fact I think it was just Elaine, who is so extremely brilliant but to this very day has never become the easiest person to collaborate with. Clearly she managed it really well in this recent *Waverly Gallery*, but almost anything she was involved with beforehand, whether she had written it or directed it, was a very complicated experience for everyone involved.

DOUGLAS WICK (*producer*): Mike was walking down the street with Leonard Bernstein, and Leonard Bernstein said to him, "Mike, you're so great. I'm just not sure at what."

ROBBIE LANTZ (*agent*)[2]: When I entered the scene, Mike was in a state of deep depression, to which he's given. We were social friends with Dick Avedon. He was a frequent visitor at Avedon's house on Fire Island, and we had the neighboring house. After the separation with Elaine, he really wasn't functioning. We all talked about him. Everybody was greatly concerned. Nobody saw him. He was in total isolation.

My wife and I thought he would make a wonderful director. Because he can't write. He can only talk. He literally, virtually can't write. If somebody has a full note from Mike to the milkman, "Leave two bottles of milk," it's a collector's item.

TONY WALTON: I had been selling Mike as a director for quite a while, because he was so uncertain as to where his career was going to lead him once he and Elaine broke up. He started sending

2. Courtesy of the John Lahr collection at the Howard Gotlieb Archival Research Center, Boston University.

pieces to *The New Yorker* and things like that. I kept screaming at him, "You're a fucking director!"

I was a frequent observer of the Nichols and May Broadway show, and I could see the degree to which he was shaping things. I didn't think that Arthur Penn's sensibility was part of that evening in any way. I blamed Mike for it. And also we were close enough friends that I was desperate for him to have a career that would be fulfilling and at which I knew he would be successful.

Probably a lot of it was also because we would go to see *Jules et Jim*, or whatever it was—it was a very lively time in terms of the break-throughs that were happening and the French avant-garde—and in talking about it afterward, it always struck me that he was incredibly savvy about what the directorial intentions had been and to what extent they had succeeded.

I had just produced [J. P.] Donleavy's play version of *The Ginger Man* and got very close to him, and also was doing caricatures for Kenneth Tynan for his *Observer* theatrical revues before he came over here. I thought, what a good idea it would be to have a revue writ-ten by Donleavy and Kenneth Tynan and my very good friend, with whom I shared an agent, Jules Feiffer. I told Mike about this and he said, "Maybe we could start it out in Chicago, perhaps even at the Compass." So that was the plan. One of the people involved was a very young Stephen Sondheim, who wrote a version of "Passionella" for *The Apple Tree*, which was one-third of that production.

JULES FEIFFER: Paul Sills in Chicago wanted to adapt my car-toons for the stage. I didn't like it much. I thought they worked better on paper. He had discovered that my cartoons were all about a min-ute or less, and said we should have something longer. So I flew home to Brooklyn Heights and over the weekend I wrote *Crawling Arnold*, which was my first play. Sills hated it. But I showed it to Mike, and Mike loved it and wanted to make that the centerpiece of the whole show.

It was the first time anybody had seen Mike direct. What amazed me from the beginning is how he created this instantly intimate bond between himself, the actors, and the entire company. It was a combination of insight into the script, and a way of talking to actors, coaxing through affectionate prodding, which I never learned to do.

At one point he was working on a scene between the two lead characters, and he asked me to leave the room. After ten minutes, I was invited back in, and they ran the scene. It was entirely different from what I ever thought that scene was all about, yet as soon as I heard it, I thought: *It's right. It's the only way to do this.* I said to Mike, "Where'd this come from?" And he just pointed to the script. I knew goddamn well it wasn't my words, but what he knew instinctively about men and women and relationships. *Crawling Arnold* was not *Carnal Knowledge.* This was pure off-the-wall satire. But he made it real.

He got a wonderful cast. And he got Steve Sondheim to write some songs which were knock-your-socks-off. Sondheim was not Sondheim yet. He had done one play that was unproduced, *Saturday Night.* As the rehearsals went on, I began to think there's only one part of this threesome who doesn't belong in this company and that's me; I don't deserve these guys. I felt that if this show went to New York and was a hit, it could be a disaster for me. I might never write again, because I would have felt it was because of the talents of these two guys.

So I canceled it, afraid that they'd be mad at me, and they weren't. I may have lied to them about why I was doing it, but that's the real reason.

TONY WALTON: I was still listed as a producer, but I was not around for it very much at all. Lewis Allen gave it an encouraging but not terrific review in *Variety.* It was actually Mike's directorial debut, though never remembered as such, because then Saint Subber came along with *Barefoot in the Park.*

ROBBIE LANTZ[3]: Saint called and said, "I have a play by Neil Simon," who had only written *Come Blow Your Horn.* He said, "Help me find a director. There are no comedy directors." I read the play, which was called *Nobody Loves Me.* I believe to this day, Doc [Simon]

---

3. Courtesy of the John Lahr collection at the Howard Gotlieb Archival Research Center, Boston University.

starts all his plays calling them *Nobody Loves Me.* I read the play, and I said, "I think you should talk to Mike Nichols." I said, "I think that would pull Mike back to life."

My best recollection is he did read it. How quickly, I can't remember. And then he said, "Yes, this is funny. I could do that, I guess. If I can direct at all." And I said, "Well, you should go and direct somewhere. I'll set it up for you. Go to Canada, do two plays. The important thing is you must pick plays you can't trifle with. You can't rewrite, you can't cut scenes." He did *Saint Joan* and, I think, a Wilde. Every night at midnight he called and said, "Get me out of this. I don't want to do this." I said, "This is precisely what the doctor ordered." He hated me, I think. But he did stick it out. And of course he realized all the practicalities because he's so quick—what the problems are, and so on. I did not get the courage to go see those productions.

ELIZABETH ASHLEY (*actress*): I had won the Tony or something for *Take Her, She's Mine* with George Abbott, and then while I was in that play, I'd gotten a call from an agency: "I'm sending over this play. It's an idea of a play. Ten pages are written. It's by this television guy, Neil Simon." He'd written for Sid Caesar, and he had one play, which was *Come Blow Your Horn*, which ran for a little while. "If you like it, he will write it for you, and Saint Subber will put the money into developing it." I read it in the taxi going downtown to meet Doc Simon—he was Doc Simon then—at Saint Subber's very grand house on the East Side. I liked it. I thought it was funny. Then Doc went out and wrote a draft of the whole play. There was another meeting, and that's when it was decided by Saint that we should take it to Bucks County under another title. They were trying to do that thing they did back then, which was hide it, so that it could be developed away from the vipers.

They were talking about who would play Paul and they said there was this actor who had just been in *The Pleasure of His Company* named George Peppard, who I didn't know from Adam. I remember Doc said, "Yeah, but is he funny?" Saint said, "Well, that play was a big hit." I said, "Well, what about my buddy, Bob?" meaning Bob Redford. Redford and I had the same agent. We made our Broadway debut together in a 1958 play by Dore Schary called *The Highest Tree.*

Simon, I don't think he knew who Redford was at the time, but he said, "Well, that's interesting."

Then they talked about directors. There were the Joe Anthonys and the covey of guys who directed hit Broadway comedies. Saint is the one who said, "Well, I want to put another idea out there. Mike Nichols wants to direct." Now, Mike had not directed anything. Nobody was a bigger Nichols and May fan than me, because I'd seen their show onstage, and also on television and everything. That was the smartest, funniest thing I'd ever seen in my life. I didn't know if he could direct traffic, but I didn't care.

ROBERT REDFORD (*actor*): Before Broadway, there was a try-out in Bucks County, Pennsylvania, and it had a different title, *Nobody Loves Me*. I was aware of Mike, because I had the album he did with Elaine May, which I thought was just terrific, very modern humor. But he hadn't really done anything else yet, so there was a certain amount of insecurity which, of course, went away after *Barefoot in the Park*.

I had done some theater, but I was doing mostly television in California, and I was getting tired of it. For some reason, I had done an episode of a show called *Breaking Point* where I played kind of a psychopath, and Mike liked it and requested that we meet in New York, which I thought was kind of odd. *This is a comedy. Why does he want to talk to me?*

So I went in and met with him, and what I encountered was a guy who was beyond smart and extremely witty. But he had one other quality that was rather rare: He was psychologically astute. He could cut down into the heart of things.

NEIL SIMON (*playwright*)[4]: We sent Mike *Barefoot in the Park*, and he called or wrote back and said, "Love it, I want to do the play." It wasn't my idea, it was Saint Subber, the producer. I said, "But Mike's a comic, he's not a director."

When I met him and sat with him in Saint Subber's office on Sixty-

---

4. Courtesy of the John Lahr collection at the Howard Gotlieb Archival Research Center, Boston University.

Third or -Fourth, right off Park, within ten minutes I said, "He's perfect," because the intelligence came out. He pinpointed things within the script that I questioned myself even while I was writing it. I've never worked with anyone in my life nor will I ever work with anyone in my life as good as Mike Nichols.

The first day of rehearsal, we went to Saint Subber's house, and Robert Redford and Elizabeth Ashley, Kurt Kasznar, and Mildred Natwick came and sat around a table and read the play for me so I could know what to rewrite. I was so used to having actors at a reading laughing at the material, if it's a comedy, because they're hearing it for the first time too. But there was not one laugh at the table. I'm saying, "Oh my God, this is deadly, just deadly." I asked Saint Subber to cancel the play. It was just a horror.

Mike says, "Relax, Neil. It's going to be all right." I said, "Why? Nobody laughed." He says, "They're too worried about themselves. Robert Redford doesn't want to do anything that looks like he's trying to get a laugh." I said, "Okay."

It's the only time I ever didn't sit in the rehearsal room. I stood out in the hall, waiting, and suddenly I heard a roar inside. I said, *Thank God, they must be up to a really good part.* I went inside, and it was Mike telling them a story during the break. Then we went back to the play: no more laughs.

He told the cast, "We're doing *King Lear*. You don't act it funny, you do it real." He said, "If we trust the play, the audience will come along with us." Mike always looked for the reality.

So we got into Bucks County, Pennsylvania, and we did a dress rehearsal in front of the ushers. They just stood there gaping, and about two hours after that we were going to do the first performance. I'm saying, "This is deadly, Mike," and he's saying, "Let's wait and see what happens." I mean, the calmness was extraordinary. He may have been having as much nerves as I was, except I was the one complaining about it.

ELIZABETH ASHLEY: In Bucks County, they had a first act, but no second act. All I can tell you is from day one, Redford and Nichols was a marriage made in heaven. Redford has many, many talents, and he's very, very smart, but as a performer, he has a dry humor, and he can make that funnier than almost anybody, given the right material. It's deeper than delivery; it's a point of view. Mike saw what Redford had and saw that nobody else had that. I think Mike also recognized that Redford had big star quality.

One of the biggest regrets of my professional life was, by that time, I'd done *The Carpetbaggers* and gotten involved with George Peppard. I had him in one ear saying, "Mike is giving the play to Redford." It was not in my nature to think that way. I was Lee Strasberg, Sandy Meisner, Stella Adler, Bobby Lewis, Harold Clurman. But George was this older guy, and I'd always wanted a father figure who knew things. He would tell me notes to give to Mike, who knew what was going on.

At one point, my insecurity just got so huge that I remember just breaking down and crying to Mike in a rehearsal break. I said, "I don't know who to be. I don't know this character. I don't know what I'm doing." Mike said, "Well, it's something that you've never been allowed to play before. Everything you've played, you've been something extreme. This time, you're a girl that's madly in love with this guy that you've just gotten married to, and you've found this place to live, and every dream of yours has come true. But you're just a girl."

He said, "Do you know why Doc wrote this play for you?" I said, "I have no idea." In my secret heart of hearts, I thought, *Well, it's because I won a trophy*, but Mike said, "It's because you're so pretty, and pretty girls have never been funny." So he did two things. He gave me the kind of compliment that when you're that young and stupid gives you confidence, and he made it okay that I was coming apart at the seams.

ROBERT REDFORD: After the tryout in Bucks County, I hit a dark zone in my life, where I wasn't sure that I wanted to act anymore. I was thinking, *I don't know that I'm satisfied with this.* I really didn't want to come to Broadway and do *Barefoot in the Park*. But I had to, because it was contractual, so I tried to get myself removed from the play. I would lie down, and I wouldn't perform.

Mike saw that I was in a dark place, and I think probably some part of him could relate to that. He started to work on me, and it became a contest. The more I tried, the harder he kept me in. I said, "I'm telling you, I'm not good. I shouldn't be in this." But he wouldn't listen to me. We went to New Haven for a tryout, and I just performed horribly, and the reviews were terrible for me. They said the rest of the cast was good, and if it wasn't for this guy, this would really be a good play. Mike took me for a series of meetings in the afternoon. He was trying to work me, and I decided, *Okay, I'm going to battle him.* I would go on the next night and be even worse. But still he kept me in.

Finally, he said to me, "Listen: You want to lie down, you can lie down. I'm not going to fire you. On opening night, you can lie down on the floor. I don't care. But let me tell you something. You seem to be somebody who carries something secret within you. Some part of you wants to hold something back for yourself." I'd never heard that before. I had not been in psychoanalysis, so I didn't know what to make of that. And he then said, "Look, I'll tell you what. Why don't you use that, carry a secret knowledge of some kind and use that so it creates a kind of mystery?" I got really intrigued with that.

So that next night I came on the stage and I just whistled. Of course, it drove the rest of the cast crazy, because I wasn't saying my lines. What I was saying was, *I'm carrying a secret.* And then suddenly, something broke, and I just came alive. I had the chance to try to sabotage this, but I wasn't allowed to, and then finally I accepted the fact this is what I should do, and, therefore, I'm going to really do it. From that point on we went forward, and I had the best relationship I could ever have with any director, because of how he handled me. It was so psychologically astute.

There was some darkness there, way down deep, where he had witnessed some pain in his life. You didn't know what that was necessarily, but he had experienced something that left him in a much deeper, darker place. But he overcame it with comedy. He incorporated that darkness into his comedy.

ELIZABETH ASHLEY: Mike knew how to use Redford. He identified with Redford. He got Redford's character. The guy who was attracted to this wild-child girl, who's not a wild child himself and who has to think about earning a living and keeping his job, and he doesn't really see the charm when he has to sleep on the floor, because the furniture's not there, and it's snowing through the skylight on him, and he gets pneumonia. Mike and Redford, I can't think in my entire career of a more perfect marriage between director and actor.

My regret was that George got in my ear. I never stopped trusting Mike, but I was convinced Mike didn't really like me, that I wasn't the good one in the play, that Redford was the genius. I was convinced after a while that Redford didn't like me much either. I never did anything bad to Bob. I always just felt inferior to him.

JOHN LAHR: Redford complained in *Barefoot in the Park* that Elizabeth Ashley was upstaging him, and also embarrassing him, by raising her leg when they kiss. He couldn't stop her, and he didn't know what to do about it, and so he asked Mike. Mike said, "Oh, that's easy. Raise your leg."

NEIL SIMON[5]**:** There was a moment when—it was a scene onstage between Elizabeth Ashley and Robert Redford, and it was a fight scene. They had just come back from Staten Island, they were both a little drunk, and she gets into a huge fight with him, and she wants a divorce—it's one week after the marriage, and you know in your heart that there's no way they're going to get a divorce—and she's screaming at him, and it's very funny and very touching at the same time. I was watching it in the back of the theater, and I said to Mike, "I don't think we should be watching this." He said, "Why not?" I said, "It's too personal." He said, "Good, I'm glad you like it."

JACK O'BRIEN: Mike was always on the train ahead of me. I was at the University of Michigan when he and Elaine were just hitting it, and we were wetting our pants in our dorm rooms. We had never seen anything like this. It was just a whole new voice. It's like walking into

---

5. Courtesy of the John Lahr collection at the Howard Gotlieb Archival Research Center, Boston University.

Hamilton and thinking, *There is a future!* Then, when I got to New York, I was teaching at Hunter College, and one of the other teaching assistants, his best friend was the company manager for *Barefoot in the Park*, so as a baby director I'm hearing all about Mike's genius.

WOODY ALLEN: I saw *Barefoot in the Park* at a preview before it opened. Mike had a fabulous gift for staging, an instinct for what would work on Broadway. He was maybe the best comedy director ever on the stage. He would've always been the director of my dreams for anything I ever wrote for the theater, but he was never available. And Neil was so good at what he did. Comic dialogue just poured out of him, and he kept doing it, year after year. People just sort of took it for granted. It was again, like with Elaine, a very auspicious coupling.

FRANK RICH (*writer*): Mike Nichols and Neil Simon both came out of two parallel tracks on which modern American comedy was being invented: one track was Chicago and Second City, and the other track was Max Liebman's writers' room on *Your Show of Shows* and *Caesar's Hour*. Chicago was the world of improv, and *Show of Shows* was very scripted, but basically these were two factories of humor that were considered daring and brave. Essentially it's New York Jewish, even though Mike wasn't born in New York. Neil Simon's characters are obviously Jewish, although they aren't presented as Jewish until much later in his career. If the mother in *Barefoot in the Park* isn't a Jewish mother, I don't know who is.

ROBBIE LANTZ[6]**:** I went to see the first performance, I think alone. My wife was too afraid. I came back at four in the morning, and I said, "The era of George Abbott is over"—of that kind of caricature comedy. It was real, it was human, it was affectionate. He had enormous affection for every character in that play.

JACK O'BRIEN: I don't know when in my life I've laughed harder

---

6. Courtesy of the John Lahr collection at the Howard Gotlieb Archival Research Center, Boston University.

than I laughed at *Barefoot in the Park*. Well, yes, there have been times; I'm given to excess. But Mildred Natwick, who was a classy woman—she wore fucking *gloves*—coming through the door of a sixth-floor walk-up, leaning against the lintel and wheezing, sliding down the wall, because she couldn't walk—it was just killingly funny, the things Mike had invented for them.

ELIZABETH ASHLEY: It's like a seven-floor walk-up or something, so everybody who makes an entrance—the mother, the telephone man, Redford's character, the weird neighbor who keeps jumping across—Mike really had us all go up and down the fire escape. He tells you who every character is before they get in the door.

Mike was the one who told Redford that he had not just a cold, he had pneumonia, and sleeps on the couch in the overcoat in the hat with the flaps. Redford can do death-rattle pneumonia better than almost anybody, because he doesn't play it, he *gets* it.

NEIL SIMON[7]**:** While we were still doing *Barefoot*—I think we were still in rehearsal—we were walking along the street, and I said, "I have another idea for a play, Mike." And he says, "What is it?" I say, "Well, it's these two guys who break up with their spouses, and they move in together and they have the same fights with each other as they had with their spouses." And he said, "I'll do it." That was it. I said, "Really?" He said, "It can't miss." He trusted me that I was going to write it right, and he promised me to do it, and he did, and *bang*.

ROBBIE LANTZ[8]**:** I watched a rehearsal of *The Odd Couple* once. And Walter [Matthau] began to improvise, real vaudeville schtick. When it came to the end of the scene, everybody was still laughing. Mike was virtually on the floor. And then came Mike's loving, but absolutely ice-cold comment: He said, "You will never do it again."

---

7. Courtesy of the John Lahr collection at the Howard Gotlieb Archival Research Center, Boston University.

8. Courtesy of the John Lahr collection at the Howard Gotlieb Archival Research Center, Boston University.

Because it was out of character, out of reality, and became comedy for comedy's sake.

When they were in New Haven, we went to see it: Neil Simon, his then wife, and Mike and I. And there was one joke, one line, it literally stopped the show. The house came down. At the end, we went across the street to the terrible Taft Hotel and sat down in the lobby and ordered something to eat. And Mike said to Simon, "You realize what has to be cut." Simon said, "The big laugh." Mike said, "Yes, it's a terrible tragedy, but it has to go. It's against the evening." And the two men, there and then, excised it from the show.

FRANK RICH: *The Odd Couple* was one of the great learning experiences in the theater for me. I was a ticket taker at the National Theatre in Washington, DC. In addition to taking tickets for the two- or three-week run, I could see it for free, and did, repeatedly. It opened with not much of an advance. You've got to remember that at that time Neil Simon was not a famous playwright. He had had one big hit. Walter Matthau was not yet a star. Art Carney was a star whose celebrity had passed him. And Mike was still early in his career as a theater director. So when *The Odd Couple* came to Washington, it was not a hugely anticipated thing. It didn't start selling out until the business caught up with the reviews.

The way he staged the first act, to this day, is the funniest staging of anything I've ever seen in the theater. I still remember that they open a little can of beer and somehow it worked that the beer spurted the whole length of the proscenium. The only thing that comes close is Jerry Robbins's staging of the opening number of *A Funny Thing Happened on the Way to the Forum*, and Michael Blakemore's staging of the second act of *Noises Off*.

There were three shows that tried out in Washington within a several-year period: the original productions of *Hello, Dolly!*, *Odd Couple*, and *Fiddler on the Roof*. All of them immediately got rave reviews, and if they weren't selling out, started to. People went crazy to get into the third week of a three-week run—they were fighting to get into the theater.

These shows were obviously hits the moment I saw them, they got the great reviews which confirmed my impression, audiences were loving them, and yet in all three cases, their perfectionist creators kept working on them throughout the tryout. They didn't freeze them and take them to New York. You saw people like Gower Champion, David Merrick, Jerry Robbins and Hal Prince, and Simon and Nichols keep working on something even though all the outward signs were: *It ain't broke, don't fix it.* It was a really useful introduction to craft and professionalism. It was exciting to be around. I could go to see it every night and watch them put in changes and take them out.

MARSHA MASON (*actress*): At one point, Art Carney burst into tears because he had to learn a whole new act while they were out of town.

DAVID GEFFEN: If you saw those original Neil Simon productions and all their revivals, the one thing you see is the difference between having Mike Nichols and not having him. Because Mike put into all of those shows a gigantic amount of business that's not on the page, and when you revive it, it doesn't have any of that business, and they did not do as well in revivals.

BOB BALABAN (*actor*): On the first day of rehearsal for *Plaza Suite*, Mike said, "To get this started, let's simply imagine you guys are coming into a hotel room for the first time. What do you do? Do you hang up your coat first? Do you sit on the bed to test it? Do you look out the window? Let's just get used to being in the space." He was a great behaviorist. He knew that rarely do people simply sit and talk to each other. In life, everything in life is triggered by physical actions, even if it's as simple as tying your shoe.

Neil's plays are really demanding, they need a certain rhythm. But Mike found a way to get into them. He didn't try to turn them into dramas, but he really understood how serious comedy was. He brought as much attention to detail directing *Plaza Suite* as he would if he was directing *Long Day's Journey into Night.*

DAVID HARE: Mike has an unerring sense of where the story is taking you. That's how he turned Neil Simon into the most successful playwright on Broadway. The laughs Neil could provide, but the story is what Mike worked on and worked on and worked on.

JON ROBIN BAITZ: I think that the Neil Simon shows could have been directed by someone else in a way that would just have been about their comic timing, but Mike managed to excavate the agony and anxiety underneath.

EMANUEL AZENBERG: Nobody had three comedies—three giant successes—on Broadway before at the same time. How come Neil and Mike didn't do more? What happened? It's a very valid question. They were not enemies. *The Sunshine Boys* would have been so logical for Mike to do but maybe Mike asked for too much money. That's possible. Or maybe he decided that he was now an auteur and doing more important things than Neil Simon plays.

Mike with Richard Burton and Elizabeth Taylor on the set of *Who's Afraid of Virginia Woolf?* "You know who's a genius?" Taylor said to producer-screenwriter Ernest Lehman, who was looking for a suitable director. "Who?" "Mike Nichols." (© *Bob Willoughby/mptvimages.com*)

CHAPTER 5

It All Started in the Alley

TOM FONTANA: I asked Mike once, "How did you direct *Who's Afraid of Virginia Woolf?* as your first movie?" He said, "I sucked up to Elizabeth Taylor."

TONY WALTON: When he was doing his evening with Elaine, Mike had adjoining stage doors with the Majestic Theatre where my ex Julie [Andrews] was then in *Camelot*, and I used to go half an hour early every night to pick her up so that I could watch the final, fully off-the-cuff, improvised chunk at the end of Mike and Elaine's show, which was just staggering, absolutely extraordinary.

DOUGLAS McGRATH: The Golden Theatre shares this back alley with the Majestic Theatre, where *Camelot* was, with Roddy McDowall and Julie Andrews and Richard Burton. After every show, they'd be with Mike out in the alley, smoking and drinking, or in each other's dressing rooms, smoking and drinking.

TONY WALTON: *Virginia Woolf*, despite what he said about Elizabeth Taylor, was actually Richard Burton's doing, as a result of how close they had become during these postproduction dressing room gatherings, which were always alcoholically fueled and hilariously funny.

DOUGLAS McGRATH: Having become friendly with him, Burton asked Mike, "Would you mind looking after Elizabeth for a little bit?" because Mike was going to be in Rome, and Mike said, "If it'll help."

So, in Rome, Mike takes her out for a day in the country, and they just have the best time together. He was a bewitching person, and she just adored him, so when he read that Warner's was going to make *Virginia Woolf*, he called his publicist, John Springer, who was also Elizabeth Taylor's publicist, and said, "You should tell her that I should direct that movie," and she loved the idea. You could say it all started in the alley behind the Golden and the Majestic.

NANCY SCHOENBERGER (*writer*): When Burton was plucked from the lead role of King Arthur in *Camelot* to play Antony in *Cleopatra* in 1962, Mike came to Rome where they were filming and visited them in their villa. This was around the time when Taylor and Burton's love affair burst onto the scene. Burton called it *"le scandale,"* because it made international news. At one point, Elizabeth Taylor was condemned by the Vatican for "erotic vagrancy." Taylor was married at the time to Eddie Fisher, her fourth husband, and Burton was married to his Welsh wife, Sybil, and they had two daughters. Once Taylor met Burton and acted in those passionate love scenes with him in *Cleopatra*, they genuinely fell in love.

BOBBIE O'STEEN (*writer*): She kept breaking up marriages. She broke up Debbie Reynolds and Eddie Fisher, and then she dumps Eddie Fisher for Richard Burton, who was married, too.

NANCY SCHOENBERGER: It was the beginning of the paparazzi relentlessly chasing down celebrities. Mike Nichols and the wonderful, then number one top model, Suzy Parker, posed for a series of photographs taken by Richard Avedon, in which they pretended to be Richard Burton and Elizabeth Taylor in hiding. Burton and Taylor loved that spoof. Though embattled, they had a great sense of humor about themselves.

AUSTIN PENDLETON (*actor*): Mike flew over to see Elizabeth just to hang out during the making of *Cleopatra*. She came out in her limousine to meet his plane, and then as soon as he got in, she collapsed in sobs and poured out her heart about how she's having an affair with Richard Burton, she's in love with him, she's betraying her husband. And Mike said to Barbara Harris, "I just kept wanting to say, 'I know all this.' Everything she told me has been in the paper."

NANCY SCHOENBERGER: Ernie Lehman, who wrote *Sweet Smell of Success* and adapted *The Sound of Music* and *West Side Story* for film, produced and adapted *Who's Afraid of Virginia Woolf?* He wanted Elizabeth Taylor because he knew she would create a huge sensation.

Richard Burton wasn't his first choice. Peter O'Toole was considered, and Arthur Hill, who had played George in the stage version. Lehman even offered the part to Jack Lemmon and Glenn Ford, but they passed on it, feeling that the role of George, a henpecked, emasculated college professor, would hurt their image. It was Elizabeth Taylor who whispered in Ernie Lehman's ear, "How about Burton?"

BOBBIE O'STEEN: Sam [O'Steen] felt Burton was miscast, and looking back, I understand what he was saying. Burton was way too macho. Martha is after him, she's after him, she's after him, and then the tables turn and suddenly George is running the show. That's much more surprising when you have a milquetoast-y guy like Arthur Hill playing that part.

NANCY SCHOENBERGER: Once they decided, yes, we can have Elizabeth Taylor and Richard Burton, and this will be a huge success just because of their names, they then turned to wondering who would direct. The first choice was John Frankenheimer, who had directed *The Manchurian Candidate*, *Birdman of Alcatraz*, and *Seven Days in May*, but Frankenheimer insisted that his name appear above the title, and Elizabeth Taylor was not going to have any of that. Elizabeth thought for a minute and said, "You know who's a genius?" and Lehman said, "Who?" "Mike Nichols."

MAUREEN DOWD: Liz and Dick were a giant, worldwide circus. Mike really loved them because they were willing to put all of that passion and fighting and loving into the film. They didn't want to separate the characters from their own lives. They were going to give him this gift of putting their own crazy relationship on-screen.

GEORGE SEGAL (*actor*): Elaine was a good friend of Ted Flicker, who created The Premise on Bleecker Street in New York. They had worked in Chicago together, and at the Crystal Palace in St. Louis, instigating a system for improvisation which Flicker used to train us in. Elaine came to see it, and I think she liked me very much. She must have told Mike about me. Mike was always the smartest guy in the room. I think what bound him to Elaine was, he thought she was the one person smarter than he was.

They held auditions for a Jules Feiffer one-act called *Crawling Arnold*. The main part of the audition was me crawling around on the floor as Mike sat in a chair, and what I remember was his handmade boots. But I also remember thinking, *Here's this hotshot guy from The Premise crawling around on the floor.* Then I was called in for an audition for *The Knack*, and I got it.

Elizabeth had cast approval, and she came to a rehearsal of *The Knack*. There were no seats in the house, so she sat on folding chairs with her then husband and agent Michael Wilding, and we did the play for them, and I passed muster. I think she went to see Sandy [Dennis] in whatever she was doing on Broadway.

When *Virginia Woolf* came along, Mike wanted Redford, whom he knew from *Barefoot in the Park*. Apparently Redford thought the part was too unpleasant, and I certainly understand that, from where he was going, so it fell to me.

BOBBIE O'STEEN: In Ernie Lehman's script, when George Segal and Liz Taylor are fucking upstairs, Burton takes a walk and comes upon two dogs fucking. Nichols took that out. Also in Ernie's script, their imaginary son really existed, but had committed suicide— another idea Nichols threw out.

Mike had Burton try on glasses. Ernie was whining, "I don't like his glasses." Mike said he did, and they fit Burton's character. Ernie said, "Well, what if it comes down to that last day and we have to go one way and I don't want him to wear glasses?" "Well," Mike said, "I'll kill you."

PETER LAWRENCE: Mike watched *A Place in the Sun* a number of times before he directed *Virginia Woolf*, just to get a sense of Elizabeth Taylor. He would reference that George Stevens could do two things at once: he could be a great artist and a commercial director at the same time, and I think that was the thing that Mike admired the most.

GREGORY MOSHER (*theater director*): When I was about to do my first movie, I said to Mike, "What do I do?" He said, "Watch *A Place in the Sun* twenty-five times, and then watch it twenty-five more times, and then call me and we'll talk," and I did. I watched it fifty times. I said, "Why that? Why not *Citizen Kane*? Or *Seven Samurai*?" He said, "Because everything you need to know about the movies is in that film." Where's the camera? What's happening? The ways Stevens shot the movie is just kind of perfect, and, indeed, it was like going to film school, between watching the movie fifty times and talking to Mike about it.

ERIC IDLE: Mike went to see Billy Wilder, and he said, "Tomorrow I am directing my first film, with Richard Burton and Elizabeth Taylor. What shall I wear?"

NANCY SCHOENBERGER: The first thing Mike did, because he came from theater, was insist on a sit-down read-through of the play before filming. Burton was very accustomed to that, because he came up through the London theater, but Elizabeth Taylor was a studio-trained actress. She would learn her marks, her lines, where she had to stand, but she wouldn't really give a performance until the cameras were rolling.

GEORGE SEGAL: We rehearsed for six weeks. We could have opened that play. The only one that was a little impatient with the rehearsal was Elizabeth, who didn't come from the stage like Sandy and Richard and me.

Where, in movies, do you get six weeks of rehearsal? Mike got everything he wanted, because he had Elizabeth backing him up, and she was the queen of it all. She got anything he wanted, plus she got everything she wanted.

JOHN CALLEY[1]: Jack Warner had agreed that they were going to do the film in black and white, and suddenly realized that it was a commercial mistake. So he said, "Look, kid, it's gonna have to be in color, that's all there is to it." Mike said, "I can only wish you all the luck in the world, Mr. Warner. I hope that at another time in the future we'll be able to work together." And Warner went, "Okay, go shoot it in black and white." He knew he'd lost.

TONY WALTON: Mike was taking forever to set up the initial shot and you could see people getting wiseacre, thinking, *This guy doesn't know what he's up to.* He finally said, "Look, I imagine all of you must be quite anxious working with this first timer, and you're right. You should be. I barely know what I'm doing at all. But I'm going to get it right with your help, and anybody who's uncomfortable with that should leave now." And I think a small handful of people actually did.

Soon after that he had to fire Harry Stradling, the unimaginably famous cinematographer, because he was making Elizabeth beautiful.

GREGORY MOSHER: One of the first questions Mike asked [Stradling's replacement,] Haskell Wexler, was, "When the door opens, why doesn't it hit the camera?" Wex had to explain what a long lens was. But then Mike was fearless.

BOBBIE O'STEEN: Nichols didn't want Sam [O'Steen]. He wanted some big-time editor, but he had to hire a Warner Bros. editor, and he

---

1. Courtesy of the John Lahr collection at the Howard Gotlieb Archival Research Center, Boston University.

picked Sam because he was the youngest. They were both very young. Then, in their very first meeting, Mike said, "Can you cut overlaps?" Mike wanted to have overlapping dialogue, because there's a reality to it, especially on a film like *Virginia Woolf* where George and Martha are constantly talking over each other. Sam said, "If you shoot it, I can do it." Mike's response was, "That's interesting, because other editors said they couldn't."

What Sam did was, when George and Martha were talking at the same time, he coded each of their tracks and mixed them together. "It didn't matter if they overlapped," he said. "They would always be in sync. I could cut anyplace I wanted to." Sam basically invented that technique, which was especially ballsy in the Moviola days, because making any changes would require going back to the soundstage and remixing, which was time-consuming and expensive. Now, with digital editing systems, it can be done easily in the cutting room. But the truth is, Sam didn't make many changes after his first cut.

When [consultant] Doane Harrison, who had worked for Billy Wilder, quit on *Who's Afraid of Virginia Woolf?*, Mike started calling Sam down to the set, because he just didn't know about how to stage a scene. It was his first movie. "What do you think about this, Sam? Do you think this angle works?" "No, we can't really use that, but maybe if you . . ." He would give him all these suggestions, and then over time he would just keep coming down to the set.

As a result of Sam being on the set, there wasn't much wasted footage, and the transitions were amazing because Sam was helping control them. I've interviewed so many editors, and I don't know of a single example of an editor who was on the set with a director for the entire shoot.

NANCY SCHOENBERGER: They filmed on the Warner Bros. Studio 8 lot in Los Angeles, and at Smith College in Northampton, Massachusetts. Warner Bros. rented a number of campus homes in Northampton, and Elizabeth went around and checked them all out. She decided the one she liked the best was the one given to Mike, so he very graciously packed up and moved out and let Elizabeth and

Burton take the house that he had set aside for himself. Mike later thought he made a big mistake filming on location. He decided he could have done the whole thing on a set.

Mike was very much the man about town, dating various famous people, like Gloria Steinem and Mia Farrow. At one point, they had to close down and lose an entire day of shooting because Mike had to fly into New York to have lunch with Jackie Kennedy.

GEORGE SEGAL: When we first got there, my then wife and I and my kids, we were all in one big house with Richard and Elizabeth: the Burtons and the Segals. We got up in the morning and had breakfast together. I can tell you that Elizabeth Taylor getting up in the morning with those violet eyes and those double lashes and the hair—she was just beautiful when she would come to breakfast.

TONY WALTON: Like Mike, Richard was a very funny guy. They were similar to the extent that no matter who was in any room, if one of them happened to be there, everything tended to gravitate toward either Mike or Richard.

NANCY SCHOENBERGER: Mike and Richard loved playing word games. They tried to one-up each other. Burton challenged Mike Nichols to identify the author of poems that he would quote at length, such as "Fear no more the heat of the sun nor the furious winter's rages," from *Cymbeline*, which actually stumped Mike. There was a lot of this playful show of erudition back and forth.

GEORGE SEGAL: There was a list that went out to all personnel at the studio entitled, "How to Treat the Burtons." One of the points was, do not greet the Burtons unless they greet you first, and do not refer to Elizabeth Taylor as Elizabeth Taylor but as Mrs. Burton and so forth. But they weren't like that at all. Their one extravagance—which I loved—was Chasen's, a big restaurant where all the stars went, would often cater their lunch.

I will say that Richard is far and away the best actor I've ever worked with. He was breathtaking, and he had Elizabeth doing e. e. cummings and whole Dylan Thomas poems, committing them to memory like he did. She became as much like him as she could, although she ran the relationship, and he was delighted in that.

I think we all gave the performances of our lives in that thing, and that's because we were working around Richard. It raises your game, working around somebody who's that good, that effortless, and no ego, none of that movie-star stuff. He was a worker in the field.

NANCY SCHOENBERGER: Elizabeth just adored Mike. She often rode a bicycle from Studio 8 at Warner Bros. to her dressing room. At one point, she fell off her bike, and Mike Nichols rescued her and carried her back to the studio in his arms. Elizabeth said, "I want you to do this for me every day." And Mike said, "I'll have to get into training," because at Ernie Lehman's suggestion, she had put on ten pounds for the role. Sadly for Elizabeth, from then on she would have a hard time losing the extra weight.

GEORGE SEGAL: At five or six p.m., no matter where we were in the shooting—if he had one more shot to make, it didn't matter—a guy came in with two Bloody Marys: one for Elizabeth and one for Richard. That was the end of shooting for the day. And she didn't come in until ten. Those were the good old days. Never had that before or since.

BOBBIE O'STEEN: Burton and Taylor had it in their contracts that they couldn't work past six o'clock, but when they were called back to the set after lunch, they often wouldn't come down from their dressing room, sometimes not until five o'clock. Meanwhile, Sam said, "Mike was going crazy, he'd walk around saying, 'Cocksuckers, I hate their fuckin' guts,' and crying to me that they were costing him time. When they finally came back late, they'd just ignore it all, be real nice. 'Hey, Mike, old buddy, sorry we're late, let's shoot.'" There was nothing Mike could do about it, and he ended up being thirty days over schedule and doubling the budget.

NANCY SCHOENBERGER: Burton would later say, "He was one of the best directors I ever had, and he didn't give me a lot of direction."

I think Mike Nichols knew how to get out of Burton's way when he was in a black mood. He knew how to let Burton be Burton.

GEORGE SEGAL: The first assistant director Mike had was kind of a bully. He got rid of him. Mike had no patience for that kind of behavior. He wanted it all to be smooth, and it always was. Everybody always had a good time, and it was always a little ironic, and it was always funny. There was a moment where Richard was pouring drinks, and he coughed a real cough, and Mike kept it in, and it just added to the reality of everything. Another director would have said, *Let's do that again without the cough.*

Elizabeth had a mouth on her that was really funny, all unprintable stuff. She was down and dirty. Everybody was raw in that thing. Everybody was defenseless, and that's Mike, too. He's right there. He's present. Everybody on that picture, the cameramen, everybody, they were *present.* It was a gift, the whole radical project.

BOBBIE O'STEEN: Mike got into a fight with Jack Warner about the composer. Ernie Lehman had already hired Alex North, but Mike didn't care, he wanted André Previn. Jack Warner threw Mike off the lot. He was banned from the mixing stage. Sam would hold up the phone and play the mix for him. People would never understand this now, but if word had gotten out that Sam did that, he could have been blackballed by every studio in town, because in those days a studio really had power.

NICK PILEGGI: Jack Warner went back to the silent movies! He did *The Jazz Singer*—I mean, a cultural chasm. And yet Jack Warner, the son of a bitch, in the end, he let the movie go through. He knew something.

TOM HANKS: They were fighting the censors. The Catholic Church was going to ban the movie. And so Mike brought Jackie Kennedy along for the screening with the monsignor or the bishop—whoever was going to pass judgment. And as soon as it was over, Jackie leaned forward with her head between the monsignor and Mike and whispered, "Oh, Jack would have so loved your film."

LIZ SMITH: Elizabeth knew that it was her greatest performance, and I think she was terrified all through it that she was going to win the Oscar and Richard wouldn't, which is exactly what happened. She said, "Liz, you've seen a lot of women play Virginia Woolf." And I have, Elaine Stritch among them. "Tell me the truth, was I the greatest?" And I said, "Well, you had Mike Nichols."

NANCY SCHOENBERGER: The film was nominated for thirteen Academy Awards. Not bad for a directorial film debut. In fact, it was one of only two films nominated in every eligible category. All four actors were nominated, of course. Elizabeth Taylor and Sandy Dennis won.

FRANK RICH: *Virginia Woolf*, along with *Angels in America* and *Streetcar*, are I think the best adaptations of serious American plays into movies.

GREGORY MOSHER: Is there a better-acted film than that film? I don't know.

JAMES NAUGHTON (*actor*): In 1980, I was in rehearsal for a production of *Whose Life Is It Anyway?* with Mary Tyler Moore when I got a call from Mike saying he and Elaine were going to star in a production of *Who's Afraid of Virginia Woolf?* at Long Wharf Theatre up in New Haven, and would I play Nick? I thought, *Hey, do a production of* Virginia Woolf *with Nichols and May, how do I say no to that?* So I walked into our producer Manny Azenberg's office on the afternoon of opening night and gave him my notice. Manny said, "You know, you're not going to make any money up there." "I know, Manny. I'm not doing it for the money." Mary Tyler Moore couldn't have been more understanding. In fact, she rented a van and took the whole company up to see our production.

SWOOSIE KURTZ (*actress*): I saw the original—that's how old I am—and I just always wanted to play Honey, for years and years. So I had a meeting with dear Arvin Brown, who ran the Long Wharf. He said, "Mike may have people in mind. I've got to check with him." And by God, I got offered the part.

JAMES NAUGHTON: I went into rehearsal with Elaine and Swoosie and Mike and Arvin Brown. It was sort of a thankless task for Arvin. Mike and Elaine asked him to direct it, but then you have three directors in the room. They didn't really give him a whole lot of room to do much of anything. It was the Mike and Elaine show.

SWOOSIE KURTZ: Mike looked at the set the first day, and in that sardonic, passive-aggressive manner he had mastered, he said, "So . . . she's the daughter of the college president . . . he's an academic . . . and they have, let's see, *how many* bookshelves? Two. Hmm, four people, three places to sit. Interesting . . ." Just lethal.

It was always cold in the rehearsal room. One time I said to Mike, "It's so cold—don't you just want to kill yourself?" And he said, "Myself second."

JAMES NAUGHTON: At one point, Mike said, "Couldn't you be a blond?" I said, "No, I don't think that's a good idea. I tried it once. With my coloring and my beard and everything else, I look sort of like a transvestite." He laughed and said, "Yeah, okay, forget it." A little while later, he repeated the suggestion, and I said, "Why?" And he starts to laugh and he said, "Because then it would be the only production of this play where all four actors were wearing wigs." Finally it got to the point where I said, "Why do you want me to be a blond so badly?" He said, "Well, I just wanted you to look like a little Nazi."

SWOOSIE KURTZ: Elaine and I shared a dressing room, because at Long Wharf it was a resident theater, so we were the boys and the girls. Mike would poke his head in every so often before curtain and say, "Eileen?" or "Arlene?" or "Irene?"

They were a little reluctant to buckle down and learn lines and actually rehearse. They kind of reminded me of children who want to do anything but their homework. They'd go off on some tangent—*That reminds me of the time*—and they'd tell some amazing story. But they totally came through.

JAMES NAUGHTON: That third act is very, very dark, and Mike and Elaine being Mike and Elaine, they mined the first two acts for every laugh and smile and hint of humor—and there is a lot of humor in Albee's writing—so they weren't spent when they got to the third act. We all had something in terms of the emotion left to give.

Whatever the dynamics of that crazy-ass couple in that play are, they are bound by some kind of intellectual capacity that they share, and you got that from Mike. You're in the presence of a really, really smart guy here. There's Mike's personality, which is huge, and there's Elaine's personality, which is huge, but when you get them together, it's like there's another person in the room, and so it was complex.

SWOOSIE KURTZ: Everybody was coming up to see it. Because it's such a long play, we wouldn't finish until eleven, eleven fifteen, and nothing was open in New Haven. There was this one little cocktail-lounge place that didn't have food, and the people who had come up to see Mike and Elaine, he'd bring them to have drinks, and he would invite Jimmy and me along. I would find myself sitting at that piney little cocktail table across from Lillian Hellman, and next to me would be Richard Avedon. I ended up actually playing Lillian years later in Nora Ephron's play *Imaginary Friends*, so it was cool that I actually met her.

Cut to about three weeks into the run. Mike had not been feeling well. Jimmy and I took his temperature, and it was 103. Turned out he had pneumonia. That was the last performance we ever did.

JAMES NAUGHTON: You know the economics of off-Broadway and regional theater. It's pretty close to the bone, so it cost Long Wharf a lot of money.

SWOOSIE KURTZ: Elaine was the first sexy Martha I've ever seen. You think of Martha as being a little bit earthy, a little bit matronly, but Elaine's Martha was sort of a seductive snake. She would slink around and put her legs up on the sofa, inviting Nick to come closer.

George is very civil and gracious on the outside, to begin with, and then this thing comes out in him that she brings out, this venom. Mike could really shift into that from the charming exterior that he presented when we first come in. Mike dug down to a deep hurt and pain. The balance was less on the humor and the laugh and more on the *I'm going to kill you—I'm saying it in a slick, clever way, but I mean it, and I'm ready for war.*

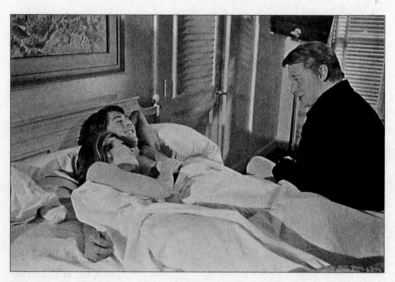

Mike with Dustin Hoffman and Anne Bancroft on the set of *The Graduate*.
Hoffman didn't feel he was right for the part of Benjamin Braddock, who is
described in the novel on which the script was based as an athletic blond WASP.
"[Nichols] said, 'You don't want to do it because you're Jewish,'" he recalled.
I said, "Yes." And he said, "Well, maybe Benjamin's Jewish *inside*." (© *Bob
Willoughby/mptvimages.com*)

CHAPTER 6

The Citizen Kane *of Disaffected Youth*

LARRY TURMAN (*producer*): I read a review for the novel *The Graduate* by Chuck Webb. The review caught my attention. It sounded like Webb would be a good screenwriter. So much of the screenplay, taking nothing away from Buck Henry, is right from the book.

The book haunted me. I identified with it personally. Two scenes in particular really got to me: one, a boy in a scuba suit in his own swimming pool; and then, that same boy on a public bus, shirttail out, with a girl in a wedding dress. I liked the book so much, I took out an option with my own money, something I counsel my students not to do.

KATHARINE ROSS (*actress*): *The Graduate* was a great marriage between Old and New Hollywood, I think. It was a generation that was kind of between Old Hollywood and New Hollywood—a no-man's-land, in a way. Things were going through a big transition. The studio system was almost out. The fact that I was put under contract was really a dying thing. There were vestiges—it was still sort of there—but it was going rapidly.

LARRY TURMAN: Mike Nichols was an intuitive hunch. The book is funny but mordant. Nichols and May humor was very funny, but edgy, mordant, and it seemed like a hand-in-glove fit to me. I didn't know the guy from Adam, but I found out who his agent was, a man named Robbie Lantz in New York, who also represented the Burtons.

I said, "I'm a producer. I've made some movies. I have a book. I would like Mike Nichols to read it."

I had another friend in New York, he was very chic, knew everybody, and he took me to a party at Richard Avedon's apartment. It was a small gathering: Sondheim, Bernstein, Mike Nichols—very heady. We played a game called Dictionary. Playing with those folks is really intimidating. They're all wordsmiths. That evening, I was introduced to Mike. He said, "I got your book." A few weeks later, I was coming back from the theater to my hotel, and they hand me a telephone message: "A Mr. Nichols called and said he likes the book."

We got together, and I gave him candor, which is who I am. I said, "I have a book. We both love it. I don't have any money. I don't have any studio. I have nothing. Let's do this. We'll make this movie together, and whatever money comes in, we'll split 50/50." I don't know if we literally shook hands on it, but we agreed.

No one else thought the book was funny. No one thought it was good. No one had any interest. Plus, who was Mike Nichols? At the point I sent the book to Mike and we agreed to do it together, he had only done one Broadway play, *Barefoot in the Park*, and no films. Who was he? They learned over the decades. That's what producing is about: your own taste, your own judgment.

BUCK HENRY: I always thought *The Graduate* was the best pitch I ever heard: This kid graduates college and has an affair with his parents' best friend and then falls in love with the friend's daughter. But give that to twenty writers and you've got twenty scripts. It's just odd to me that it hadn't been done a hundred times. But it is possible, too, that shortly before we started, that would have been a taboo subject. I think part of the reason all the studios passed on the film was the incestuous nature of it, which, of course, is what makes it interesting, more than anything else.

KATHARINE ROSS: I think what I responded to is the kind of confusion that you feel when you're young, particularly when you get out of college. *If I make the wrong decision, my life is over.* Even though we don't all have affairs with our parents' business partner's significant other, there's something classic and basic about it.

LARRY TURMAN: Who else is out there who has money? It proved to be Joe Levine, who was an enormously successful schlockmeister. He would buy junky films, have an imaginative, aggressive ad campaign, and plaster his own name all over it. "Schlockmeister" is an apt description for how he functioned in business, but it's colored with a touch of admiration for a great flamboyant throwback salesman. He flogged his pictures; he got them out there and made a lot of money for himself in the bargain. I don't even know if he "got" the book, but he climbed aboard.

CANDICE BERGEN: Mike had a cat named after Joe Levine, whom he hated. I remember once going to the house in Connecticut. He kicked the cat aside. "Get out of here, Levine, you bastard!"

LARRY TURMAN: By now Mike had done maybe a second and third play. He had cachet, which Joe didn't have. I think one of the main reasons Joe got aboard was to be in business with Mike Nichols. In fairness, I wasn't chopped liver. I had done a couple of movies. I had done *The Best Man*, which was a succès d'estime. But Mike had that New York chic. Also, in fairness, I told Joe—not producer bullshit, because I really believed it—I said I could make the movie for a million dollars. The film ended up costing three.

At some point along the way, Ernie Lehman, a dear friend of mine, calls me to ask about Mike Nichols. I said, "Why?" He said he was doing *Virginia Woolf*. I said, "I think he's super smart, that's why I chose him." In my secret heart of hearts, I thought, *Let Mike get experience directing* Virginia Woolf. *Then he'll come to me on* The Graduate—I wasn't ready anyway—*as an experienced pro.*

BOBBIE O'STEEN: Larry Turman actually signed Nichols for *The Graduate* before *Virginia Woolf*, so Mike only got $25,000 even though he had already gotten $50,000 for *Virginia Woolf*. But Mike eventually got 6 percent of the net profits of *The Graduate*, so he ended up making $6 million.

LARRY TURMAN: I suggested a well-known writer named Calder Willingham to adapt it. He turned in a script, and it was vulgar. The sexuality in *The Graduate* was strong for its time, both in the book and in the movie, but Calder added some gratuitous sex and homo-sexuality. I gave it to Mike to read, and I said, "Mike, read this, but I don't like it, and here's why." Mike called me a few days later and said, "I agree, I don't like it at all." Mike then suggested Buck Henry. Willingham failed, so I thought, *Let's go with Mike's guy.*

When the film was over, I wrote a letter to Calder, saying, "I just want to give you advance notice that Buck Henry is getting the sole screenplay credit." I got back a letter from Calder, saying, "I'm going to have the Writers Guild arbitrate it," and they arbitrated it. Calder Willingham not only gets credit; he gets first position. Order of credit is very important. The old Hollywood line was, "Have you heard of Barnum and Bailey?" "Barnum, sure. What do you know about Bailey?" Being in second position ain't so good.

Yet every person you would speak to said it's Buck Henry's script. Which it is, by the way, it's totally Buck Henry's script. I told Calder the truth: "Buck never read your script." Calder was there first, so he gets the credit, but it's all Buck's.

BUCK HENRY: George Segal and I were in an improvisational the-ater together in New York in the early '60s. We were longtime friends, so when he did *Virginia Woolf,* I'd hang around. I saw a lot of Nichols in that year. And one day he said, "Read this book. Tell me what you think." I had heard of it, but I hadn't read it. So I read it, and I thought, *It's a movie.*

Nichols and I related to it in exactly the same way. I think we all thought we were Benjamin Braddock. It was very much the story of part of our lives. Plus, it's an absolutely first-class novel, with great characters, great dialogue, a terrific theme. Who could resist it?

BOBBIE O'STEEN: Sam loved it until the second half when Ben-jamin was driving up to Berkeley. "He kept driving back and forth. I mean, come on." He said to Mike, "What do you wanna do that for? After *Virginia Woolf* you gotta do something that snaps your head around." But Mike said he felt something, he identified with that boy a lot. And the main reason he wanted to do it, he told Sam, was because he loved *The Catcher in the Rye* but he couldn't get the rights and thought this was as close to it as anything he'd found.

CANDICE BERGEN: Mike and I became friends when he came to LA. He was the quintessential New Yorker in LA, which, in those days at least, was just defined by dopey. I remember him saying, "People in LA don't know what houses are supposed to look like or how you're supposed to lead your life because nobody's told them."

. The first house he rented was where David Selznick and Jennifer Jones had lived, and it was the most glamorous old Spanish house, way up at the top of the canyon. He had a Spanish chef who traveled with him named Roberto. The dining area was almost like a tree house. It was a long, narrow, mirrored room with trees outside. Mike would have dinners and invite anybody who was any kind of presence.

DAVID GEFFEN: Mike was complaining to me about how when he was first in Hollywood he didn't know anybody and never got invited anywhere, *blah blah blah*. Anyway, a friend of mine says, "Oh, did you see these movies on YouTube of summers at Roddy McDowall's house at the beach?" So I'm watching these movies, and there's Mike Nichols! So I called up Mike and said, "What are you talking about? There you are with Natalie Wood!" He said, "I was never there." I said, "I'm looking at you."

HANNAH ROTH SORKIN: There's some footage that I saw, I think on YouTube, of him at a pool party in the '60s. It just captures everything because he's odd man out at the party. He's fully dressed. He isn't going in the pool. Ever.

BUCK HENRY: When we started, we were talking about actors who looked nothing like the final result—they were all tall and blond. But it wasn't as interesting.

ROBERT REDFORD: He wanted me to be in *The Graduate*, because *Barefoot in the Park* had been so successful, and he wanted to continue the relationship. I said, "Yeah, but, Mike, I'm not right for that guy. I see this character as it's written: a guy on an escalator who can't get off." I said, "If it was me, I could get off the escalator. I'd just jump over it. I think that's what I project, and I don't think the character should project that." We went back and forth. He just wouldn't accept what I was saying. Finally I said, "I'll show you. I'll do a screen test." So I did a test with Candy Bergen. I did everything I could to seem like a schlub, but when it was over, he said, "I get it. You're right," and that was the end of that.

DOUGLAS McGRATH: Mike's version was that even though on the surface Bob seemed right for it—because in the novel of *The Graduate*, Benjamin is described as looking exactly like Bob Redford—it's also about a guy who's not so lucky with girls, and so when Bob was pestering him for the part, Mike said, "Let me ask you a question. How do you react when a girl turns you down?" and Bob said, "What do you mean?"

LARRY TURMAN: We saw a million kids. Redford tested with Candy Bergen. We tested Tony Bill. Charles Grodin came in for a reading, and it was a terrific reading. I've heard or read a couple places that Charles Grodin says the biggest mistake he made was turning down *The Graduate*. Well, he was never offered *The Graduate*.

At one point, Mike turned to me and said, "Turman, you SOB, you got me into a movie that can't be cast."

KATHARINE ROSS: Before doing *The Graduate*, I think I had done four movies. But the one just prior to *The Graduate* was a movie called *Games*, with Simone Signoret, who was a good friend of Mike Nichols's and put in a good word for me.

I did two tests. I tested with Dustin [Hoffman], and I tested the next day with Charles Grodin. Mike let the test be borne out of the interaction between the actors. It wasn't like he had Dustin and Charles Grodin doing the same blocking, the same everything. So it was two very different tests.

I remember meeting Dustin in the office a couple of days before. He was from New York, all dressed in black, and you know, we're all tan out here. Those were the days when all the leading men looked just like Robert Redford. Dustin looked like he had crawled out from under a rock. He was in some off-Broadway production. Not at all interested in being in a movie, or at least that's what he said. He was very outspoken about that.

I gave him a ride home. He had no car, didn't want to have a car. And he was staying at his parents' house!

DUSTIN HOFFMAN (*actor*): I had just gotten an apartment for eighty dollars a month, and I was painting everything black. You're living to pay the rent. We never went to bars or clubs. I didn't even have money to buy records. Nichols and May had performed on Broadway, but I kind of wiped Broadway off my mind. That was like a foreign land.

I auditioned for *The Apple Tree*, a musical about Adam and Eve that Mike was directing. I was reading for the snake. I didn't know how to sing. I'm bad at auditions anyway, so I'm very nervous, but I'm doubly nervous because I knew Mike was there. Sometimes, if I didn't think I had a chance of getting it, I'd do the scene in such a way that they would at least remember me. I heard him laughing, and he came forward and complimented me. I didn't get the part, of course.

Eh? is what really brought me to the attention of Broadway. Before that, I had been fired three, maybe four times by directors. Always the same reason: me telling them, *I really don't think this is working that way, I think it works better this way.* I thought that was a great perk to being an actor.

The first director on *Eh?* wanted me fired, and for some reason, the legendary Ted Mann, who ran the Circle in the Square Theatre, said, "No. Hoffman stays, you go." I don't know why he was taking a chance on me. Then they hired a second director. Same thing happened after a week. I said, "Why are you firing this guy? Why aren't you firing me?" Then he hires this guy by the name of Alan Arkin. Alan and I had the same humor.

On opening night, the usual *Times* critic was on holiday or something, so they sent the book critic Christopher Lehmann-Haupt, and he gives it a fucking rave. Before that, people had been laughing in the previews. After that, they came in laughing at the wallpaper! They're so conditioned.

That weekend or two weekends later, because nobody tells you anything, I pick up the *Sunday Times* and my face is all over the front of the Arts and Leisure section. It's by Walter Kerr, and he compares me to Buster Keaton. I had never seen a Buster Keaton movie, but I went to see one afterward, and I understood what he was talking about: the body language. I think Nichols must have read that and told somebody to go see the show. I don't think he ever saw it.

Suddenly I'm getting some off-Broadway plays. If I could work off-Broadway for the rest of my life, I'd be delighted. And then my agent, Jane Oliver, calls me and says, "They want to audition you for this movie called *The Graduate* with Mike Nichols directing."

LARRY TURMAN: Dustin had a thirty-second scene in *The Tiger Makes Out*. Somehow we arranged to go see that thirty-second scene, and off that, we decided to test him too.

BUCK HENRY: I'd seen him onstage. He was stunning. I also had known him in passing because he'd been around the Village and the theaters there that we were all around.

DUSTIN HOFFMAN: I cannot honestly remember if I read the book first or the script, but I know I read both. I said, *What the fuck is going on? I'm not right for this.* A five-foot-eleven-inch WASP with blond hair and blue eyes? I'm a character actor, but there's a limit.

It's funny what you remember. On my little coffee table was *Time* magazine. It said, "Man of the Year: Twenty-five and Under," and there was a drawing of a guy that looked like Benjamin. There he was: Mr. Gentile. I said, "Mr. Nichols, take a look at that cover, because that's who you want: somebody like Robert Redford." I didn't even know Redford had tried out. I later found out that Mike wanted someone who would have trouble getting a date, and Redford wouldn't.

I was living with Gene Hackman and Robert Duvall. We had no money. This was a different time—the Beat Generation, '60s coffeehouses. It was: *Fuck 'em. I am not going to compromise my work.* You didn't take a commercial, even if you were broke. You didn't take soap operas. If you got nominated for something, you didn't go. It was a thing. But my agent said, "You can't do that! They want to audition you."

Mike called again. I think he was kind of intrigued because this unknown actor is saying, *I'm not right, sorry.* He said, "You don't want to do it because you're Jewish." I said, "Yes." And he said, "Well, maybe Benjamin's Jewish *inside*." I said, "Okay, I'll audition." I had to get permission to leave the play for a few days. Coincidentally, Elizabeth Wilson was in the play, wonderful woman, and she wound up playing my mother in *The Graduate*.

LARRY TURMAN: *The Graduate* was a book written by a WASP, about Pasadena, at a point in time where it was really a WASP community. We filmed it in Beverly Hills, putatively a Jewish enclave. The picture was produced by an atheist that was Jewish. Mike Nichols is Jewish. Buck Henry is Jewish. The leading character, Dustin Hoffman, is Jewish. The guy who put up the money, Joe Levine, is Jewish.

BUCK HENRY: We decided to switch it and make nouveau riche Beverly Hills Jews out of them. It's my theory of California genetics: Jews from New York came and within one generation the Malibu sand had gotten into their genes and turned their children into tall Nordic powerhouses.

BOBBIE O'STEEN: The book is sort of sardonic, but Benjamin is more finger-wagging and judgmental, more obnoxious. After Mrs. Robinson traps him in the bedroom and proposes the affair, he goes on a road trip and sleeps with hookers, so he's not a virgin, which I think is so much a part of his vulnerability with her in the movie. They made really good changes to the book.

DUSTIN HOFFMAN: Before I fly out, my agent tells me, "You have to sign a contract before you audition." I said, "What kind of contract?" "You agree to the money, which is scale." "Okay." "And Nichols, Turman, Levine, all three have options on using you for two films." "What are they?" "They don't know, whatever they want." I said, "No, I won't do it." Later, people said that's maybe the smartest business move, but it had nothing to do with that. The best thing about acting is that you don't have to do anything that you don't want to do. She said, "Well, you're not going to get the audition then." I said, "Fine." I told Neil Simon this whole thing, and he used a lot of it in *The Goodbye Girl*. Anyway, she calls back, and she's shocked: "They said okay."

I did it for minimum and didn't get per diem, so the movie *cost* me money because I had to keep my apartment; I couldn't rent it out. I stayed at the Chateau Marmont. Four months later, whatever it was, I went on unemployment. I was broke. I like to think that that was their way of getting even, because I wouldn't give them two films apiece.

I go out there for the test. I remember Nichols was very nice. We read it first in his office, Anne Bancroft and me. I thought I probably was terrible, but I think he thought it was interesting. The screen test was like ten pages. I thought, *How am I going to memorize this before I go out there?* I'm a terrible memorizer, always very bad in school. And now I was struggling because Mike wanted to do it all in a master, so you have to get those ten pages right. I did three or four pages and then got a line wrong. I fucked up. You can't be more nervous than this. You don't sleep in New York a night or two before, you don't sleep on the plane—you're just a wreck. I remember sitting in the chair when they're making me up, they're shading my nose. He comes in—he said it kindly, but he's Mike—he said, "Can't you do something about the nose?" And they did it already! I thought, *Why am I here?* I already told him this is the reason I shouldn't be testing. And I just started sweating all over. Jews are paranoid just to survive. Jews cross a one-way street and look the other way first. The prop man, the cameraman, the makeup person, the lighting people—I didn't know anything about movies, but I can feel from them that they thought that even screen testing me was a great mistake.

I sit down on the edge of the bed next to Katharine Ross. I screw up. She screws up. I think my screwing up, it was screwing her up more. At one point I reached over, and she said, "Don't you ever touch me!" I said, "Let me out of here! Please let me out of here!" The whole crew was looking. Then Mike says, "I want to talk to you for a minute."

So I walk over to him. I thought he was going to say, *You can go, thanks.* But he doesn't. He says, "What's the matter?" I say, "I don't know, I thought I had it memorized. I couldn't sleep for a few days. I'm nervous." He says, "We're not making a movie, it's just a screen test." And he puts out his hand to shake, and his hand is so sweaty that my hand comes out like *that*. He's acting like he's very relaxed, but something is grievously wrong.

We finish. I thought, *Fuck, I'm glad this day is over*. I take my hand out of my pocket to shake the prop man's hand and my tokens fall out, about seven or eight of them—and they were big then. He picks them up and as he hands them back to me he says, "Here, you're going to need this, kid." At the end of the film, he gave me a frame with the tokens. I have it in my study.

I don't know how much time passes. It wasn't the next day. My agent told me to call Nichols, and I thought, *Oh, fuck. He's going to tell me, You almost got it but you weren't right*. I remember walking to my girlfriend's apartment, trudging up the middle of Columbus because there was a lot of snow. I walked from Eleventh Street all the way up to the seventies. She was about to make me a nice Sunday breakfast, and I said, "I've got to make this phone call." Mike answers, "Hello?" "Mr. Nichols, I'm sorry—what time is it?" I woke him up. They said to call at ten. That made it seven in the morning his time. There was a long pause. "Well, you got it." Those were the words. No *I've got great news for you*. He said, "Hello? You don't sound very excited." I said, "No I am," thinking, *They must have made a mistake—this is a bad joke*. I hang up the phone and look across to where my girlfriend is cooking the eggs. She looked at me and I looked at her, and I said, "I got it." She said, "I knew you would," and it wasn't happy. She knew it meant we were going to be separated, because she was a dancer in the New York City Ballet.

I've heard—and I underline that because it doesn't mean it's true; Turman might have said it—they're sitting there looking at the test. It's over, and one looks at the other and there's silence. And finally, one of them says—because we were the last they had tested—"Well, I don't know, what do you think? We go with them, or we don't do it." And Mike says, "Okay, we go with them." I'm convinced, if that's a true quote, that if we had auditioned in the first two weeks, it would never have happened for me.

LARRY TURMAN: When we saw Dustin and Katharine, it's not like either one of us said, "That's our couple!" We said, "They'll be okay." "Yeah, let's use them." No magic bell went off saying, *Eureka, we struck gold*, as we proved to do.

JULIAN SCHLOSSBERG (*producer*): Joe Levine had an office on Sixth Avenue. Mike's in for a meeting, and the guy comes in to clean the windows. Joe says, "So who have you chosen?" And Mike said, "This guy." Dustin was cleaning the windows.

WILLIAM DANIELS (*actor*): Mike's a pretty independent guy. He wanted Dustin, who nobody knew. I heard he was a very good actor off-Broadway, but this was his first film, and Mike insisted on him to Paramount. So Mike was in a pretty strong position to do that and turn down an already established movie star. And I think he was right.

DUSTIN HOFFMAN: I had grown up in Los Angeles always despising it. And that's not an overstatement. I lived in anti-Semitic neighborhoods, and I never felt a part of it. I used to go to the Saturday matinee movies to see the Dead End Kids jumping into the river, and I wanted to be one of them. When I turned twenty and got out of theatrical college, where I met Gene Hackman, I quickly went to New York and I felt I was home.

My father was always trying to better his image, so he moved around a lot. He went up and down like the stock market. The one year we were in Beverly Hills—before he went broke—I went to a school there called Hawthorne. I met someone there named David Parent. I bring it up because the house that was the exterior of Mrs. Robinson's house was next door to his.

The truth is, I've never felt very attractive growing up in LA, and I never felt as unattractive as I did while making *The Graduate*.

LARRY TURMAN: For Mrs. Robinson, I was interested in Doris Day, because she's Miss All-America. I sent the book to her manager, who was her husband. He hated it and wouldn't even pass it along to her. Mike had expressed interest in Patricia Neal. The only other person was Annie Bancroft.

WILLIAM DANIELS: Larry Turman thought I was too young for the role [of Benjamin's father], because there's only about nine or ten years' difference between Dustin and me. But Mike was just interested in having the people he wanted, so they aged me up.

LARRY TURMAN: Mike and I had some adjoining offices at Paramount. I'm in my office and Mike says, "Larry, come on in for a minute." So I walk in and Bill Daniels is sitting there. And Mike says to me, "Larry, tell me again: *Why* don't you want Bill Daniels in the movie?"

WILLIAM DANIELS: I remember they had a little party at Larry's place before we started shooting. My wife, Bonnie, was there with me. When I introduced her to Mike, she said, "We've never met," and he said, "Of course we have. I was a student with you in Lee Strasberg's class."

DUSTIN HOFFMAN: Once they cast us, we all met around the table, and Mike says, "Okay, let's read it," which is what you do when you're doing a play. And I remember he said, "It's a comedy, but please don't try to be funny—just read it straight." And we did. He later said he was ready to throw up because he thought it was a flop. We took him too literally.

We rehearsed four weeks. It was the best rehearsal I ever had in my life. The shooting was tense.

LARRY TURMAN: We cast Gene Hackman to be the girl's father, and then after three weeks' rehearsal, Mike fired him. It was a little bit tricky emotionally, because he and Dustin were roommates. Gene Hackman was replaced by Murray Hamilton. It was Mike's choice, not mine.

BUCK HENRY: Gene Hackman was Mr. Robinson. We had been rehearsing for at least a week. I came to the studio, and Larry or somebody said, "There's been a little change of plans." Mike had asked Gene to step down. I was nonplussed. It was a complete and total surprise to me. Then Murray came in.

Many years later, I heard from a mutual friend that Gene thought *I* was the cause of his being fired, and I was so shocked at that! I still am. I'm the wise guy hanging around that gets blamed for a lot of stuff. It's strange, but it was a good move for everybody because then Gene went immediately to *Bonnie and Clyde*, and has worked for Mike subsequently. So I guess he's okay with it, unless he still blames me.

But Mike is ruthless when it comes to artistic decisions. He will shut a film down, he'll throw a film away, he'll fire someone, he'll do some really mean stuff in the editing.

DUSTIN HOFFMAN: Gene and I are old friends, and we went to take a piss together. He's four urinals away, and he looks at me and says, "I think I'm getting fired." "No, *I'm* probably getting fired!" "No, *I'm* getting fired!" And at the end of that day, he got fired. So getting fired was a possibility. And we weren't allowed to see any rushes, so we never knew how we were doing. Katharine also thought she was going to get fired.

WILLIAM DANIELS: Mike was very demanding of Dustin, because a lot was riding on him.

DUSTIN HOFFMAN: It's not that he wasn't comfortable with me: he wasn't comfortable making the choice. Anyone who would make a radical move like that would be uncomfortable. I don't know of another director at the height of his powers—the most respected director at that moment in time—who would take a chance and cast someone like me in that part. It took enormous artistic courage.

I remember one time doing a scene, sitting in a car with Katharine Ross, talking about my feelings, a kind of short scene—I heard him whisper to Bob Surtees, "He's like Montgomery Clift."

I think he wanted the character on edge. What he was always doing—and looking back on it now, I wish every director would—he was never satisfied. He was always looking for the exquisite take. I was dubbed a perfectionist for years and years, and all I could think was, *I learned from Mike Nichols.*

BUCK HENRY: Dustin—who, in later years, has been spoken of as being sometimes difficult to work with—was, in my estimation, brilliantly well behaved, always interesting. He picked up all these Nichols habits, which he used in the character. Those little noises he makes are straight from Mike. And he kind of walks like him, too, in the film.

DUSTIN HOFFMAN: We were rehearsing, just me and Bancroft, and Mike told her to take a half hour off, and he sat me down. I'm always thinking, *Uh-oh, here it comes, I'm going to get fired.* And he says, "How old are you?" I said twenty-nine. He says, "Benjamin is twenty-one. Do you think Benjamin is a virgin?" I said, no, but I don't think he's learned it, and he certainly has never screwed his mother's best friend—which I thought was one Oedipal step away from screwing his mother—and he agreed. Then he said, "What were you like in school in terms of girls?" I said, "Oh, forget it. I was on the periphery. My grades were bad, I never went to college. I was never part of the great guys' club. I was always hanging back with the black and Mexican students on the fences." I said it's one of the worst memories I have, that period of my life.

He says, "Did you have any movie heroes?" I don't know where he's going with this, and I said, "Yeah, Gregory Peck in *The Yearling.* When I was a kid I thought, *God, I'd love to have a father like that.* And I loved John Garfield." "Anybody else?" I never had dates, but my older brother did. He was an A student, varsity football, he was in a fraternity, very popular. And sometimes girls would call, or his friends, and I'd answer the phone, and I would imitate him and get away with it. And I told Nichols that, and he said, "Do the scene again and try to be your brother." And I did. Then he says, "Did you ever see your brother get nervous or tense?" I said yeah. He said, "Does he ever do something that exhibits that tension?" I said—it hit me—yeah, he stops breathing, he realizes he hasn't breathed in a long time. Mike said, "Do the scene again as your brother, very tense." And I did. And then he said, "Okay, let's do it again, and don't do your brother; just try to keep the essence of what you were doing without imitating him." I did it again, and instead of a sigh, it came out as a [*whimpering gasp*]. That doesn't happen if he's not rehearsing the way he rehearses.

I had told him that the first physical thing I'd done with a girl was, when I was sixteen, I grabbed one breast. We were waiting to do an assembly, and she was playing Al Jolson, so she was in blackface, so I couldn't get too close. Mike told me, "I want you to go up to Anne Bancroft and take her breast in your hand"—and he doesn't tell her that I'm going to do it. So I did, and she's brilliant: she barely acknowledges it, doesn't take my hand away. Instead, she's rubbing something out of her sweater, and that made me laugh. The worst thing you can do, we're taught, is to break character. You don't break; you incorporate it into the scene, like she did. But I couldn't. I turned from her and from Nichols and I just walked away—I thought, *If you ruin the scene, you're in big trouble.* I start banging my head against the wall—*Don't laugh, don't laugh*—and Mike breaks out laughing, he can't stop. It's all in the movie.

BOBBIE O'STEEN: One of the things Mike did to create a backstory for Mrs. Robinson and Benjamin was he had Dustin and Anne play out a scene where Benjamin is twelve, and he goes over to the Robinsons' house for a barbecue. Sam said, "That way Anne and Dusty would know more how they felt about each other when they both got older."

DUSTIN HOFFMAN: *The Graduate* was a one-hundred-day shoot. They built the house in a soundstage. That wasn't a set; that was a *house*. If you opened the door to the bathroom, where there were no scenes planned, it was totally outfitted, because maybe Mike will change his mind.

LARRY TURMAN: We shot on the USC campus because [UC] Berkeley turned us down—they thought the movie was too dirty or something. So just like they used to say in Old Hollywood, "A tree is a tree, a rock is a rock. Shoot it in Griffith Park instead of Texas." So we shot it at USC. The exterior of the nightclub was on the Sunset Strip, the interior was a soundstage. San Francisco was the streets, Berkeley was Berkeley, the zoo was their zoo. But the house was built.

BUCK HENRY: The original script began with the graduation. At some point, Mike said, "What's the point?" And we never shot it. He was completely right, of course. The airplane and airport is much more interesting, much less pretentious.

I don't know whether this came out of an opium dream or not, but Mike had this idea that we're in the plane, Dustin's coming back to California, and we look down and we see swimming pools from very far away, and then we're down another 10,000 feet, and there are more swimming pools, and suddenly all the swimming pools congeal into one huge swimming pool. I don't know what the hell he was talking about, but it was very funny at the time. And I think he was seriously considering trying to find a visual way of doing it, to make some sort of aesthetic point which is now lost to time. I remember thinking, *How can I try to write this—the pools congealing all over Southern California?* But the idea was dropped immediately. He just may have been stoned!

The only word that's improvised in the movie is Dustin saying his name to Mr. Robinson, because Murray couldn't remember the character's name. I love that! That was the only non-scripted moment that I know of. I wrote the "plastics" scene in probably five minutes. I was improvising. He made this little gem out of it. So much so that the Peace Corps copied it for an ad.

DUSTIN HOFFMAN: Everybody knew their lines. We could have opened it on Broadway. But Mike would open it up a little bit when we were shooting and say things he hadn't said in rehearsal.

In my memory, we never rehearsed the scene where I have to walk to the front desk of the hotel. Mike never said what most directors would say, which is, *This character is really scared, his heart is beating.* He didn't do that. Instead, Mike said, "Did you ever take a girl to a hotel?" I said no, I hadn't. "Have you ever been nervous about anything sexual?" I said, "Well, I remember"—and it just came to me—"purchasing condoms." We didn't call them condoms; we called them rubbers, and the fancy word was prophylactics. He said, "Okay, let's play the scene like you're getting a dozen prophylactics." So I say to Buck, "I'd like a room," and he hits the bell on the desk. And without thinking, I moved my hand to stop the noise, and Mike broke out laughing.

There's two categories of directors, I've found. Those who have a vision, right down to the way the lines should sound. I've been standing aside watching a scene that I'm not in and I glance at the director and he's mouthing the lines, and I think, *Oh, boy.* And then there's the other type—like Mike—who want to be surprised. You rehearse, but they're in the moment, never mouthing the lines; it's a new experience.

KATHARINE ROSS: I depended on Mike a lot. We did many, many takes of the scene when I run up the stairs and burst into Benjamin's room. For whatever reason, I wasn't getting it. Maybe he just wanted to wear me down to a certain point.

BUCK HENRY: Katharine couldn't figure out the sequence where Dustin comes to Berkeley and kind of comes storming up the steps and into that apartment and he's banging right into her. She couldn't get a handle on that scene at all. So Mike said, "Katharine, get up off the chair and walk to the bed for that first line and then walk to the window on the next line and then open the window in the next line and then close it, and walk back to the—" He had her criss-crossing the apartment in every conceivable configuration. It takes the burden off the actor in terms of meaning. They can't do meaning *and* do all this physical stuff. And the scene is terrific and she's wonderful in it.

BOBBIE O'STEEN: Sam and Mike were both worried about her acting, and Sam definitely had to edit strategically to cover up key moments where she didn't make it. For instance, when she finds out her mother is having an affair with Benjamin and Benjamin says, "Please don't cry," she doesn't really cry. But Sam played most of the scene on Benjamin. Also the scene where she busts into his apartment in Berkeley, he and Mike were both worried she wasn't making it. Sam suggested Mike use a very long lens with her walking around, have a big close-up of her, so the audience would be captivated. "It's one of the most spectacular shots in the movie because she looks so beautiful." So even though Mike and Sam sweated her acting, he said, "She ultimately worked like gang-busters. Every guy in America was in love with her."

BUCK HENRY: We were all in love with Katharine, of course. She had a boyfriend at the time, some nice school-type kid who used to hide behind trees and bushes when we were on location.

LARRY TURMAN: Haskell Wexler had shot *The Best Man* for me, which got him in the union, and Mike used him wonderfully well on *Virginia Woolf.* He's a fabulous guy, but really hard-nosed. Wealthy family. He didn't believe in the script, so he quit us.

BOBBIE O'STEEN: Bob Surtees took a look at *Virginia Woolf* before he shot *The Graduate* and said to his camera crew, "Be prepared, because you're going to be doing some way-out shots." After they finished *The Graduate*, he said to Sam that he used every trick he learned in thirty years.

BUCK HENRY: I remember thinking, *Boy, Mike's doing some extraordinary work.* Interesting stuff we take for granted now. All that stuff at the beginning, up and down the stairs and out in the yard. It was rare that a long, handheld sequence would be done in that formal a film. He had these great ideas that you could really write toward, like the jumping on the raft cutting to the jumping on Mrs. Robinson. It's really avant-garde for a big movie at that time. Well, it wasn't a big movie like that: it wasn't that expensive, and it wasn't loaded with movie stars.

TOM STOPPARD (*playwright*): Ben announces to his parents that he's going out with this pretty girl whom they know, and the toaster pops up. I have always been fascinated by that. It is the perfect cinematic, psychological, symbolic moment. It bothers me to this day, that were I writing a screenplay it wouldn't occur to me to put that in as an event. I asked Mike about it and he said, "You mustn't go into directing a scene knowing everything that's going to happen in it." But it's as though he had already edited the scene in his mind and he realized it needed an end-stop of some kind. He was ahead of the curve in that way. In the years subsequently I've been in a cutting suite many, many times wishing that there was an end-stop.

LARRY TURMAN: In the book, Benjamin Braddock arrives at the church before the wedding ceremony is consummated. I remember when we were already shooting, Mike said to me, "You know, I think maybe he should get there after the ceremony is completed." I was stunned. It really was shocking to me because I still had the 1967 sensibility.

BUCK HENRY: I wrote the church scene the way it's in the book, which is that the ceremony had not been finalized when Dustin got there, so he is able to drag Elaine away before she's formally married. And Mike said, "No. It's too much like, *The cavalry's here*. What if the cavalry doesn't get there until the ceremony is done?" Charles Webb was not pleased by that. To him, Benjamin is the only moral person in this universe, and that behavior is immoral. He strongly objected to it.

That thing at the end on the bus—the two of them just there, uncomfortable—was not planned or written. I think I had a couple of lines which may be in the script, like, "What do we do now?" But Mike felt, why say it when you can show it? So he just let the camera run out on them, when they really did have nothing to say or do as actors. I don't know whether there was more than one take or what, but to me it's a great ending. It doesn't button it up. It says that life is going to be just as tricky as it was before. It's a Bergman ending.

KATHARINE ROSS: They get on the bus, and Mike let the camera roll. And roll. And roll. You learn when you're making movies that unless something is really terribly wrong, you let the director cut. You should stay in character, in the moment, until you hear the word "cut." So it was kind of like doing an improv. I'd have to say that was my favorite piece of the whole movie.

BOBBIE O'STEEN: As Sam tells it, "Mike said 'action' when he started that scene, when we were all outside and then Dusty and Kathy ran onto the bus, came down the aisle, and sat down in the back. The camera swung around and everybody on the bus reacted to them, including me. I was on the bus because Mike would have been recognized in that shot." But when the scene was supposed to end, Dusty and Kathy just sat there for a long time and looked at each other, not knowing what to do, because nobody was saying "Cut." Mike had forgotten to tell Sam to do so. But finally he did. So when Sam and Mike saw Dusty and Kathy look at each other indecisively like that in dailies, Mike said, "That's a hell of a moment."

When Sam asked Mike what he thought would ultimately happen to them as a couple, Mike said, "She's gonna end up like her mother."

BUCK HENRY: I once asked Mike, what is it that Benjamin's going to do? And Mike said, "He isn't going to do anything. He's an intellectual." That became our secret.

BOBBIE O'STEEN: If you watch the movie, the average shot length is over seventeen seconds. That's very, very unusual. For most movies it's three or four seconds. There were some scenes, like the church scene or the scene where she traps him in the bedroom, that are very fast cut, but there were a lot of shots where they just held on the master with very little cutting. I thought they must have shot the movie that way, but it's not true. When you look at the line script, they shot everything with lots of coverage. They protected themselves and shot conventionally, and then didn't use it. My guess is that that was Sam's first cut for the most part, and it just worked, and Mike never changed it.

ROBERT NICHOLS: Music is 50 percent of the effect of a movie. Watch the opening scene of *Chariots of Fire* with the sound off: it's just a bunch of guys running in their underwear. It doesn't look like anything. With the music, suddenly it's inspiring, it's uplifting, it's fabulous.

Mike was a classical-music announcer for a while, so he knew a lot, but he was more into books than music, whereas I was always more into music than books. I was in the Columbia Record Club where they sent you a record every month, and you could choose, and one of them was Simon & Garfunkel. I was just struck immediately by how great they were, especially by Simon's lyrics. He's a great poet.

I was staying with Mike overnight at one of the places he rented when he was making a movie, usually in Beverly Hills or Bel Air, and he was just beginning on *The Graduate*. I said to Mike, "You've got to hear these guys, Simon & Garfunkel," and I quoted the lyrics from one of their songs called "The Poem on the Underground Wall": "In the dark deserted station, restless in anticipation, a man waits in the shadows." Mike was intrigued. He said, "Why don't you go to Tower Records and get me the album?" The Tower Records on Wilshire and La Brea, or something like that, was always open, twenty-four hours, so I went at midnight, and I got him the record, and we played it, and he said, "Maybe I'll put them in my movie."

LARRY TURMAN: Mike said, "What would you think about Simon & Garfunkel?" I said, "What would I think? I tried to get them for my last picture"—*The Flim-Flam Man* with George C. Scott—"and they turned me down."

WILLIAM DANIELS: I felt the film was a light comedy. Then Mike said, "I have these two kids—one's very tall, and one's very small—I'm thinking of them to do the music for the picture." He played us "Sounds of Silence." I think it was the first time most of the cast had heard it. I remember thinking, *Wait a minute: this movie is not what I thought it was going to be.* These are young guys that represented a whole movement in our country. There was a far more serious intention from Mike's viewpoint than I had envisioned, simply because I knew him from *Barefoot in the Park*.

PAUL SIMON: Mike contacted us and asked if we were interested in writing and performing the score for this movie that he was about to make. I don't think he had the script yet. He sent the book. I didn't like it. I thought it was sort of a bad *Catcher in the Rye* imitation, but I wanted to work with him, and so did Artie. It was a little intimidating at first to be around Mike. We were twenty-five, twenty-six, maybe, and we were fans of his. He had just been nominated for an Oscar for *Virginia Woolf*.

ART GARFUNKEL: Boy, *The Graduate* has had an amazing ride in the last fifty years. People bow down to it. Did we think it was that important when we made it? Not quite. Paul had gotten to know Mike. Mike commissioned Paul to write three, or was it four, songs for

The Graduate. I saw a rough cut of the film. The movie didn't impress me. I had a hard time going with Dustin as the hero.

LARRY TURMAN: I made a deal with Simon & Garfunkel to write three new songs. While we're making the movie, they were getting hotter and hotter, touring more, and not writing the new songs. So Sam and Mike laid in "Sounds of Silence" and "Scarborough Fair" while they were editing. Mike one day turned to me and he said, "Larry, we are going to be so used to those old songs, we won't like the new ones." I said glibly without really thinking, "So we'll use the old songs."

ART GARFUNKEL: Paul wrote "Punky's Dilemma"—"Wish I was a Kellogg's Cornflake, floatin' in my bowl takin' movies"—while Dustin is in the swimming pool wondering about his future. And Mike rejected it. He was living with Simon & Garfunkel tunes that already existed as placeholders and learning to love "Scarborough Fair" right there and what it was doing for that scene.

BUCK HENRY: All of the songs Paul was writing fell by the wayside, except for "Mrs. Robinson." In theory, I don't like it. Simon & Garfunkel would never have been my choice. I probably would have used jazz. But I must say, once "Sounds of Silence" gets into your head, it's very hard to get rid of it.

LARRY TURMAN: Levine said to us, "You can't use those old songs! Every kid in America will laugh you off the screen!" Well, anybody can be made insecure, and Mike and I were made insecure. So we slept on it, and the next morning we met and said, "To heck with it. We love this, we're going to do it."

PAUL SIMON: He used our older songs as a temp track while I was working on new ones. And then at a certain point he said, "I love these songs so much, I think I just want to keep them."

BOBBIE O'STEEN: Sam edited the whole movie to the record. He assumed it was temporary but it grew on Mike, and they kept them all in. Paul Simon kept telling Sam, "I can't get over how that music fits," and Sam said, "I cut the picture to *make* it fit!"

PAUL SIMON: The only new song was "Mrs. Robinson," which I was fooling around with. I hadn't finished the song, I just had the structure and the chorus. Art told Mike that I was working on a song called "Mrs. Robinson," and Mike came to me and said, "You're working on a song called 'Mrs. Robinson' and you haven't told me?" And I said, "I don't know if it fits the movie. Sometimes I sing 'Here's to you, Mrs. Robinson,' sometimes I sing 'Here's to you, Mrs. Roosevelt,' and I haven't decided which one is more appropriate." And he said, "Mrs. Robinson." So that was that.

We sang it live to the movie as it went along. I would play the guitar and slow it down as different things happened, like when he runs out of gas. We didn't know it at the time, nor did Mike, that it was going to become a cultural artifact. It would have been a burden.

We'd take a break every once in a while and go outside and smoke a joint, which Mike didn't do. One day he said to us, "I'm wise to you, you know." And then we turned him on to smoking pot.

ART GARFUNKEL: Paul gave Mike his first joints. I'm so jealous that I wasn't there. I remember in those days, actors were ten years behind us musicians. They were straighter. Mike must have gotten crazy, a clever mind getting stoned for the first time.

ROBERT NICHOLS: My so-called contribution was just telling Mike [Simon & Garfunkel] exist and that I like them. Putting it in the movie was his stroke of genius, not mine. I had the occasion to tell Paul Simon about it at one of Mike's horse auctions, which were fabulous productions. I said, "I played a role in your career," and I explained how, and his eyes widened. He said, "You did play an important role in our career." It's my one claim to fame.

We lived in London for three months, and we were walking into the Underground and some busker was playing "Mrs. Robinson," and

I had a funny feeling that artistic people must feel all the time. I said, "That song wouldn't exist if it weren't for me."

Mike was never shy about crediting me. At one point, it might have been the AFI thing, he turned to me and said, "Thank you, Bob"—not for the world to hear, just me—when the subject of Simon & Garfunkel in *The Graduate* came up.

LARRY TURMAN: Back in Hollywood, we had a screening at the Directors Guild, which was sort of de rigueur. Mike and I were in the back row and the laughter was just polite. He wanted to turn the sound up, because you're very nervous with your peers. I remember Mike turned to me—this was only twenty minutes in—and said, "Turman, you son of a bitch, I told you we shouldn't have had this screening." Afterward, one or two top writers came up and said, "Oh, nice little picture."

BUCK HENRY: One of the first screenings of the film was a private screening—"the friends screening," as we used to call them. A lot of people said, "Loved the film. Very good. Very funny. Very interesting. Something awfully weird about that kid."

DUSTIN HOFFMAN: Turman said the *New York Times* people who had seen the film in previews were telling him, "Do you know what a great film you would have if they hadn't miscast the lead?" I thought my suspicions were correct.

ROBERT NICHOLS: I saw a very early screening of *The Graduate* before it was released, and Joe Levine was there and asked me what I thought of it—because I was young, so I was in the audience they were reaching. I thought it was great, but I thought Hoffman was all wrong for the part. It turns out I was all wrong.

DUSTIN HOFFMAN: Joe Levine had been talked into the fact that the film was going to be unsuccessful, so he decided he would release it as an art-house film, which meant soft porn. I got a phone call that he wanted me to come in and pose with Anne Bancroft. She would be sitting on a bed, and I would be facing her, standing up, naked, and she would have her hands around me, holding my buttocks. The only reason that didn't happen was that Nichols found out. I think Anne also said nothin doin'!

LARRY TURMAN: When I finally saw it all together for the first time—the rough cut—I thought, *Wow, that had a heavier, stronger, darker impact than I had envisioned.* Mike brought a little more depth to it. Didn't lose any of the fun, but he brought a little bit of a darker tone which I think makes it a better film.

PAUL SIMON: I saw the movie in a screening room with Mike and Joe Levine. Levine was sitting in the front row by himself—this is the first time he's going to see it—and Mike and I were closer to the back, near the projectionist. The movie finishes, and the lights come up. And there's a pause. And Levine says, "I smell money, Mike. I smell money."

DUSTIN HOFFMAN: There was a sneak preview, before it opened, on Eighty-Sixth Street. I go with [my girlfriend] Anne and we sit up in the balcony, and I'm sitting really low in the seat. The first shot—oh my God—it's a close-up of me on the whole screen, and I think, *Oh, fuck.* And I'm panicked that I'm going to not be good. It was mostly young people, and of course they didn't know what they were going to see. And my memory was they were slow to take it in.

And then something happened. I don't know what it was, but suddenly you could feel it. I had done enough stage stuff to know that you know when you've got the audience, and we've got them, I felt. We're getting laughs when we should and it's quiet when it should be quiet. Now I'm running to the church, and I get the cross, and the first six rows stand up! And they're yelling at the screen! "Go! Go!" And then I put the cross through the door, and they applaud! I thought, *Holy shit.*

The movie ends, and I sink back down in my seat. I say to Anne, "Let's just wait until everybody goes, and we'll go out last." I was afraid I'd be recognized. So we wait ten, fifteen minutes, and we go. Everybody has left the theater, except for one person who is walking with a cane, holding on to a railing. And she looks at me, and says,

"You're Dustin Hoffman." And I said, "Yeah." And she points the cane at me, and she says, "Life will never be the same for you from now on." It was Radie Harris, the Broadway columnist.

Anne and I leave the theater. We're going to get a cab—we're going to splurge. And Anne looked at me and said, "I thought it was good. I thought you were good." You know, understated. And the snow starts to come down and I looked up and I said, "See that? *That's* real. Nothing else."

I called Mike or he called me. He wanted to know what I thought, and I said, "My God, I thought it was incredible." And he said, "What about yourself?" I'm sure I'm not the first one who has ever said this to him, but I said, "I think you got the best out of me."

JOHN CALLEY[1]: Mike has the gift as a person, as a director, to take things that are interesting and doable, and elevate them in some way to some other dimension of quality or interest. *The Graduate* in hands other than Mike's and Buck's at that time would have been a kid movie. Mike, somehow or other, with his astonishing intelligence, was able to make it a kind of emblem for something, questions that a generation felt and responded to, and it was therefore a phenomenon. The first night it played, on Eighty-Sixth Street, the theater was *shaking*. People were going crazy, it was like an insane asylum. It wasn't a good preview; it was a metaphysical experience for them.

JULES FEIFFER: When I wrote *Little Murders*, I sent it to Mike to direct, and I never got an answer from him. I stopped speaking to him. For two years, I didn't say a word.

And then I went to a screening of *The Graduate*, hoping madly it would be lousy, wanting nothing but bad things for him. There hadn't been much advance word. And from the first shot of Benjamin, I just inhaled this entire movie the way I inhaled Nichols and May on *Omnibus*. By twenty minutes into the movie, I was thinking—instead of, *I hope it fails*—I was thinking, *Don't fuck it up. Don't fuck it up. Don't fuck it up.*

---

1. Courtesy of the John Lahr collection at the Howard Gotlieb Archival Research Center, Boston University.

I went home and wrote a love letter to Mike telling him that this was a revolutionary film, and it seemed within five minutes I got a hand-delivered letter back, wildly grateful, and we were on again.

DUSTIN HOFFMAN: Three or four weeks later, the movie opens at the Coronet. Much older crowd—fat cats, tuxedos. I don't remember a single laugh. They did not take to it. Maybe they thought they were being laughed at, but they had already given their kids cars instead of love.

The reviews weren't that exemplary. That was a day in which you could build with word of mouth. After the film had opened, to build the audience, Joe Levine paid me $500 a week, which was more than I got for shooting it, to promote the movie on the college campus circuit. He felt it had a shot but that it needed help. I put $3,000 in the bank after making that movie, more than I had ever earned in a year.

BUCK HENRY: By the time I came back to America, it had been playing more than a few minutes in the theater. I saw it at the now-defunct place on Fifty-Seventh Street, between Sixth and Seventh. I think Joe Levine owned it for a minute or two. Anyway, I went, and it was full. That was my first surprise. So they put us up in the balcony. There were kids sitting on the steps, and they were saying the lines, which I found incredibly distressing, although I suppose in the abstract it's complimentary. I think that was what the balcony was for: people who'd already seen it. That was the beginning of a period of young people going to see films over and over again, particularly *The Graduate*, *Easy Rider*, and *Bonnie and Clyde*.

I don't think any of us thought it was going to be a significant social event. Not Nichols, certainly not me. What it seemed to be was a really good story about people sort of like us. But it's like rock and roll: a whole generation changed its idea about what guys should look like. Bogart: they called him ugly, until one day he wasn't.

For the next ten or fifteen years, I wrote a script, it became a movie—one after another. I wasn't subjected to the pitfalls and the hardships that a lot of writers went through, because of the success of

The Graduate. Now, there are God knows how many scripts wandering around with my name on them that haven't been made.

LARRY TURMAN: After a few weeks, I asked a theater owner, "How's it doing?" The guy I spoke to said, "It's doing great. I think the picture is going to do $20 million." Now, the film cost $3 million. Standard procedure in those days was two-and-a-half times that cost, you start seeing a profit. So $20 million, I was on cloud nine.

One studio head, I saw him in line at one local theater to see the movie. He later said to me, "Larry, why didn't you make me make *The Graduate*?" I'll never forget the phraseology: Why didn't I *make him* make it?

About ten years later, *The Graduate* was rereleased. The ratings system had come in by then, and it only got a PG. How swiftly the society moves.

TOM HANKS: Three years after it comes out, they're saying, *And here's the film that defined a generation.* It was already the *Citizen Kane* of disaffected youth.

DUSTIN HOFFMAN: When he was asked about this again, Mike said that he didn't realize this consciously, but he had cast me because I was his alter ego, meaning that he always felt that he was the outsider, born and raised in Germany; he came to this country at whatever age, and always felt that he was odd-looking like me! Or at least in terms of what we call the leading man. He guided me in such a way that I was, literally, a younger version of him. He saw himself in the role.

LARRY TURMAN: Later, I vividly remember walking down Fifty-Seventh Street with Mike, on the south side of the street, and Mike turns to me and says, "You know, Larry, *The Graduate* is the story of a boy who saves himself through madness."

Mike in Guaymas, Mexico, for *Catch-22*, with eighteen B-25 Mitchell bombers lined up behind him for use in the film. "It was like the fourth largest air force in the world," Bob Newhart remembers. *(© Bob Willoughby/mptvimages.com)*

CHAPTER 7

Icarus Was Falling

ROBERT NICHOLS: I think it was Joe Papp who said of Mike, early in his career, "Mike Nichols is not a success." The person he was talking to said, "Why not?" And Papp answered, "Because he hasn't had a failure yet." When Mike was asked about it, he thought for quite a while without comment, and then he said, "Absolutely true." You have to prove yourself by rising from the ashes and going on to bigger and better things. That's why his company was called Icarus Productions. He sailed so near the sun at the very beginning.

JULIAN SCHLOSSBERG: The very first play he does is *Barefoot in the Park*, and he wins the Tony. The next play he does is *Luv*, and he wins the Tony. The next play he does is *The Odd Couple*, and he wins the Tony. Then he makes a movie, *Virginia Woolf*, gets five Academy Awards. Then he makes *The Graduate*.

I remember him saying—and it was really funny—he kept saying, "I've got to just get this failure out of the way. I know it's not going to keep going." And while it was said jokingly, I'm sure it really meant something. No one could keep doing that. I'm sure part of him liked being the golden boy, but a lot of it he didn't like.

DUSTIN HOFFMAN: After *The Graduate* opened I was getting awful scripts, quasi-*Graduate* parts. I had never gotten scripts before. I kept saying no, no, no. They said, "You've got to work," and I said, "I don't care, I want to do something onstage." I think a year went by, and I heard about this thing, *Midnight Cowboy*, and I read it, and that was my meat and potatoes. Nichols called me after I got the part and said, "I hear you're going to be in *Midnight Cowboy*," and I said, "Yeah." He said, "Are you playing the cowboy?" I said, "No, I'm playing the other guy, Ratso Rizzo." He was stunned. He says, "But that's not the lead. I made you a star." And I said, "Yeah, but I like this part—much easier part to play for me than being a Gentile." That's the toughest character act, a handsome Gentile. He said something about how he made me so attractive in *The Graduate* and now I'm going to ruin it.

I heard he was doing *Catch-22*. I read that book because I wanted to work with him again, and I loved it. I wanted to play Yossarian. Then I hear Alan Arkin got the part, and I said, "Well, he's perfect." I did get a call from Mike, and I think maybe he's going to offer me Milo Minderbinder, but he doesn't. He offers me a smaller part, Captain Orr. I'm devastated. *This is nothing.* And I said no. I would never have done that again if I had it to do over. But I didn't think I could do anything with the part. And that may have affected our relationship.

Later, I asked him to do *Straight Time* before Ulu Grosbard came in, and Mike read it and he said no. I remember seeing *Carnal Knowledge* and thinking, *Why didn't he ask me to do that?* We actors are like that. And then he calls me, I don't know how many years later, and he says, "I read this book, I want to do it, and I want you to play the lead." I read it, and I can't believe the violence in it; you don't expect that from Mike Nichols. I mean, it's really gory and violent. I said, "Mike, I can't do it. It's against everything I feel." I was against the war, I had taken one of Senator Eugene McCarthy's daughters to the Academy Awards, I campaigned for him. I just thought this was so bloodthirsty. It was called *First Blood*. Somehow he got disentangled from the project, and it wound up as *Rambo*, a kind of exploitation movie. It wasn't written that way, and Mike wanted to do it the way it was written. He wanted to show the real post-traumatic stress.

We never got to work together again, and it makes me sad. I bumped into him once at a restaurant. I hadn't seen him in a while, and we're always very warm and very affectionate to each other. He looked up and he whispered to me. I said, "What?" He said, "Why didn't you ask me to do *Tootsie*?"

ART GARFUNKEL: I was talking with the nuns outside my brownstone on Sixty-Eighth Street on the Upper East Side. And Mike pulled up in a limo. He rolled down the window. I hadn't seen him since *The Graduate*. He hands me a script and says, "Arthur, read the script. I see you as Nately in this." "Mike, I've never acted." "I know. Read it anyway."

PAUL SIMON: After we finished work on *The Graduate*—or maybe even before we finished—Mike said, "My next movie is *Catch-22*." He wanted Artie and me to be in it, and we said, "Yeah, of course." We were thrilled.

And then, in the summer of 1968—I was renting a house in Stockbridge—he called me up late one night and said, "We've been working on the script, and it's so long that we're going to have to write your part out. So I guess that means Artie will be out too." And I said, "No, no, no, don't be silly. You don't have to take Artie's part out." The idea of being in a movie, at that point, was so beyond what either one of us imagined, that it wasn't a devastating loss.

AUSTIN PENDLETON: It was a project that a lot of people wanted to do. Orson Welles had wanted to direct it, and of course he wasn't asked to.

BUCK HENRY: I love the book, so did Mike. We knew it had been owned and was being fiddled with by the Kirk Douglas family and we were appalled at the idea of anyone trying to make it except us, because we really thought we knew it in a way that nobody else would be able to, although we assumed that somebody would make it someday and it probably wouldn't be us. So we pushed ahead a little faster and got there a little quicker.

ART GARFUNKEL: During *Catch-22*, Mike had a print of the Bruegel painting, *Landscape with the Fall of Icarus*. In Mexico, Icarus was falling.

BOB NEWHART: I was really surprised that Mike wanted me in *Catch-22*, because you were surrounded by really great actors—Alan Arkin, Jon Voight, Orson Welles, Richard Benjamin, Paula Prentiss— and I was a stand-up comic. I really wasn't known as an actor, so I took that as quite a compliment. They asked me to play Major Major, and so we went down to Guaymas, Mexico, where they built an airfield over the Sea of Cortez. I was also offered a part in *M*A*S*H*, which I turned down, because I felt a loyalty to Mike and his confidence in my abilities.

I remember one of the first things was, Mike got us together, the entire cast and crew, and he said, "You have to understand that you are figments of Yossarian's imagination," which was certainly a departure from the book. I just played it for laughs. But then the making of the movie started to take on a kind of surreal quality.

BOB BALABAN: At first, *Catch-22* was filmed only during magic hour, which allows you three hours a day of shooting. The location was so difficult to get to. There were like two planes a week, and then you had to drive for about eight hours after the plane landed. On our off days we would sit by the pool. People ran, jogged, played tennis a lot. You couldn't go anywhere to eat or anything because we were so scared of getting poisoned. It was beautiful, but there was nothing to do. Once in a while, they'd bring in American candy bars. That was a big deal. I'm not kidding. They had food from Zabar's flown in occasionally, special stuff for Mike.

BOBBIE O'STEEN: Mike was the first director since Orson Welles to have been given a contract by a major studio that specified he didn't have to show his dailies to anyone.

BOB NEWHART: There weren't great feelings between Paramount and Mike. Later, I got to know Marty Ransohoff, and he told me Mike wouldn't show him anything. Mike went back to Hollywood to look at some of the rushes. When he came back, he said, "I question my genius. I shouldn't ever do that."

There wasn't a hell of a lot to do in Guaymas. We weren't even *in*

Guaymas; we were outside of Guaymas. It was almost a moonscape, the location.

BOB BALABAN: It was a tremendously lonely place to be, but for Mike it didn't matter. When you're directing six days a week and looking at dailies on the seventh day, you could be on the moon.

BOB NEWHART: They had so many B-25s, it was like the fourth largest air force in the world. The planes would take off, and Mike would yell, "Cut!" When he cut, all the planes had to land and line up again. If something was wrong, well, that took half a day.

BUCK HENRY: We had two fabulous pilots. They looked like the characters they would have played had they been in the film. They both were named Frank and they both had lost a leg in some war or other. They went back as far as *Wings*, which one of them did the choreography for.

It became apparent on the first day, the first takeoff and return, that we were doing something very dangerous, because none of the actors had trained for the rigors or the dangers of flight. Every air force person who knew what they were talking about was talking about it, because it looked like we were planning our own death.

BOB NEWHART: I wasn't supposed to shoot for a week or something, and so I went in the cantina with Marty Balsam and Norman Fell, and we had several drinks. I get up in the morning and they say, "Oh, they're shooting you today." I had a terrible headache from the night before. We did the scene where Yossarian is naked up a tree. I'm thinking, *Everybody remember your lines. I've got to get back to my trailer or I'm going to throw up.*

About a week later, Mike showed me the scene, and he said, "See, that's the kind of quality that I'm looking for in Major Major." I thought to myself, *Oh my God, I'm going to have to get drunk every night to match.*

Stacy Keach was originally going to play the colonel, and then I think Mike fired him. I never knew the reason, but some of the old-time directors, they would fire somebody just to keep everybody on pins and needles. Everybody was walking around saying, "Did Mike seem funny to you today? He seemed funny to me."

Then they went to Chuck Grodin. They tried to age him up, did some screen tests. Then they said, "Well, let's try him with a mustache." So they flew a mustache—just a mustache—down from Hollywood on a private plane. You pictured the pilot and the mustache sitting in the other seat.

A little later, Jack Gilford said, "I'm going into Guaymas. Does anybody want to go with me?" And Tony Perkins said, "Yeah, I'll go, because I haven't been since the elephant's funeral." I said, "Hold on. I read a lot, so I know elephants are not indigenous to Mexico." And they said, "Oh, that's right. You guys were out of town." They had a circus come through, with this elephant on the flatbed truck, and they went around this curve, and the elephant leaned out, and this bus hit the elephant and killed him, and they had a big funeral in Guaymas. Again, where does the movie end and the surreal begin?

AUSTIN PENDLETON: Mike and I wound up having a common adversary, who was Orson Welles. Orson had said the only way he would agree to play General Dreedle is that all his scenes had to be in a clump in two weeks, so I was there for two weeks also. But the shooting just went on for months and months and months. Orson brought all this baggage to it. He was so angry he wasn't directing it.

BOB BALABAN: Orson was a pile of trouble basically. It was really hard because Mike couldn't just say "Cut the shit" to the world's greatest director.

BOBBIE O'STEEN: Once when Mike asked for an alternate, Orson said he didn't like alternates because "some drunken editor might put it in."

AUSTIN PENDLETON: Orson was enchanting, but he was making trouble. He would say outrageous things to Mike—"I'm not sure you understand comedy"—just outrageous things. He would redirect the scenes. He wouldn't alter the camera position, because it was all lit, but the way the scene was supposed to be played by everybody. They weren't as good as when Mike would direct it, but Mike went along with it to get the shots. Although maybe Orson was directing them that way just to undermine the movie.

He would blow take after take after take. At one point he said, "Mike, I don't understand. I never blow lines. There must be something wrong with the scene." Unforgettably, Mike said, "Well, Orson, *you* know what's wrong, and *I* know what's wrong, but who are we against *Pendleton*?" Orson didn't know what to do with that. The next time he got the take.

BUCK HENRY: The only scene when all of us are together is the scene when Yossarian gets his medal. So we were all standing in line, and Orson does a long throat-clearing: *"Aagghagghagghagghahhh."* And he says, "Mike, listen, there's a lot of words in this scene and a lot of them don't really mean much, they're just gags. What would be really helpful and make us move twice as fast, is if you hold the book and say the line the way you hear it in your head and then I will repeat it."

ART GARFUNKEL: He said, "Mike, often directors struggle to put into words what they want of me. Don't struggle. Give me the exact line, will you? Don't be embarrassed."

BUCK HENRY: I thought, *Jesus, what will happen if Mike gives a reading that Orson thinks is stupid? How messy can this get?* But it didn't. Mike started reading the scene and Orson repeated every one of Mike's lines to the T: every syllable, every uptick, every downtick. It was fabulous. Line readings, you know, are generally poison to any actor, but Orson thought it would go faster and he'd get back to the hotel sooner—and to the bottle of brandy that was waiting for him.

I realized Orson may have figured out that this would ensure him getting close-ups on all the pieces, because the camera can't go anywhere if Mike is reading the lines.

AUSTIN PENDLETON: When shots were being lit and stuff, we'd all sit in those chairs out in the desert. We would throw out the name of any film director, either living or dead, and Orson would expound. It was like throwing fish to a seal. He loathed Stanley Kubrick, because Kubrick was original like Orson, but he figured out how to game the system. *2001* had just come out, and Orson said, "I'm not going to go see that. Life is too short." He had been offered to teach a course in film at Columbia University, and he said, "What I would do is I would take *Paths of Glory* and point by point I would make them understand how horrible the script is, the acting, the editing." Mike finally said, "Orson, promise me you will not come to see this movie."

JEFFREY SWEET: Subsequently, even though he thought Orson was an asshole to him, Austin wrote a play called *Orson's Shadow*, which was a posthumous apology to the man.

AUSTIN PENDLETON: I was trying to make up for all the smart-ass things about Orson that I said to the press.

BUCK HENRY: Mike and I and [John] Calley went up on an excursion to Rome by way of several of the big islands. We were looking for locations for the last sequences, and while we were there we got the news that Frank Tallman, perhaps the more seasoned of the Franks—what happened was, there was a plane beneath him and it rose up, it came up too far and bumped the bottom of his plane, and to recover he had to overcompensate to get the plane to recover. But the bump bumped him out of his seat and he rose up in slow motion and went out the back of the plane, down into the water a mile below. It's not a good landing, as you can imagine. We tried to pick his body up out of the water, but if you drop a mile into the welcoming arms of the water, your body just flattens out, and so you have to be siphoned up. Calley got the film and a few of us looked at it. And there it is: he just loses his grip, floats out over the machine gun, out the back. It's very beautiful in its own horrible way. He filmed his own death.

BOB BALABAN: When he saw the first day of rushes, Mike said, "It's like I'm giving birth to a dead child."

You know what happened with *Catch-22*? *M*A*S*H* opened about three months before. The studio was going to scrap it, but they had this Directors Guild screening in San Francisco. The audience was quiet at first, but at the end of it, people were standing on their chairs, screaming and throwing things for a twenty-minute ovation. It was so radical—the way Bob [Altman] shot, the way he used improvisation, the combination of funny things with awful things. I think it stole a lot of thunder from *Catch-22*. It couldn't be judged alone.

BOB NEWHART: *M*A*S*H* came out before *Catch-22*, and I think it took a lot of the edge off *Catch-22*. I think that if *Catch-22* had preceded *M*A*S*H* it might have gotten more recognition.

AUSTIN PENDLETON: I saw an industry screening, maybe two weeks before it opened. When Orson Welles's name appeared, the place went wild, people screaming and yelling. At the end of the credits, when it said "Directed by Mike Nichols," they clapped very slowly. It was chilling. At that point, Mike had never had either a play or a movie that wasn't a hit, so they were lying in wait.

JON KORKES (*actor*): I remember Buck saying something like they knew which critics would like it and which critics would not like *Catch-22*, because they knew which ones liked Mike and which were waiting for him to fail. I'm sure *M*A*S*H* had something to do with it too, but there were articles, a big to-do about how much *Catch-22* cost, and I think there was some critical resentment of Mike. All that stuff worked against him.

AUSTIN PENDLETON: I called Mike up after I'd seen it. I said, "I think this is brilliant." He said, "Really?" He was holed up somewhere in the country terrified to be getting calls about it. And he hadn't gotten that many calls. For years after, he would kind of disown the movie publicly.

I think it's one of the great movies of the '60s—like *2001* or *Lawrence of Arabia*, sort of epic, abstract, not exactly the movie you would think that Mike would make of that material. Over the years, the reputation of *Catch-22* has really grown. Every decade there's a whole new set of young people who are interested in the film, and they don't know the cynical feeling everybody had about Mike when the movie first came out.

TONY WALTON: Mike was very fearful of how *Catch-22* would be received, and when it got panned, it cheered him up immensely. I remember him saying on the phone to me the morning those reviews came out, "It's everything I've been fearing, and nothing terrible has happened. I still have my home, my marriage, my horses. It simply hasn't changed anything." I think his nature was to fear the worst, and so when it happened, he almost embraced it.

JULES FEIFFER: When I wrote *Carnal Knowledge*, I offered it to Arkin, but he didn't like it. So I sent it to Mike, and Mike called me up twenty-four hours later and he says, "I want to do it, but I think it's a movie, not a play." And I said, "Give me thirty seconds."

He said, "There's a guy named Nicholson in *Easy Rider*. Have you seen it?" I said no. So I went. I didn't like the movie, and I didn't like Jack Nicholson. Mike said, "Trust me, he's going to be our most important actor since Brando," and I trusted him. I worried if Candy Bergen was good enough, and he said, "Trust me," and I trusted him. Over and over again I would have my doubts, and over and over again he proved right. I realized that I can write them, but I can't cast them.

BOBBIE O'STEEN: Mike and Jack's nicknames for each other were "Nick" and "Nick."

JULES FEIFFER: He had rented Jennifer Jones's house in LA, and I remember I'd get up in the morning and the World Series was on. I'd watch the game, and then Mike and I would work for about three hours, and I was exhausted at the end. He would grill me like a prosecuting attorney on who these characters were and why. I wondered why Mike was banging away, and I realized he's got to figure out how to take them off the paper and make them living, breathing people.

And so he gives them a backstory that I never thought about. It was truly an education.

RITA MORENO (*actress*): I read the script, and my husband read the script, and he said, "You are not doing this." Well, remember the time. It was a very, very bold script, and it was kind of a pornographic film. I was a little nervous about it, but I said, "Come on, it's Mike Nichols. I have to see him, at the very least." So I went to see Mike at his penthouse apartment on Central Park West. We were in his library, which was a very vibrant red. We talked about the script. I said, "Frankly, my husband tells me he's going to kill me if I do this," and Mike looked shocked. He talked to me and talked to me and talked to me. I was there the whole afternoon. He said, "I just think you'd be great for this. I think you would understand this woman." I said to myself, *He thinks I think like a hooker?* It was not going well.

I finally went home. My husband said, "You told him no, of course," and I said, "I did not tell him no. I really think the script has something amazing to say that nobody has said before." I said, "I really want to do this, Lenny," and he said, "Well, I have to think about it." I said, "No, I'm telling you that I need to do this. I think it's very important."

Mike was a perfect person to direct that film. I think he had an icy kind of heart.

CANDICE BERGEN: *Carnal Knowledge* was written in two sections. The early section was shot in Vancouver, a completely idyllic location. You'd work French hours, and there would be this running buffet of lobster. And then at night, he would have screenings. I think one was *War and Peace*, another was a great Garbo movie. I stayed in a house with Jack and Artie, and we would come home still wearing our college costumes. And then they wrapped in Vancouver and moved to New York, where it took a much darker tone.

RITA MORENO: Because it was being shot in continuity, everyone was so fucking depressed by the time I got there. I had never seen such a dark set. Everyone was kind of not quite themselves.

When I went to makeup the first morning, Jack was sitting in a chair getting made up while I was getting made up, and it turns out that Art Garfunkel and Jack had formed a very similar relationship to the one in the movie. Jack had gone out with some girl, and I guess got laid or something, and Art said, "How was it?" I almost started to laugh.

BOBBIE O'STEEN: To quote Sam: "It was a picture about fucking and everybody on the crew was fucking like apes. I don't know what happened to us."

JULES FEIFFER: The one trouble spot was the night before we were to shoot the big fight between Jack and Ann-Margret. Mike said, "I don't think we can shoot this, it's just too ugly. We're gonna lose the audience." And so I just let him talk and talk and talk about all the things that could go wrong and would go wrong. And then we got into the car to go to this Chinese restaurant where we were shooting, and the last thing he said before we got back was, "No, I have to shoot it, because that's what would happen." He'd won the argument against himself.

I had a line in the script where Jonathan, the Nicholson character, says, "We all think boys hate girls when they're kids and grow out of it, but we never grow out of it. We just grow into liking pussy." Mike cut that out because he thought that was the story of the film. With Mike it was always about the work and never about his ego, never about his sense of importance. It was about storytelling. It was about the relationships. It wasn't about a laugh, but if you could get a good laugh, why not?

RITA MORENO: "It's as though she is descending forever"— that's how the writer described the scene. We had one entire wall in this soundstage of wallpaper, and the hydraulic system kept getting these bubbles. We did the scene a million times. Jack was so good. He was very generous to me in that scene. He didn't even have to be there, but Jack lay down under the camera, fully dressed, and leered at me between takes to just help me out. There was one point where I was doing one of many takes, and tears came to my eyes, because I got so angry at Jack's character. I was so inside the scene. Mike loved that. He saw what it was: tears of hatred and humiliation.

When the film was going to be cut together, Mike called me up and said, "Rita?" I said, "What?" He said, "We're going to have to do it again." I had to do it without Jack this time.

BOBBIE O'STEEN: About halfway through the first preview, Mike leaned over and patted Sam on the shoulder and said, "This is the best movie we ever made."

RITA MORENO: I remember going to see a screening of it in a private screening room in New York, and Arthur Penn was there too. I knew him well enough to say hello, and I said, "What did you think?" He said, "Oh my God, that was the most depressing thing I have ever seen in my life."

JULES FEIFFER: We had a Directors Guild screening of the film, and Billy Wilder and William Wyler and half a dozen other names who weren't big anymore came to see it. At the end of the movie, the first great director said, "Uncompromising." And the second great director said, "Like open-heart surgery." I leaned over to Mike and whispered, "We're dead."

And as a matter of fact, although the film had great reviews and did great business, Hollywood hated it. The only nomination they gave was to Ann-Margret, one of their own. And I didn't get an offer to write another movie for ten years, until Robert Evans called me up and asked me to write *Popeye*. Ten years.

RITA MORENO: My husband and I went to see the movie at the RKO-something on the West Side, and in front of us were two older New York Bronx Jewish ladies. He and I sat in the mezzanine up above, because I didn't want anybody to see me. We watched the scene, and while we were watching the scene, these women are saying,

"That is the most *disgusting* thing I have ever seen in my life. Rose, look at that. Look what she's doing. *Oh my God.*" They went on and on. But they didn't leave.

DAVID HARE: In my opinion, *Carnal Knowledge* is Mike's masterpiece. I think it's one of the great American movies. People say *Carnal Knowledge* is a very bitter film, but it's actually intensely pleasurable as well.

JOHN CALLEY[1]**:** I loved *Carnal Knowledge*. I remember a reviewer talking about, Yes, it's brilliant, yes, it's this searing look at . . . but how can Nichols do a movie about that time without dealing with Vietnam? That sort of view of his work recurs from time to time. It's all about the reviewer having an implied agenda for Mike that Mike isn't following and therefore is disappointing the reviewer, and I don't feel it works like that.

CYNTHIA O'NEAL (*friend*): I was having dinner at Acme, and this man came over to me and introduced himself as James Grissom, who's just written a book about Tennessee Williams. He said, "You know, Brando was obsessed with *Carnal Knowledge*." I said, "No!" Just the thought of Brando watching *Carnal Knowledge* . . . He said, "Yeah, if you give me your email I'll send you the part of my interview with him where he talks about it."

JAMES GRISSOM: Here is what I sent Cynthia:

"What [Mike Nichols] did was take the themes and the obsessions of [Michelangelo] Antonioni, and there are the creamy, bare walls, the prisons we call homes and jobs and pleasure, but he opened the windows, so there is air and there is blood and there are people we've passed on the streets.

"I would find it hard to find a better graph or study or image of seduction—thwarted—than that scene where Jack [Nicholson] sets his

---

1. Courtesy of the John Lahr collection at the Howard Gotlieb Archival Research Center, Boston University.

sights on his friend's wife. Pussy is pussy is pussy, and in he goes to claim it. But this is not a woman prepared or willing to be a victim of his priapic charms; his forced charms; that stale, stained apartment. She may be a victim—she is absolutely a victim—but she has chosen the terms and the conditions, and Cynthia [O'Neal] was an elegant obelisk that remained immobile but nonetheless shattered the fragile globe in which Jack lived and operated. How fragile that is! Tenn[essee Williams] might have wondered. That woman knows the terms, the score, the cost, and she came with better tools and a better game. What a brilliant and smooth scene—the turning of tables as if by magic. Evil magic. We were talking about adjectival acting and how Tennessee hated it. How I hate it. You want to get the adjective, of course: You want the audience to say 'Magical' or 'Evil' or 'Glorious,' but the actor can't be seen applying, like thick paint, the adjective that is called for. What is applied is emotion and memory and an homage of gesture and sound from past experience that lets you know what's going on, what's been felt, what's being shared. That's a brilliant scene—clean and smooth—and you see the machinery of the people, and you never, ever see the effort to have it given to us—a great gift. They got in by stealth, which is what acting should be. Acting is stealth. So is sex. So is humor. That is a sexy, stealthy, funny scene—until it tears your heart out."

When I told Mike all this, he was just agog. And then he went, "Everything Marlon is saying is correct, but I wasn't aware of it. I wasn't thinking it." It went to Mike's theory: Don't be the ornithologist, be the butterfly.

ART GARFUNKEL: Mike could be thought of as the man who broke up Simon & Garfunkel, the world-loved duo.

PAUL SIMON: When he offered Artie a role in *Carnal Knowledge*, Artie didn't tell me. I heard about it from Chuck Grodin. I asked Artie if it was true, and he said yes, and I said, "Why didn't you tell me that?" He said, "I was afraid that if I told you that you would stop working on *Bridge over Troubled Water*." And I thought, *I don't want to deal with this.*

Many years later, Artie and Chuck Grodin, who met when they were making *Catch-22*, did a talk at the Museum of Television and

Radio. I don't know which one said it, maybe they both did: that Mike broke up Simon & Garfunkel. I was sick with the flu when Mike called me. He said, "Is that true?" I said no. But in fact, it's partly true.

Even though I think that is true, it had no effect on my friendship or my feelings about Mike. No, that's not so. I still really liked Mike, but I thought he disregarded—no, that's not the right word, because that would imply that it was an act of volition—I think he just didn't bother thinking about the consequences. I think Artie wanted to be a movie star, and Mike said, You can be a movie star. And so that was the last album we made together.

ART GARFUNKEL: I got invited to come to the Paley Center as part of a seminar with Chuck Grodin. In the course of this thing, he suggests that Mike Nichols had no business dropping Paul [for *Catch-22*]. He brings that up and I acquiesce to the notion—yeah, that's fertile ground for examination. But *The Hollywood Reporter* wrote it up as: Art pins the blame. I blame myself for hurting Mike, though maybe he didn't care. The last time I saw Mike was at a party. He said, "I know, I'm the troublemaker." He threw it off, but the whole thing embarrasses me. I love Mike. I don't know of anything he's done wrong. He has been a Santa Claus in my life.

PAUL SIMON: I think in the same way that Mike and Elaine broke up, we would've broken up anyway, but that set it into motion earlier. I never said any of this to Mike, even when he asked me directly, because he would've just felt terrible, and it was years later, and it wasn't like I regretted it. Artie and I were fighting a lot then. I didn't regret leaving. I think Artie has a different feeling about that.

DAVID GEFFEN: When John Calley was the head of production at Warner Bros., he offered Mike *The Exorcist*, and Mike read it and decided it wasn't for him. John said, "You really should do this, Mike, because it's going to be a giant, giant hit." And Mike said, "Well, I suppose so, but I can't see how to make a movie of this that I would be interested in making." Anyway, the movie gets made with Billy Friedkin, and Mike is driving in Westwood, and he sees the longest line he's ever seen in his life—literally, he said it was blocks long—and he follows the line to the theater, and it's *The Exorcist*. And he calls Elaine on the phone and he says, "Elaine, I am such a schmuck. I just passed the longest line I've ever seen for *The Exorcist*, and you know I was offered it and turned it down." And she said, "Don't worry, Mike, if you had made it, it wouldn't have been a hit."

JANET COLEMAN: According to Frank Shaw, he and Michael Elias had written *The Frisco Kid*, about a rabbi who takes on a new congregation, and they sent it to Nichols. And Nichols was sitting on it and sitting on it, they'd had no word, nothing. Finally they got a telegram from Nichols: "Kill the Jew, we're going with the fish."

BOBBIE O'STEEN: Mike did *The Day of the Dolphin* to get out of his three-picture deal with Joe Levine. Roman Polanski was originally supposed to direct it. He was in London doing rewrites on the script when Sharon Tate was murdered in LA.

JON KORKES: It was unbelievable. We were a couple of weeks in Miami, and then we were three or more months in Abaco, and then another three or four weeks on Nassau. We stayed in these bungalows by this hotel on Treasure Cay. Mike had all sorts of visitors. Nicholson came down to hang out. It was quite a time.

When you went from one section of town to the other, it was all burned-out woods. You would turn and go down this dirt road, through these two stone pillars. Before you hit the trailers, if you took a left, they'd built a prefab commissary for us. Mike brought his own chef down there, a guy named Roberto who was a Cordon Bleu chef from Spain. The meals we would get—bread pudding with sherry for dessert—it was ridiculous. They started getting complaints from the crew that they weren't getting more basic meat and potatoes, and so they ended up having two lines with two different kinds of meals.

Before we started shooting, Mike met with each actor privately. We talked about people who turned out to be a lot worse than you think they are, which is what my character was supposed to be, and how sometimes it's out in the open and you don't see it. He mentioned a well-known woman that he had had an affair with for a year and a half—very well-known woman—and that she'd been fucking some other guy a good bit of that time, and everybody knew it but Mike. And then she was on a talk show where she openly said that she worked with the CIA, but nobody dwelled on it. He was trying to illustrate how, if you really look back at someone who turned out to be duplicitous, the signs were all there, but you realize you never really paid attention to it. He didn't say a lot on the set. Most of the work was done in private conversation.

TONY WALTON: George C. Scott was going through his meltdown of *acting is no job for a real man* and Mike was helping him through that with great intelligence and an irresistible humor, which is what I think did the trick with George.

JON KORKES: George was a troubled guy. A brilliant actor, but a tortured alcoholic who was three or four different people, depending on the day. You'd hear all the stories about him. I don't think he got that broken nose from playing chess. For the first few weeks of the shoot, he and his wife and entourage lived on this one-hundred-something-foot yacht moored off the location. One night, he invited the young people from the film to come out for dinner. He got very morbid and heavily into his cups and it got a little scary. He said something like, "Hey, I know what we're going to do. We'll stay here all night and we won't go to work tomorrow!" Ed Herrmann looked around and said, "Well, George, Jon's dog is here on the island. We can't leave his dog back there." George said, "Oh, okay. I'm sorry," and then they called for the launch. We all nervously stood around waiting for the boat to take us back as George went around to us one by one and apologized.

The next day, we're shooting a scene where I let the dolphin slide into the water on a cue from George. They had changed the cue a few times, and I wanted to make sure I knew what it was, because we're dealing with a live animal, and they're fragile in captivity. So I went up to him and very nervously asked him, "George, what would be the cue? I just want to check." He doesn't answer. He's just smoking, and he's looking at the sky. I'm a babbling idiot now, and I'm just kind of stuttering. Suddenly he swells up like a blowfish and says, "So, we'll do it *your* way! *Okay*, Jon?" And he leaned down into me, stuck his face in mine and stared at me, and I just froze. He kind of snorted and turned away, and I shot downstairs toward Mike. I said to him, "We've got to work with a maniac like this?" Mike said, "Go for a walk. I'll see what's up." We get called back to the set, and Mike is at the doorway downstairs. He says, "Everything's okay." He sees that I don't believe it. He says, "Trust me, Jon. It's going to be all right." All of a sudden, George shows up at the top of the ramp, and sure enough, his eyes are red like he's been crying. He comes over, and like a four-year-old he says, "I'm sorry I snapped at you before. I apologize." I shook his hand, and he gingerly took mine, and we stood there very awkwardly, and I just said, "It's okay. We're all right now."

MIKE HALEY: We were out in the middle of this nowhere island, Abaco, all pretty much stuck there. It was the same routine, day after day after day, and it started to get a little tense because Mike was nervous about George Scott and his behavior. I don't know why, but I just thought, we've got to break this up because we're all getting island fever.

Every day we would drive out nearly ten miles on this bombed-out limestone road to our location, and there was a little wooden booth and a guy who held the rope. So I told the guy to go get a coffee somewhere, I took his orange hat, took all my clothes off, and sat in the booth and held the rope up. As people drove by they would do the obligatory wave and keep going, but then I'd hear brakes.

JON KORKES: In the morning Haley picks up a few of the actors very early, and we're riding by those two stone pillars at the edge of this location. He turns back to me and he says, "Hey, you know what I'm going to do?" I said, "What?" He said, "When Nichols's car comes in later, I'm going to be standing on top of one of those things wearing just a jock and slippers and goggles with a spear." I'm thinking, *Have a nice trip back to New York*, because I'm thinking Mike's going to fire him. But it had the opposite effect: Nichols could not get enough of him. Every week after lunch on Thursday it became a regular thing. Nichols was giddy with anticipation.

MIKE HALEY: Every Thursday, I would come up with some kind of new mooning technique: naked in a parasail, limos showing up and me dressed as a foreign director with the back of my pants cut out. It just kept everybody's morale up. One of the great ones was a series of Polaroids that Mary Ellen Mark took of me mooning all over the set while everybody was at lunch. Towards the end of the day Mike said, "You haven't mooned today." I said, "There's twenty-four hours in a day, Mike." Buck Henry had taken all the Polaroids to where Mike was living, and put them in the medicine cabinet, in his soup at supper. The last one was on his wife's stomach.

On *Primary Colors* and *Regarding Henry*, I became this character, Don Diego Caperon y Garcia Vega, with a Zorro outfit, except the back of the leotards were cut out, who would show up on set every once in a while and do something insane, any time I could see Mike getting a little crazed. I think his core thing was, if you don't laugh, you die.

ART GARFUNKEL: I visited Mike when he was editing *Day of the Dolphin* in his Connecticut house. But he wasn't that into it. He was lazy about getting down to work and I thought, *Oh, he's not gripped by this project the way I am by mine.* Something was souring in Mike then. He was eating too much. Too many gourmet trips to France. I could feel he's making movies in more of a routine. Now he needs the moolah. I can see he's settling into a rhythm now.

CANDICE BERGEN: He was always very embarrassed about *The Day of the Dolphin*. I don't remember why he did it. I suppose they paid him a fortune. But he knew that he had to get out of Hollywood to survive. That was very clear, and he did.

STOCKARD CHANNING (*actress*): When I went to read for *The Fortune*, I got in the elevator, and I walked down this hallway, and the door opened, and there was Mike Nichols, Warren Beatty, Jack Nicholson, and Carole Eastman sitting in a room. I had met Mike before at Carole's, and he said, "The boys aren't going to act with you." Jack was just in *Chinatown* and Warren was just in *Shampoo*. They were best friends at the time. Warren was seeing Michelle Phillips, who was Jack's ex, and Jack was living with Anjelica [Huston]. They were all talking about the party they'd gone to the night before and how hungover they were. I remember that Warren had these velvet bell-bottom pants on and Jack had a mink-lined Levi's jacket and dark glasses. This is 1974. I was so tongue-tied because I wanted an autograph from these guys. I went into the bathroom, and I literally turned around three times and stared at myself in the mirror. I had not said one word to anybody. So I came out of the bathroom and they said, "Okay, let's begin." The line was, "Freddie enters, crying hysterically," and I just took a deep breath and went for it. I thought Warren was gonna jump off the couch. Mike has this line: when you want to act surprised, act as if the mailbox was speaking—it's a great image—and that's what Warren did.

We took like four months to make that movie. It was very luxurious. Even the underwear was from the '20s. Once we started shooting, it was the three of us basically all the time. It was sort of a kid-sister thing. I was really kind of upset that neither of them ever hit on me. I was like a cat and they were two big dogs who basically played with each other—there was a lot of conversation about the evening before, quite graphic conversation—and then they'd stop, look at each other, and tease the cat. Jack used to call Mike "Nick" and Warren was "the Old Pro" and I was "Stockaroo." Socially, I was not part of this circle, needless to say. But Mike didn't allow my lack of history with them to get in the way. He was very kind to me personally, and would invite me over to the house, because I didn't know a soul in Los Angeles. I was wearing the clothes I wore in college, a complete fish out of water.

The press hated the movie because Mike wouldn't let them onto the set. I don't think he wanted to have to pander to anyone. The only person he let on was Frank Rich, who gave it a negative response. In hindsight, it probably wasn't the smartest way to go about it.

FRANK RICH: As a young film critic at *The New York Times* I spent at least ten days in Culver City on the set. It involved a stellar group of people, including Carole Eastman right after she wrote *Five Easy Pieces*. Often you can't tell if a movie's good or bad from watching it being made. It was clear to me, this is dead.

PETER DAVIS (*director*): I was in a Chinese restaurant having lunch with Mike and his wife after he made *The Fortune*, which hadn't gotten terribly good reviews, and he said, "Why can't they just let me make my unimportant little pictures?"

MARSHA MASON: Neil got the idea for *Bogart Slept Here* from hearing Dustin Hoffman talk about his early experience as a struggling actor, doing an off-Broadway show, and then having Mike Nichols see it and ask him to come out to Hollywood and do *The Graduate*.

The Fortune came out when we had just started shooting and was not successful. We all went to a big audience screening in Century City, and I just remember Mike saying he just didn't know what was wrong with it. You're riding high, feeling solid, and then—*boom*. I think that was very unnerving, along with the fact that there were creative differences between Neil and Mike having to do with *Bogart Slept Here* and how it was being realized, so there was a certain amount of tension.

Mike offered the lead to Dustin first, but he never responded, or he took so long to respond that we moved on. So Mike decided next on a relatively unknown actor named Robert De Niro. He had just finished shooting *Taxi Driver* on Friday or Saturday and showed up on Monday or Tuesday to start *Bogart Slept Here*. I think it was hard coming off of that picture and then immediately jumping right into a romantic comedy.

Timing is really important with Neil's material. Each movie or play has its own rhythm, but it's a Neil Simon rhythm. Robert worked a very different way. Our rhythms were not in sync in terms of the way we worked, and it cost us a lot of time to try to work it through and try to deal with it, and I suppose that's when Mike began to realize that this mix wasn't going to work. He called me one day and said that they were going to recast, and then he left the movie.

ANTHEA SYLBERT (*costume designer*): After we reviewed the footage already shot on *Bogart*, I was walking down the hall and as I passed Mike's office, he called out, "Ant! Come in." He then asked, "What did you think?" I shrugged. "You're right," he said. "It's a shrug. What should we do?" "Cancel" was my one-word answer. "But what about the three million dollars we've spent?" My response was, "Think of the three and a half we haven't spent yet."

MARSHA MASON: We had a new director for a short period of time, Howard Zieff, and that's when I remember being asked to come out to the studio to do a reading with Richard Dreyfuss. Neil said after the reading, "Well, I realize now what was wrong with the script. Give me three weeks." He told me on the drive home that he realized that a story about being successful isn't nearly as interesting as a story about struggle. That's how *The Goodbye Girl* came about.

I assumed Mike leaving the movie was also because he and Neil were not getting on. Neil had stopped coming to the shooting. They kind of grew up together, but their styles are very different, and, consequently, how they ultimately see the world. Both men came from very difficult childhoods filled with various kinds of trauma—of course, comedy always comes from something very deep and painful, some of the best comedy does, anyway—but I think Mike's voice was more intellectual and satiric and ironic than Neil's was.

You have to remember, gossip was not as prevalent, and everybody had reason to keep the story under wraps. John Calley was a dear friend of Mike's, as Neil was. But it was a painful situation for everybody. It wasn't really anybody's fault. Creative differences are creative differences, and there's nothing personal in them. None of us were quite right together, I guess, myself included.

Robert [De Niro] was hoping to have a second chance at it, but Mike had decided to move on from the picture entirely, and it became, I think, a moot point for everybody. I always felt really badly about it, because there wasn't anything I could really do. I was caught in a very delicate and difficult situation being married to Neil, but also understanding the issue of how an actor works and what they can and can't do at a certain time. Years later, I wrote Bobby a letter, and he called me. I told him how terrible I felt, and he said, "Listen, I totally understand." He was very sweet and very understanding. He knew that it wasn't only his fault because Mike left the project, and then he didn't make another movie for eight years.

DAVID HARE: I think Mike felt that work should be enjoyable, and he had a gut feeling about whether things were going right or going wrong. That occasion when he walked off that Robert De Niro picture after five days, he always said that was the most liberating thing he did in his life. He said, "There was a moment when I realized you don't have to grind it out if you're not enjoying it. And that if you're not enjoying it, it's just better to face the fact of it and walk away. To realize I had the strength to do that and that I had no obligation to Hollywood to turn out a bad picture was the most freeing thing I've ever done artistically." I thought that was beautiful. I loved him for that.

BARRY DILLER (*executive*): It wasn't as if Mike couldn't get a job after that. For certain, I didn't devalue him at all, and I think people in positions such as mine, who were able to say yes or no to making movies and who would be in them, would have felt that way as well. I think Mike actually withdrew himself. He was really in exile.

CANDICE BERGEN: Mike left Los Angeles and stepped back from the business for a while. For someone who's not an LA person, and who doesn't love working there, they see it as very dangerous to the creative process. He moved back to Connecticut and he focused on theater and he focused on his horses.

*

Mike and Meryl Streep at a diner in Texas during the filming of *Silkwood*, in 1983. Based on the life of the labor activist and whistleblower Karen Silkwood, who died under mysterious circumstances, *Silkwood* was Nichols's first film in eight years. He would often tell friends, "Meryl woke me up." (© *Mary Ellen Mark*)

CHAPTER 8

We Must Work Together

TONY WALTON: Mike invited me to design *Annie* when it was about to come to Broadway. I had seen it and said, "Mike, why do you think it's going to work?" And he just said, "Trust me. If we get it right, it'll be your annuity." I had a similar experience on *Star Wars*. George Lucas asked me if I would do it, and I said, "I'm not really very interested in futuristic things." I added that if all these high-tech wonders were rusting and falling to bits, I'd find that in some way appealing enough to get onboard and, cheeky bugger, he actually ended up using that idea. After the success of *Annie*, Mike never tormented me about it. But George did, every time I saw him.

TOM STYRON (*former assistant*): Mike was living in the Carlyle. I was his gofer. He was always driving some beautiful, top-of-the-line, very souped-up Mercedes. I think the one he had that year he actually had imported from Germany, because it had some bells and whistles that were not yet allowed in the States. *Annie*—I don't know if it was still on Broadway, but it had three touring companies. I don't know the numbers, but I was aware that there were vast sums of money entering that office every day, just based on *Annie* alone.

JOHN LAHR: Mike knew how to fix things. He was famous for that. *Call Mike Nichols in.* He fixed *Annie*.

MARTIN CHARNIN (*lyricist*): There was a compilation book of *Annie* strips that was being sold at Christmas of 1970 or '71, and upon reading it, I thought it could be turned into a musical. I had no collaborators at the time, so I had to put this entire package together myself. First, I optioned the material. Then I approached Tom Meehan and talked him into doing the libretto. We wrote the show and took it to Michael Price at the Goodspeed Opera House. We went into rehearsal in the summer of '76, and it went through all of the things that musicals go through. Musicals are rarely written, they're usually rewritten.

Once it really looked good, we decided to find a New York producer to invite into the piece, and Mike was an old friend of mine. We'd play charades at my house in New York. I called him at the end of that summer and begged him to come up and see it, because I really believed that strongly in it. He and his wife and his then partner Lewis Allen came up on a weekend and saw the show, and we went out and had a cup of coffee afterward. Mike said, "It's sensational. It needs certain fixes, but we really loved it." Then the bomb was dropped. He said, "I direct shows, but I really don't produce them. I wish you all the luck in the world," and drove back to New York. The next morning, I got a telephone call from him, saying that he and Lew had spent the entire ride talking about *Annie* and that they did, indeed, want to produce it.

Raising the money was not the easiest thing, because there was a sense that comic-strip musicals simply would not work. There had been a number of attempts and they'd basically failed. As a matter of fact, our composer Charles Strouse himself had attempted to do Superman as a musical. Mike's existence in the project validated it. Once he was listed as the producer, things really fell into place quite quickly.

Mike said to me early on in the rehearsals, "I'm going to be the kind of producer that I've never had," and I said, "What does that mean?" He said, "All I've had are producers who butt in. I'm going to raise money and be your lead man on trying to sell it, to get it on. You guys go about the business of making it happen, and come to me if you need me." Mike was responsible for an idea here or a joke there, and they were all, with very few exceptions, things that worked and remained in the show, but he was more somebody who was encouraging us to hold the fort—*don't lose the point of view that you have about the show, listen to yourselves*—and he was absolutely right, because most of the suggestions that came at the beginning were outrageous. People would say things like the dog should be played by a person in a dog suit. Basically Mike was there putting his stamp of approval on what we had originally intended to do and convincing us not to lose our way. I think if every musical had a mentor of that kind, every musical would be successful.

Truth be told, he didn't "save the show." If saving the show meant that he would turn around and say, "Well, that's a stupid idea, do what you intended to do," then he saved the show, but he didn't write one song. I have a rehearsal script that I look at every now and then. I'll go and compare it with the final script that's printed. It's not a lot different. I think his being there saved the show. The fact that he was a part of it saved the show.

Three or four nights before we opened, he took me aside and said, "I have to apologize to you," and I said, "For what?" We'd been getting standing ovations, people were screaming. They would walk away from the theater whistling the score. We had a record deal. But he took me aside and he said, "I have to apologize to you." I said, "For what?" He said, "You're not going to win the Tony," and I said, "Okay. Why?" He said to me, "You're going to win a lot of awards, but you're not going to win Best Director. Because my name is on the program, the theatrical community will assume that whatever good there is in that show has come from whatever I have contributed, and I apologize." This is the first time I've ever told that story.

He was right. I didn't win it. When Mike won as the producer, his entire speech was an ode to me. It was his only way of publicly apologizing and telling the world basically what he had said to me. Funnily enough, I never resented that conversation. I understood it completely. Nevertheless, every now and again the whole subject is a little pinprick that comes and sticks me in the ass. Then I get up, and I've got a new musical that's being done somewhere, and that pain goes away.

My instinct is that we would not have gotten on had Mike not attached himself to the piece. Or maybe we would have gotten on, but it would have been a year or two later, and who knows whether or not we would have had the same kind of impact. I thank Mike—and I blame him, in the best sense of the word—for being there and for helping get us on.

ANJELICA HUSTON: They wanted me to test for *The Fortune* and I didn't want to because I'd already worked for my dad and I didn't want to get all hung up working with Jack. This was before I realized that's how you get work! And so the part gently went to Stockard Channing—who, by the way, knew what she was doing, as opposed to me at the time.

Mike often said, "Let's do something together." And I'd think, *Oh my God, it's Mike and it's the stage and it's New York—what would it be?* I was always a bit scared of him. And then he discovered Meryl Streep, so what are you going to do about that? They even looked so much alike. It was a perfectly symbiotic relationship.

PAUL SIMON: Mike and Meryl used to kid around that they had the same nose, which they do.

TOM STYRON: I have never thought that it was anything other than a platonic, powerful, professional relationship, but I have no question—and I don't think that Mike would say otherwise—that he was completely smitten and madly in love with Meryl, both for her extraordinary artistry, and because she was this gorgeous, incredible woman. I think Mike had a predilection for falling in love with whomever he was working with. I remember him bringing Matthew Broderick up to our house in Connecticut after they made *Biloxi Blues*, and it was clear that he was completely taken with this fabulous young actor. So I think it was male and female, but I think Meryl probably was at the top of that list of all time. Mike was in some state of worship, and I'm sure it was mutual.

MERYL STREEP (*actress*)[1]: My dad had all the Nichols and May records, but the first time I saw Mike not on an album cover was in

---

1. "Mike Nichols," *American Masters*, directed by Elaine May, produced by Julian Schlossberg, season 30, episode 1, aired January 29, 2016, on PBS.

1979 when he came backstage at a play called *Taken in Marriage* at the Public Theater. Elizabeth Wilson, one of his favorite actresses in the whole world, came to my dressing room and said, "Mike Nichols is here and he wants to meet you." I said, "Oh my God." He said, "We must work together." I said, "Oh, yes, we must." And I thought, *That'll never happen.* He called me over the next couple of years for readings of things. I remember after one he sent me a Tiffany pen as a thank-you, and I thought, *This is the most elegant person I've ever met.*

Nora [Ephron] and Alice Arlen sent *Silkwood* to me through Sam Cohn, who was Mike's agent. In those days, they packaged things, so the studio would be—ahem—*encouraged* to employ ICM clients. So that's why I was there. But I was thrilled to be able to play this part. It was so different from other things I had done.

NICK PILEGGI: Nora was fascinated by the business, and she asked Mike if he would help her. He just put her on a chair next to him while he was directing *Silkwood* and, this is according to her, explained everything he was doing: the cameras, the lenses, the drama for a scene, what makes a scene work in a movie that doesn't work in a book and vice versa. She was a sponge. She absorbed every bit of it.

CHER: When I walked in to audition for *The Fortune*, Mike was very blunt. He just said, "You're not that woman." When he was casting *Silkwood*, he was about to get rid of my part when someone said, "You should go see Cher in *Come Back to the Five and Dime, Jimmy Dean, Jimmy Dean*, she's really good." So he saw a matinee, and he came backstage and said, "How would you like to do a movie with Meryl Streep?"

In New York, when you're driving downtown under what used to be the Pan Am Building, and then it curves around, there was a huge black graffiti reading "Who killed Karen Silkwood?" No matter how many times they marked it out, it was always there: "Who killed Karen Silkwood?" I guess it was destiny. I actually was the only one who'd ever met Karen Silkwood. She was a Sonny and Cher fan. Her boyfriend, the guy Kurty was playing, he came and visited us and told me, "We went to see you once and got an autograph."

KURT RUSSELL (*actor*): When Mike asked me, "What would I have seen you in?" I said, "Nothing." He nodded, and then he said, "Well, would you like to read a little?" I said, "Not really. I'm not much of a cold reader, but if you want me to, I'll do it." He said, "Nice meeting you." An hour later, they told me, He wants you for the movie.

About three weeks into shooting, somebody said, "Why did you hire Kurt?" Mike said, "Oh, that was easy. I needed to have someone who I knew the audience would always believe."

MERYL STREEP[2]: I finished *Sophie's Choice* in Yugoslavia, got on the plane, and came to Texas to start *Silkwood*. The night I arrived, I still had my hair and eyebrows bleached white-blond. Cher was there, and Mike took the two of us out to dinner. And he said, "I love this. The two: the dark, the light." I thought, *I have a surprise for you, because tomorrow I'm going to be Karen Silkwood.* And my hair and makeup man darkened my eyelashes and brows and cut my hair all off in a mullet shag and dyed it dark. When I walked onto the set the next day, Mike just turned bright red. And then he started to laugh. And then he started to cry—which was his favorite thing to do. Actually, he would say that was his third favorite thing. The second favorite was to cancel. And the first was . . . *you know.*

CHER: Meryl and Mike would go into a corner together and talk and talk and talk. Kurty wasn't like that very much. He'd just want to go and act, but they would delve into the scene. That was a relationship of equals. I wasn't in his league, but I never felt left out.

KURT RUSSELL: It was a tight-knit group, very family-oriented. We lived in very close proximity to each other. It was easy to talk to everybody. We were very open and honest with each other about whatever our questions were.

CHER: We all stayed together in the house. We spent all of our days in that house together once we got out of town, hanging out. Meryl

---

2. "Mike Nichols," *American Masters*, PBS.

was knitting—she made the worst sweater ever—and I was doing a needlepoint for Christmas, so we would be talking, and Kurty would come in being his silly self.

I wasn't allowed to wear any makeup, and every day Mike would run his fingers along my eyelids to make sure. It was such a disadvantage in the beginning, but then once we started, it was great, because I never thought for a moment what I looked like.

KURT RUSSELL: Cher would come in and show Mike the hair and makeup and clothes, and he'd say, "Okay, let's bring it down a little bit." About the third time she came into the room after going back and—"bringing it down" would be a euphemistic way of saying it—she said, "How's this?" and he said, "Yeah, it's almost there." She said, "Okay, fine, I'll bring it down some more." When she came back the last time, she had no makeup on. Mike said, "I think that looks great." Cher, who was used to a more glamorous appearance, was pretty distraught. Kiddingly, I said, "What are you complaining about? All you've got to do is show up like that and you're going to get nominated for an Academy Award."

CHER: Right before you started the shot, Mike would come up and tell you a story. He had the best stories of anyone I've ever known. A lot of times it was a sad story, and tears would be coming out of his eyes at the end of it. I started to learn the stories were not just stories for no reason. He never said, do this, or don't do that. He allowed you to be. I really wish everybody was like that as a director, because acting is hard. It's not manual labor, but it's hard to be in the moment and to be honest and to be good.

KURT RUSSELL: We rehearsed this one scene all morning long, maybe five, six, seven times, and now it was noon, and he was still walking around the room, thinking to himself. I saw him say something to the assistant director, and the word was: have lunch. So we broke for lunch, and we hadn't shot a thing.

I was sitting in my room by myself, eating lunch and thinking, *I don't know what it is, but I'm doing something wrong in this scene.* As I'm thinking that, there's a knock on the door, and Cher comes in and says, "I know I'm the problem. Nobody's going to tell me, so what am I doing wrong?" and I said, "I was sitting here thinking the exact same thing." And then *bang, bang, bang*: another knock on the door. It's Meryl. She says, "I'm out to lunch in this scene, and I don't really know why."

We went back to rehearsal, and Mike said, "Okay, run it again," and we did, and then he said, "Okay, run it again," and we got about halfway through the scene and he stopped us and said, "Okay, we're done for the day." We all said, "What do you mean?" He said, "Everything that's in this scene has already been said. There's no point in shooting it because it's not going to be in the movie."

CHER: When the trailer came out, Mike called me and said he wanted me to go see it. So I went, and I was really, really excited. At the end of the trailer they said, "Meryl Streep," and everybody in the theater applauded, and then said, "Kurt Russell," and everybody applauded. Then they said, "Cher," and everyone laughed. I just bit the inside of my cheek. I called him when I got out and I told him what happened, and he said, "They might be laughing at the beginning, but they won't be laughing at the end. They'll be clapping."

BOBBIE O'STEEN: Karen Silkwood's boyfriend came to a screening. Afterward, he said, "It brings it all back to life so well. I can't get over it."

ROBERT GREENHUT (*producer*): On *Heartburn*, I started to get wind of how much Mike had a crush on Meryl. She was married, but that didn't prevent Mike from at least trying to hit on her a bit.

MERYL STREEP[3]: On *Heartburn*, he let somebody go very early on. Then Jack [Nicholson] came in.

---

3. "Mike Nichols," *American Masters*, PBS.

ROBERT GREENHUT: We hired Mandy [Patinkin] with full confidence, and Meryl was happy about it. Everybody signed off on it. We had rehearsals, read-through rehearsals. He was bright, and he was brilliant, but he was a little scared, because it was his biggest thing to date.

After about a couple of weeks of dailies, there was something that just wasn't—they didn't seem complementary on-screen. The chemistry was not quite there.

Mike said, "This is not working." I said, "Boy, replacing him is going to be some disaster." He said, "Well, what about Jack Nicholson?" I said, "Fine, but he's going to be very expensive, and we don't even know if he's available." So Mike put in a call to him.

TONY WALTON: I was among those standing near him when he spoke to Jack, and it was a very quick call. I asked him about it, and Mike said, "I just said to Jack, 'I need you,' and Jack said, 'What for?'" And Mike said, "If you could be in Central Park at eight a.m. tomorrow morning, you'll save my ass," and he was. I don't think he even knew what the movie was.

ROBERT GREENHUT: As it turns out, Jack sort of had a crush on Meryl, too. I think that was magnetic for him, the chance to work with Meryl. So now came the *All right, we've got to sever ties with Mandy.* Mike said, "Can you do it?" I said, "Listen, I can do it." I've done it before. I've been through some awkward ones like Michael Keaton on *The Purple Rose of Cairo.* I didn't want to do that, but Woody doesn't like confrontation. Keaton won't make eye contact with me to this day. But I said, "Mike, you should really do it." I had a car phone. I said, "We'll make the call. I'll sit there with you. I'll hold your hand." It pleases me to no end every time I'm watching *Homeland* and I see Mandy has this great career intact, but, boy, that was awful.

The next thing we know Jack is getting fitted for wardrobe and coming to work. I don't think we actually stopped shooting. Listen, he's Jack. He's great, but, boy, he was all over Meryl, man. Between the two of them, *jeez*.

MERYL STREEP[4]: Mike was asking Nora to write more scenes for Jack. Suddenly this movie that Nora had written about an experience that she'd gone through, now the viewfinder was on the husband's side a little bit. I remember saying to Mike one day, "You know, this is about the person that got hit by a bus. It's not about the bus." And he went, "Oh. True." He had no trouble living through the female protagonist of anything I've done with him. It was only in *Heartburn* that he was tempted to look at the film through the viewpoint he was more familiar with.

PETER LAWRENCE: Mike always said that Meryl woke him up. After *Silkwood*, he did two plays in New York, *The Real Thing*, and then *Hurlyburly*. I believe that virtually every show he ever did after that was to work out moral themes. Mike made everything personal.

TOM STOPPARD: I was living and working in Bristol in the west of England, and we had the vinyl 33⅓ revolutions per minute of Nichols and May in the household. It was a period where really funny Americans were suddenly part of the culture: Mort Sahl, Bob Newhart. By the time I met Mike, he was famous. He was a glamorous figure to me.

I did the thing one mustn't do, really, which is to agree to write something entirely because of the person whom you might be working with. Mike asked me to adapt a novel, *Innocent Blood* by P. D. James, which is a good novel, but it wasn't my thing, really. He came to where I lived with my wife in the country outside London, and his charm and intelligence and humor—you couldn't possibly defend yourself against him. Of course, it was never filmed, but we stayed close. I found very quickly that we shared so many frames of reference. I had read what he had read, and he had read what I had read.

ERIC IDLE: Mike said, "I'm going to do *The Real Thing* on Broadway." I said, "Oh." I wasn't mad about it. He said, "I know how to

---

4. "Mike Nichols," *American Masters*, PBS.

make it work." And then it was a huge hit. If you can help Stoppard, you're pretty much in a league of your own.

PETER GALLAGHER: My wife and I saw *The Real Thing* in London in '83, on our honeymoon. It was still the play, but it was an entirely different production. Mike made it almost cinematic, as much as you can make Broadway cinematic.

EMANUEL AZENBERG: Everyone and his brother was asking for the rights because it was a hit in London. Then Frank Rich wrote a bad notice for it, and everybody else went away, and we were the only ones left.

FRANK RICH: There was no way it would have transferred from London, no matter what I had said about it, without Nichols taking it over and overhauling it. It had no stars, and Stoppard was box-office poison in New York. He had had one commercial and critical success, which was *Rosencrantz and Guildenstern Are Dead*; then he had had productions of his plays that had basically failed. The one exception was *Travesties*, which was a succés d'estime. Some of them I'm sure got good reviews, but none of them ran, and none of them got their money back, and that's the only criterion that counts in the commercial theater. More than fifteen years had passed between *Rosencrantz* and *The Real Thing*. My guess is no one was interested unless there was some, as Bill Goldman would say, muscle, and that muscle would have been Nichols.

TOM STOPPARD: Mike put out a feeler. So I talked to Peter [Wood], and he saw the point, and so he stepped aside. It was the first time with a play, going from London to New York, that we started from scratch.

JACK O'BRIEN: Mike's great gift to *The Real Thing*, I think, was to give it momentum. I don't think Tom's work had had an American pace prior to that. The difference between his plays here and his plays there, they're very leisurely over there, very sort of fusty and intellectual, and here we don't do that. Mike streamlined it. He made the show burst forth, brought it to the audience. I love Tom, and I think he's one of the most seductive, sexy, potent, compelling people I've ever known. You don't see that on the page when you read his material, but when you hear it spoken, it's there, and I think that Mike and I shared that appreciation of blood.

I think the directors in England who have worked with Tom are all Oxbridge guys, and Tom's an autodidact, he never went to college, and I think there's a thing about the British where they want to one-up him or meet him on his level. I don't want to meet on his level. I don't think Mike did either.

EMANUEL AZENBERG: Because, I suspect, Frank Rich had already pissed all over it, Tom—who is one of the great honest gentlemen in the world—was amenable to rethinking the entire physical show, rethinking the casting.

Mike wanted Christine Baranski and Glenn Close, and I must say it was my suggestion that we get Jeremy Irons because he had just done *Brideshead Revisited*.

JEREMY IRONS: I'd been asked to do it in London, and I couldn't, because I was filming *Betrayal*, and then I went off to Australia to make a picture with Liv Ullmann. I went to see the production in London, which I didn't like. I felt it was passionless—didn't work for me at all.

Having read the play before that, I knew that it was a fantastic play. I heard that Meryl and Kevin Kline had been to see it in London, so I called my agent, and I said, "If I don't play *The Real Thing* in New York, I'm leaving you." He came back with an offer to do it with Meryl, and then Meryl pulled out, as she tends to do from Broadway shows, and Glenn came onboard.

It was a very snug fit for me, that role. I felt it was one of those God-given parts which happen every now and again in your lifetime, if you're lucky, where the character is you. I thought, *This is extraordinary. I don't know Tom Stoppard, but he seems to know me.*

EMANUEL AZENBERG: There was an actor who was hired to play a smaller part and we all questioned it, and Mike said—it's like the *Pygmalion* moment—"I'll make him great." But it didn't happen, and Peter Gallagher took his place.

PETER GALLAGHER: I was initially not cast in *The Real Thing*. They cast a kid who was still at Juilliard, and then they asked me to come up when they were out of town, to see the play in Boston, and to think about replacing him for the New York previews. Thank God I had my wife with me, because I told her there were certain things I'd do entirely differently, and she just said, "So why don't you tell him that?" "What? Tell Mike Nichols that?" And then I realized of course she was right. And so I said, "Well, Mr. Nichols . . . I see it like this." "Great, try it!" I thought, *Oh my God, those are words I've always wanted to hear.*

A lot of times in the theater, you have a sense of, there's the grown-ups and the kids, and the kids couldn't possibly know as much as the grown-ups. Whereas with Mike, we were standing shoulder to shoulder, trying to tell this story. With all the great directors, from Altman to Soderbergh, the focus is on the story we're telling, not who came up with what.

JEREMY IRONS: With a good director, the process of directing is to feed the actors' creativity, and so one is never quite sure where an idea comes from sometimes, whether it's come from the actor or whether it's been placed in the head of the actor by the director. That whole process of creating a production is very delicate. Of course, Mike was an incredibly feeling and delicate man, an artist himself, and he must have learned so much with Elaine about how you create drama, how you create interest on a stage. One really felt one was being guided through by a master.

CHRISTINE BARANSKI: When people ask me about being in *The Real Thing*, I say, "It was like going to Paris on the Concorde." It was Mike Nichols at his peak and Tom Stoppard in the rehearsal room together. Jeremy and Glenn, whose careers were red-hot; mine was in the ascendancy; the handsome and dashing Caravaggio-looking Peter Gallagher; and a young, spritely actress named Cynthia Nixon.

We went out of town to Boston. That's when you could go out of town and nobody followed you, and there were no blogs. You actually could go out of town and do your work. That will never come again.

TONY WALTON: There were quite a number of people in the company with whom Mike was really almost in love, which was his wont. It was the reverse of so much of what you usually experience. People were so knocked out with Jerry Robbins, and before him the incredible Jed Harris, whose fondest belief was the more you torture, the more you'll get out of them.

PETER GALLAGHER: When we did *The Real Thing*, Mike would speak to Glenn in one way, and Jeremy in another, and me in another. Not remarkably different, but specifically tailored. He took great responsibility for how his words would land.

GLENN CLOSE (*actress*): During rehearsals, I remember he said, "Bring your day," which was incredibly helpful. I always think about that when working, "Bring your day."

EMANUEL AZENBERG: Tom was in the room for all the rehearsals. That was his peer. Maybe greater than his peer. So Mike was at his best. If Stoppard is in the room, you behave. You can only fake so much. And we were doing it differently than in London and contrary to his original intention.

TOM STOPPARD: He was quiet, he was definite. Obviously he would explore as well, but he never tried to hit six different targets at the same time and figure out which one worked. He could see which targets should work. My impression is that he was ahead of all of us.

I was sitting in the stalls, and a stagehand walked in with a chair in either hand, and he shouted to Mike, "Which chair?" And Mike instantly said, "That one," indicating the one in his left hand. As the guy walked off, I was thinking, *Christ, I'll never be a director.* The chairs weren't that different, you know. And I said, "What was it about that chair?" He said, "Nothing, you just have to answer instantly. You can change your mind later."

CYNTHIA NIXON (*actress*): Glenn Close's character, who is having an affair with Jeremy, comes home, and she's in a rush to hear Jeremy being interviewed on the radio. She's getting her coat off and turning the radio on, and then her husband says something and she realizes that he knows. Mike had Glenn not only taking her coat off and all this stuff, but unwrapping a candy bar and taking a big bite, so that by the time she realized, she had a mouthful of chocolate. She was caught in her indulgence of her appetite, essentially, but there's also no way to have dignity talking with her mouth full.

TONY WALTON: One of the things I could kill myself for was I never kept a journal. It was just an extraordinary group of people. Jeremy was no slouch, but between the two of them, Mike and Tom, it was blinding to listen to, and I used to try and creep up behind them in rehearsals.

PETER GALLAGHER: The note sessions between Mike and Tom were astounding. We would be assembled, during previews, underneath the stage, crammed into furniture left over from various productions. Tom would sometimes get very technical, in terms of the sounds of things, the structure. And Mike, very often, had a different take. I remember Tom was explaining some aspect of the play, and Mike said, "No, no, Tom. It's about you and your first wife." He so surprised Tom with the undeniability of his observation.

CYNTHIA NIXON: He and Stoppard were just simpatico. They were both refugees. They were both from Eastern Europe, wunderkinds, very, very well-read men with tremendous love affairs, men for whom women loomed really large, men who were about love and thought more than about power.

EMANUEL AZENBERG: *The Real Thing* is about an author who writes a play called *House of Cards*. And on the set was a poster of the

Polish production of *House of Cards,* and at the bottom it said, "Directed by Mikhail Peschkowsky." That was the inside joke. Remember, Tom Stoppard was Tomas Straussler from Czechoslovakia. Each one knew who the other really was.

TONY WALTON: I thought Mike would, of course, bring that set from London, but he said, "It's problematic for Broadway, because you learn nothing about the lives of these people who are not familiar types to an American audience. We have to make it realistic so we know the kinds of lives they're leading and the society they live in. The problem is," he said, "there are fifteen scenic changes, and they all need to be virtually full stage"—because it's not like the old musicals when you could go into one and change it to the one behind—"and I can't afford to wait more than four seconds for any scene change." That took a while to figure out. I used to almost always do it in the dead of night, because it was the only time when it was quiet enough to be able to make this jigsaw puzzle from scene to scene, before a police siren or something interrupted and made me go back to square one.

CYNTHIA NIXON: Mike was a fanatic about getting those turntable transitions exactly the right length so that people had time to digest what had just happened, but not come out of the play.

JEREMY IRONS: Mike spent days working with the technical crew. He knew that if we were to keep the ball in the air, it couldn't be slowed up with all of these interminable scene changes. Once we were out of rehearsal and into technical, he would spend a couple of days just rehearsing with stage crew, and I think it paid off, because we had very slick scene changes as a result.

Opening night, we were gathered in the Ritz in Boston. Mike had provided capacious, extravagant room service, and we sat around the roaring fire waiting for the telephone call with the reviews. I remember watching him when it came through. I can see him now, standing there with that sort of impish smile on his face, nodding, eyes half-closed, and thinking, *I think they're all right.* He put down the phone and indeed they were.

CHRISTINE BARANSKI: There's a wonderful story of a woman sitting in the audience of *The Real Thing*. In the middle of the play, she turned to her husband and was overheard saying, "Oh God, I feel so witty."

GREGORY MOSHER: It was the same year as *Glengarry Glen Ross*, so it was Mike's billionth and my first. My date to the Tonys was Elaine. Elaine and I were sitting right behind Mike, and we were up against an Australian and an Englishman, and neither of them had come to the awards, because obviously Mike was going to win. Mike said, "All right, here's the deal. If I win, you'll applaud politely, and if you win, I'll applaud politely, and if either of those guys win, we have to stand on our seats and scream, 'There is no God!'"

He won, and I applauded—enthusiastically, actually. It has enormous heart, that production, and it was funny, and it was glamorous, and it was just everything you want a Broadway play to be. It had a full emotional life onstage.

EMANUEL AZENBERG: We changed Frank Rich's mind, which only happens once every thirty-eight years. And Mike won the Tony, Stoppard won best play, Christine won, Glenn won, Jeremy won.

JON ROBIN BAITZ: *The Real Thing* was a high point. He was the perfect director for it. Mike's favorite thing in it was that it argued for balance in life, and forgiveness. There's a moment in the play where someone says, "Happiness is equilibrium. Shift your weight." It's the character talking about how he sometimes writes movies for money, and he's justifying it—not all moments could be about art—and Mike loved that.

PETER LAWRENCE: A man who was the smartest—could have a conversation about anything—is finally reduced to whimpering to his lover, who is about to leave him, "Please don't." Those two words were the reason that Mike did that play.

CYNTHIA NIXON: Shortly after we opened *The Real Thing*, Mike handed me this really long script called *The Untitled David Rabe Play* with a list attached showing me all the people who would be in it. "William Hurt is Eddie, Sigourney Weaver is Darlene, Christopher Walken is Nicky"—this incredible list. And then it said, "Cynthia is Donna."

PETER LAWRENCE: I got this call from Peter Neufeld, a general manager who worked with Mike a lot. He said, "Look, I've got this play. It pays $350 a week. There's no per diem. It's going to Chicago. It has all these movie stars, most of them who have not done plays before. It's five hours long, and it doesn't even have a title." I said, "Why would I want to do this play?" and he said, "Well, Mike Nichols is directing it," and I said, "I'll take it."

DAVID RABE (*playwright*): I wrote *Hurlyburly* in this crazy state. There was some order, of course, but I had a lot of trouble trying to orchestrate it and write bridges and figure out the logic of it all. I took it to Mike because I came away from *Streamers* feeling he was brilliant. Yeah, it was hard, and it was stressful, but it was worth it. We were not on bad terms by any means. He was such a persuasive and dialectically strong person in terms of pursuing what he wanted. I came to say that even if I was mad at him, I liked him. And I was very mad at him, at one point, and rightly so, I think.

CYNTHIA NIXON: We rehearsed it in New York while I was doing *The Real Thing* at night and at matinees, and then we took it out of town to Chicago, in the ninety-nine-seat black box at the Goodman Theatre. We were kind of a hit there, although the play was four and a half hours, which is really, really long.

CHRISTOPHER WALKEN: There was this apartment-hotel thing that we all moved into, Mike included, and spent time together, kind of in a big frat house.

CYNTHIA NIXON: *Hurlyburly* essentially takes place in a living room, and Mike was trying to figure out how to arrange the furniture onstage so that it would be good for playing on, but also believable.

Obviously, this is an age-old problem in the theater. He said, "We can't have everything facing out. The people coming to see this know what a living room looks like, because they have living rooms of their own. And not only that—they've been to their friends' houses, and they've seen their friends' living rooms. If we tell them this is what a living room looks like, they won't believe us."

TONY WALTON: David's saying to me, "It's the Elizabethan theater that I picture when I'm staging it in my mind." But he also said, "If I just go to my gut and think, *Where is this taking place?*, it's some strange clearing in the jungle where a bunch of wounded animals are coming to lick each other's wounds." I mentioned this to Mike, who was thrilled at that comment, and from day one of rehearsals he had the cast improvising animal behavior. So Chris Walken, for example, was always a panther.

CHRISTOPHER WALKEN: He talked about what kinds of animals each of our characters were, who were the cats and who were the birds. Working with him was very much like kids playing. It had that freedom and exuberance. Sometimes we'd all just lie on the floor and say our lines, and we'd do it really quite quickly, kind of speed-read through, and sometimes you'd get through one of those and see the play in a different way.

He put certain people together, I believe, knowing that certain things were going to happen. He was kind of a chemist: add this to that, and then put that in relation to something else. I don't remember ever talking to him about anybody's private thoughts or motivations or anything like that. I always had the feeling that he knew stuff that he didn't even have to express.

JUDITH IVEY (*actress*): I had come in with this Valley Girl delivery. In rehearsal, he took that away from me, because I was relying on it so much. It made me find the truth of the character—to be the character rather than just sound like them. Then he said, "Now you can put it back, because it's hilarious, Jude."

SIGOURNEY WEAVER: The first day, he separated the women—me, Judith Ivey, and Cynthia Nixon—and said, "You are scrunts. You don't belong in this world, so you will always rehearse at the end of the day." But he said it with great compassion. I'm sure he had been, at times, the horrible chauvinist, but he had also certainly felt at times, whether in the business or not, like a scrunt, so you always felt like he was on your side.

CYNTHIA NIXON: If I had to pick one thing that I imagined drew him to that play, other than liking David and wanting to collaborate with David again, it would be the misogyny of the play. I think that Mike was interested in a lot of things, but nothing more than the battle of the sexes, and the harm that men and women do to each other. Mike was keenly aware of what he felt were the weapons women would use, but I think he was not in any way deluded about the realness and the power of misogyny, and that's what the play's about. He sort of encouraged the battle of the sexes within the company. Mike would get the men to act a certain way, and then the women would feel slightly victimized and react accordingly.

Mike liked to talk about love and sex and affairs. I remember him saying once, at one point in our notes, "When you're having an affair, your number one concern is to act like nothing is happening." So you *don't* light up when you're around that other person. I remember he said the biggest mindfuck of all that a woman will do is she'll take you to bed, and it'll be the greatest night of your life, and then the next time she says, "I just want you to hold me tonight." That's the thing about Mike. He's not a misogynist, but he understands it.

SIGOURNEY WEAVER: It was so much behavior and it's very easy for actors just to get lost in behavior. He really wanted to give it a structure, a skeleton, and a pace. I remember him saying things like, "When you're first having an affair there comes that moment when you're lying there wondering who will be the person to say, 'Well, I've got to call the garage.'" You know, who's going to pop that bubble? He seemed to bring so much of his own personal stuff to everything he did. We would stop rehearsal and just talk about life for hours.

CYNTHIA NIXON: He saw the ugliness in people, and he brought it out. He doesn't smooth over rough edges. I think he was a good enough artist that he could judge the character and still cut them an even break, but Mike is a person who, in things he's directed, sees people who are—*whoa, that's a bad person. That's an evil person.* Yet Mike knew well enough that you can't just make the evil person a stick figure, because then they have no power, and you don't recognize them, and they seem easy to write off.

SIGOURNEY WEAVER: At the same time as I was doing this play where men are so terrible to women, I got engaged. By the end of the summer I got married, and everyone came to the wedding. Mike was a great dancer. He came up to Jim [Simpson] and me at the beginning of the party and cut in. He looked at Jim and he said, "Droit du seigneur."

CYNTHIA NIXON: When we were in Chicago, it was a very long play in a very tiny space. It was the spring, and you had to have the air-conditioning on in that little theater, otherwise it would just be unbearable for the performers and the audience. So we had the air-conditioning on, but it was really loud. In the middle of the third act, William Hurt's character gets this phone call. He's in the midst of a fight with Sigourney Weaver, they're having this petty lovers' argument, and then he gets this phone call, and she's like, "What? What?" and he says, "Phil's dead." An important character has just killed himself very unexpectedly, and it completely shifts everything that happens after that. Mike had the stage manager turn off the air-conditioning at that moment, so that all of a sudden, you literally felt an absence. You couldn't put your finger on it. Nobody in the audience thought, *Oh, they just turned the air-conditioning off,* but, all of a sudden, things were quieter and stiller. It just felt empty. And also it meant that this very poetic last scene would not have this terrible air-conditioning under it.

PETER LAWRENCE: Mike said, "Pete, we have to make this play float. Right now it's concrete. In order to find out what it is, we have to raise this thing to the surface so that it has buoyancy. The audience cannot stand five hours." David Rabe called him the devil.

CYNTHIA NIXON: That was not Mike's usual experience. People loved him and would be falling all over themselves—*Daddy, like me, please.*

JUDITH IVEY: Mike's point of view was, how much can you ask of an audience? There were nights in Chicago where I might not even come on until ten, and there was a whole act after me. So I went back and forth, because I could see both points of view. They're both wonderful artists; Mike was just looking out for the commercial aspect of it more than David.

DAVID RABE: The problem that I had with Mike developed over the third scene of act 1, starting where Phil gets mad at Donna about watching football, and then Eddie comes back and he talks about not wanting the baby, and then gives what is one of my favorite speeches about fate. That scene did not exist in the Broadway production; he cut it. During an early rehearsal, Mike said, "You know, it's such a big play"—and it was. "Leave that out for a while." I said, "Well, okay."

I got him finally to do it in one rehearsal, and it was just pointless. He couldn't do it. He couldn't face the scene. He sat in the audience and the actors were onstage and nothing was happening. He couldn't tell them what to do, or wouldn't. If you take that scene out of the play, Phil becomes a thug and nothing more. In Mike's defense, I don't think he was cutting the scene for time or length. There was something else going on, something was happening in his own life that I didn't know about.

CYNTHIA NIXON: I've seen the play both ways. It's much better with that scene out. The play's too long, and we don't need that scene.

DAVID RABE: The play *was* too long, and we were in a situation where we couldn't cut it the way you normally would, because we had all these movie stars. It was so high profile. But to me the play kind of stopped making sense without that scene, so I really shut down. I refused to work on it anymore, and that's when I was really mad at him. I didn't care that it would have been too long. It was too long, but that wasn't the way to cut it.

In the business, it was known that I was upset about this, and I think it did me a certain amount of harm. I got a reputation of not being easy to work with, because there I was with half of Hollywood in my play, and Mike Nichols directing, and I was unhappy. So it was from the outside, without knowing everything that went on. Even if they had known, I don't think they would have thought it made any sense to be unhappy. I know it's a marker in my career. Something's been different ever since.

TONY WALTON: David said, "It's hard for me, because I'm not entirely responsible for what I write. It's coming through the ether, from the characters themselves. I don't know to what extent they're real. I only know I can't defy them. If they have presented something very clearly to me, I don't feel I have the license to mess with that." A hard thing to deal with.

I later worked on a prequel to *Hurlyburly*, which was called *Those the River Keeps*, by which time David decided he wanted to direct his own work. I would beg him from time to time to approach Mike to at least come and be his second set of eyes and ears.

PETER LAWRENCE: Cynthia Nixon, who was seventeen when we started doing the play and eighteen when we opened it, plays this street waif, Donna, and the men all use her and eventually throw her out. William Hurt's character, Eddie, takes her in. She puts her head on his shoulder at the end of the play and they fall asleep on the sofa together. It's a moment of real human contact. Well, David Rabe, who was constantly rewriting, came in one day and said, "I have a new idea for the end. Now when they fall asleep on the sofa, Donna robs Eddie and leaves."

We rehearsed it. We were going to put it in the play the next day. I couldn't sleep all night, and I called Mike early in the morning— because Mike was a famous insomniac—and I said, "I've got to talk to you before rehearsal," and he said, "Oh, good, Pete, I was hoping I could talk to you before rehearsal too." We met at the theater two hours early. I said, "Mike, I'm sorry, I cannot sign on to this, morally. The only moment of genuine human contact we have in the whole play has been taken away. I'll stay with the show through the opening, but I have to leave right after that." And Mike said, "Pete, I came in to tell you the same thing. I was going to leave the play as the director for exactly the same reason." We put our arms around each other and cried. When we finally got our shit together, he said, "Okay, when David comes in, I'm going to tell him we're going back to the old ending," and that's exactly what we did.

CYNTHIA NIXON: Why would she leave? It's not like she's at heart a thieving, two-faced person. She is endlessly victimized, and all she's looking for is a place to sleep and not be raped, essentially. The last thing she says to him is, "You want to fuck me or anything, Eddie, before I go to sleep?" and he says, "No." She says, "'Night." The street is the last place she wants to be. They're two people who are really lost and broken, and just to let them hug each other and sleep is a pretty small thing, but it's something.

There was certainly a tension between Mike and David, but Bill Hurt was also a big part of it. I'm incredibly fond of Bill and David, but they decided that Mike was taking this exquisite, beautiful play and tarting it up in a way to make it untrue to itself, taking something painful and turning it into a commercial laughfest. I think they were completely wrong. Mike did a bunch of things, like cutting the play's length, mining every laugh, and filling it with movie stars to make sure people came and were hooked, so that when the gut punches came near the end of the evening, the audience was a sitting duck, ripe for the kill.

DAVID RABE: I have no memory of this rewrite. I'm not denying it happened, but it was not important to me. I felt that the arc of the evening had become very cynical and cold by that point, and so perhaps

I thought a cynical gesture at the end would be more suitable. I think the fact that when I published the play, I always included the Phil scene, but never anything like this ending, makes clear that it wasn't important to me.

PETER LAWRENCE: When *Hurlyburly* finally moved to Broadway, the Barrymore Theatre was right next door to a porn house, and they had a marquee with these very graphic titles. I would sometimes wander out during intermission—we had *two* intermissions—and see these businessmen with their wives. The businessmen would be looking longingly at this porn house, thinking for $1.99 they could have seen *Miss Piggy Goes to Hollywood*, and instead they spent $100 to see this three-hour-and-fifteen-minute, difficult play—and they went because of the movie stars. Mike was very smart about that.

JUDITH IVEY: Whoopi always gives me credit for being the person who changed her career, because one of those nights when Mike said, "What are we going to do on our day off?" I said, "Well, somebody said we should go see Whoopi Goldberg," and he went, "Who?" I said, "I just heard she's incredible," and so he got tickets. The rest is history, because we went backstage and met Whoopi— I'll never forget watching him cross the dressing room to embrace her—and then, of course, he produced her on Broadway right after that.

WHOOPI GOLDBERG (*actress*): Mike came to see a show I was doing at the Dance Theater Workshop. One of the characters I do talks about Anne Frank, and Mike was on the last boat out of Berlin, so he connected to it. In tears he said to me, "I'd like to present you on Broadway."

JUDITH IVEY: After the Tonys, we all went to a big dance club—I want to say it was Area. It was fast and furious and loud, and everyone was enjoying various recreational substances, which of course is what went on in *Hurlyburly*.

PETER LAWRENCE: Years later, *Hurlyburly* was done in a revival off-Broadway with Ethan Hawke, and Mike called me up and said, "Pete, you want to be my date?" We went backstage afterward and talked to the cast and everything, and Mike said, "You know, Pete, I think they may have done a better job than we did."

DAVID RABE: I won't say we made up completely, but when Scott Elliott's revival of *Hurlyburly* was on, I got a phone call one night from Wally Shawn after Mike had come that night with Peter Lawrence. He said Mike and Ethan and Wally were together, and Mike had said to them, "Tell David he was right."

10. Nichols and Diane Sawyer on their wedding day at the Federated Church in Edgartown, Martha's Vineyard, in 1988. (Max Nichols, Nichols's son with his previous wife, Annabel Davis-Goff, is at right.) "After he married Diane, he was the happiest that he'd ever been," David Geffen recalls. "He always said that and meant it. He said, 'I finally got it right.'" *(© Carly Simon)*

CHAPTER 9

No New Worlds to Conquer

JULIET TAYLOR: There was a period when he was moodier. I remember thinking, *What happened to Mike?*

PAUL SIMON: That was awful, until they figured out what it was. He just was weepy, crying, and thought everything was over.

ROBERT GREENHUT: I'd call every month just to check in: *What's going on? How are you feeling?* He knew why I was calling, but it was hard to tell when he was going to get back to full function. I was worried about him.

RENATA ADLER: Long ago, I kept all sorts of pills, in case some pain or blues ever became too deep. During what seemed that worst time, Mike called from LA and asked me whether I would come out there with those pills. I said I would. We never spoke of it again.

RICHARD AVEDON[1]: I would visit him a lot at the Carlyle. I'd say, "Mike, you've got to get out of this room. Come on, we're going to walk down to the elevator. No one's going to look at you. And we're going to walk around the block, and we're going to come up the elevator, and

---

1. Courtesy of the John Lahr collection at the Howard Gotlieb Archival Research Center, Boston University.

that's all you have to do today." We got halfway around the block, and I hit him and said, "Snap out of it."

ANJELICA HUSTON: Mike went into this sort of panic where he thought he was going to lose everything and die. But oddly enough, one would never have been able to tell that he was emotionally fraught in any way. He always seemed very calm in his panic.

BARRY DILLER: I had heard about it from our mutual friends, I just never saw it. Some of my friends, it wouldn't take more than a millisecond to know they were not what they had been four hours ago—you knew they were on something not native. But Mike never appeared to be anything but Mike in all of his full flavor.

MATTHEW BRODERICK: He said, "It manifested itself that I thought I had no money." His accountants kept telling him, "You have plenty of money." He just thought he didn't have any money.

TONY WALTON: He would come sit next to me and say, "How do you ride the bus?" Suddenly he saw himself as about to be a pauper. He said, "Now I know why poor people feel so miserable."

DAVID HARE: He said to me, "I just became absolutely convinced that I had no money at all and that I was going to go broke. So I did this incredible thing." I said, "What did you do?" He said, "I started traveling coach class in airplanes," and I said, "How was that, Mike?" He said, "The state of the toilets, it's disgusting. Have you ever traveled coach class?" I said, "Well, yeah, I have, actually, Mike. I travel coach class all the time. Most of the human race travels coach class." He looked at me, completely bewildered by this. He said, "You can *do* that, can you?" I said, "Well, yeah, Mike. I'm not very rich."

JON ROBIN BAITZ: He once said to me, "I thought I was broke when I was crazy. And so I'm flying coach, and I tried to go into the bathroom, and they said, 'That's first class,'" and Mike said, "I live in first class."

JOHN CALLEY[2]**:** He thought that he was ruined financially. I'd go to Connecticut and sit with him day after day after day, and we would quantify his assets. Finally I got smart enough to realize that I had to get him to agree, almost to write it, because he would never accept what I had said. I had all the financial information, and he would agree to every single item. It was foolscap pad time. I'd say, "You see all these?" And he'd say yes, and I'd add the numbers up, and I'd say, "Now can you accept that?" And he'd say, "The only thing I could accept would be you telling me that when I go into debtor's prison, you will take care of my children."

ROSE STYRON (*writer*)**:** I remember him coming over one day— he was sure that he was going to die very soon, and that he had no prospects and no money and he didn't know what was going to happen to his children, so would Bill and I take care of them? Of course, he was making money and wonderful movies, but that wasn't his view at the moment.

TOM STOPPARD: When Mike was having his "delirium," he called me a few times for reassurance of some kind and I remember one phone call when he asked me if I would take his children in under my roof if he became incapable or dead. It was so strange I didn't realize he was serious at first. Anyway, I said I would and he was comforted by that.

SUSAN FORRISTAL: Anjelica and I went to visit him at the Carlyle, and he wasn't feeling well at all. The depression was going on, but we didn't know what it was. So we said, "Come on, lie down on your bed," and we were giving him foot massages. And above his bed hung this amazing Balthus [*The Guitar Lesson*]. We went, "You're never going to get laid with *that* above your bed," because he was single now. So we basically said, "You've got to get rid of this picture"—and he did. And he way undersold it.

---

2. Courtesy of the John Lahr collection at the Howard Gotlieb Archival Research Center, Boston University.

ANJELICA HUSTON: I remember Suze and I were giving him a foot rub under the Balthus, and there was a storm imminent, one of those storms that attacks New York every couple of years. The windows had been taped up and we were waiting for the storm, for the hurricane to hit. He was sure this Balthus was bringing him bad luck. It definitely had a creepy vibe. We recommended highly that he get rid of it, which I think he did for a quarter of what it was worth. We were his worst advisers when it came to his collection.

SUSAN FORRISTAL: The guilt! Anjelica and I still go, "Oh!"

ERIC FISCHL (*artist*): I met him after he sold all of the big stuff, after he was crazy. He talked about that time, and how horrible it was. He was very angry and disillusioned by the way he was preyed on by the gallerists who were selling his collection and misleading him about its real value. That was a big regret in his life.

SUSAN FORRISTAL: Annabel [Davis-Goff] called me and said, "Would you come up for a few days? Mike is having a terrible time." So I went up and we were taking a walk, and I said to him, "What are your medications?" He mentioned a few, including this sleeping pill. And I said, "Oh my God, don't you know about Halcion?" He said, "What do you mean?" Penny Marshall and Randy Newman were staying with me and Lorne in Amagansett, and Penny was very, very depressed, contemplating suicide. And Randy said, "What do you take to sleep?" She said Halcion. And he said, "That's the problem, it happened to me."

ROBERT NICHOLS: He was too dependent on those medications. He told me all the trouble he was having sleeping and all that. I told him over the phone, "It's got to be the medication. You've got to get off it," and I talked to Annabel about helping him get off it. I even gave a schedule for getting off it, reducing it slowly, because you can't just cold turkey it. The person who helped him turn the corner on that was not me, though. It was Quincy Jones. At least Mike credited Quincy Jones.

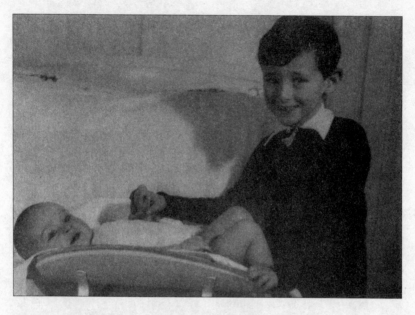

(above) Mike (né Igor Mikhail Peschkowsky) as a young boy with his infant brother, Robert, who became a prominent physician, practicing for a time at the Mayo Clinic. *(Collection of Dr. Robert Nichols)*

(left) A page from the manifest of the S.S. *Bremen* listing the names Michael and Robert Peschkowsky. They crossed alone from Germany to escape the Nazis in 1939. *(Collection of Dr. Robert Nichols)*

(top left) Mike's maternal grandfather, the anarchist Gustav Landauer, counted among his closest friends the philosopher Martin Buber and B. Traven, who wrote *The Treasure of the Sierra Madre*. *(Collection of Dr. Robert Nichols)*

(top right) Hedwig Lachmann, Mike's maternal grandmother, translated Oscar Wilde's *Salome* into German for the libretto of the Richard Strauss opera. *(Collection of Dr. Robert Nichols)*

(bottom left) Mike's father, Pavel Peschkowsky, changed his name to Paul Nichols in 1938 after resettling in New York City, where he established a thriving practice as a physician. He died too young to see his son's phenomenal success. *(Collection of Dr. Robert Nichols)*

(bottom right) Mike's mother, Brigitte Landauer Peschkowsky. "Before she was forty, she lost both parents, both sisters, and her husband," Mike's brother, Robert Nichols, said. *(Collection of Dr. Robert Nichols)*

(above) Mike backstage with Estelle Lutrell and Paul Sills during a Playwrights Theatre Club production of Jean Cocteau's *The Typewriter.* *(Courtesy of Carol Sills)*

(right) Mike and Elaine May in a scene for the Compass Players in Chicago, where they began their legendary partnership. "Elaine could improvise with anybody. I could only improvise with Elaine," he said. *(© William A. Mathieu)*

Mike and Elaine May onstage at a performance of *An Evening with Mike Nichols and Elaine May* on Broadway. A recording of the show went to No. 10 on the Billboard 200. *(Photofest)*

With a cover photograph by Mike's great friend Richard Avedon, *Nichols & May Examine Doctors* collected a series of routines performed live on the radio program *Monitor*. The last track, "Nichols and May at Work," is an on-air improvisation. *(Photograph © The Richard Avedon Foundation)*

(above) Elaine May and Mike with President John F. Kennedy at his gala forty-fifth birthday celebration in Madison Square Garden in May of 1962, where they performed. *(John F. Kennedy Presidential Library and Museum, Boston)*

(right) Mike in 1962. *(Tony Walton)*

(left) Mike and Neil Simon in 1963, beneath the marquee for *Barefoot in the Park*, the first in a string of hits they worked on together. "It was again, like with Elaine, a very auspicious coupling," Woody Allen said. *(Photofest)*

(below) Robert Redford in *Barefoot in the Park*. "Mike and Redford, I can't think in my entire career of a more perfect marriage between actor and director," Elizabeth Ashley, Redford's *Barefoot* costar, said. *(Photofest)*

(above) Mike with Walter Matthau and Art Carney in 1965 during rehearsals for *The Odd Couple*. *New York Times* drama critic Frank Rich recalled, "The way [Mike] staged the first act, to this day, is the funniest staging of anything I've ever seen in the theater." The play garnered Tony Awards for Matthau, Simon, and Mike. *(© Burt Glinn/Magnum Photos)*

(right) Mike at a gala dinner for the Metropolitan Opera, with Robert and Ethel Kennedy (left), Jacqueline Kennedy (center), and Leonard Bernstein with his wife, Felicia Montealegre (right). *(Fred W. McDarrah/Getty Images)*

MIKE NICHOLS SUZY PARKER ROCK EUROPE

PARIS SHOCKED

The decent people of Europe, and indeed all the world, were stunned last week as the tempestuous affair between SUZY PARKER AND MIKE NICHOLS

erupted in Paris, a city difficult to shock. They had arrived in Paris to co-star in *Napoleon and Josephine*, the fifteen-million-dollar epic being produced by Eleven Arts Films. Their reception had been relatively calm, as such things go, but by the middle of the week it be-

came apparent to the world that Napoleon and Josephine had carried their stormy love off the screen. They flashed like a rocket across the Paris sky.

The World Disarmament Conference scheduled at Geneva was hastily called off as the press flew to Paris and SUZY AND MIKE, who had become top news all over the world. They loved, they cried, they fought. They were mobbed, hunted and humiliated 24 hours a day as they desperately tried to avoid publicity in all the top night spots in Paris.

Left and below: Caught on the set. Right: The lovers on the stairs after dinner

AT MAXIM'S

These exclusive on-the-spot photos tell the story that has shocked, sickened and delighted respectable people everywhere—as the world, from embattled Berlin to wartorn Algeria, from Ghana to Laos to Wall Street, waits breathlessly to see what will happen next to SUZY AND MIKE.

LANVIN-CASTILLO CREPE DINNER DRESS. AT I. MAGNIN.

This 1966 Richard Avedon photo series of Mike with model Suzy Parker for *Harper's Bazaar* parodied the international *scandale* created by Richard Burton's affair with Elizabeth Taylor while filming *Cleopatra*. Burton and Taylor found the spoof hilarious.
(© *The Richard Avedon Foundation*)

(left) Mike directing Richard Burton and Elizabeth Taylor on the set of *Who's Afraid of Virginia Woolf?*, his screen directorial debut. The film was nominated for thirteen Academy Awards. Taylor and Sandy Dennis won Best Actress and Best Supporting Actress, respectively. *(© Bob Willoughby/mptvimages.com)*

(below) Mike lighting Elizabeth Taylor's cigarette on the set of *Who's Afraid of Virginia Woolf?* "You've seen a lot of women play [Martha in] *Virginia Woolf.* Tell me the truth, was I the greatest?" Taylor asked the columnist Liz Smith, who replied, "Well, you had Mike Nichols." *(© Bob Willoughby/mptvimages.com)*

(above) Mike directing Dustin Hoffman as Benjamin Braddock in *The Graduate.* "It's like rock and roll," Buck Henry said. "A whole generation changed its idea about what guys should look like." *(mptvimages.com)*

(right) Leslie Caron hands Mike his Best Director Oscar for *The Graduate* at the 1968 Academy Awards. *(Photofest)*

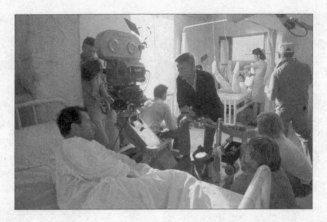

(above) Mike directing Alan Arkin on the set of *Catch-22*. The 1970 adaptation of Joseph Heller's satiric anti-war classic was something of a critical and box office disappointment, though it has since gained a cult following. *(Julian Wasser/The* LIFE *Images Collection/Getty Images)*

(right) Mike with Buck Henry in Rome, on location for *Catch-22*. Henry wrote the screen adaptations for three Nichols films: *The Graduate*, *Catch-22*, and *The Day of the Dolphin*. The two lifelong friends first met as boys at the Dalton School in New York City. *(© Mary Ellen Mark)*

Mike with Orson Welles, Buck Henry, and Martin Balsam on location in Mexico for *Catch-22*. Directing the imperious Welles was a challenge equal to adapting Joseph Heller's complex novel and choreographing a fleet of B-25s. *(© Bob Willoughby/ mptvimages.com)*

Mike with his lifelong friend Candice Bergen. "I worried if Candy Bergen was good enough [for *Carnal Knowledge*,] and he said, 'Trust me,' and I trusted him," Jules Feiffer said. "Over and over again he proved right." *(Ron Galella/WireImage)*

(above) Mike at one of his legendary horse shows, which were elaborately choreographed events. "He made something utterly memorable out of the buying and selling of horseflesh," Tom Stoppard said. *(Paul Hosefros/*The New York Times/*Redux)*

(right) Mike with Meryl Streep and Cher during the filming of *Silkwood*. Mike, who hadn't directed a movie in eight years, would later tell friends "Meryl woke me up." *(© Mary Ellen Mark)*

Mike (as George) strangling Elaine (as Martha) when they appeared in the 1980 revival of *Who's Afraid of Virginia Woolf?* at the Long Wharf Theatre in New Haven, Connecticut, with James Naughton and Swoosie Kurtz (as Nick and Honey). *(Martha Swope/New York Public Library)*

(left) Mike with Jacqueline Kennedy in New York. A longtime friend of the former first lady, he would deliver one of the eulogies at her funeral. *(© James Colburn/Globe Photos/ZumaPress.com)*

(below) Sigourney Weaver, Cynthia Nixon, and Judith Ivey, who appeared in David Rabe's dark satire of Hollywood, *Hurlyburly*, directed by Mike. Other cast members included William Hurt, Harvey Keitel, Jerry Stiller, and Christopher Walken. Nixon was simultaneously appearing in Tom Stoppard's *The Real Thing*, also directed by Mike, and her entrances and exits were timed so she could shuttle between the two plays. *(Photofest)*

Mike with Whoopi Goldberg, whose groundbreaking one-woman show, *Whoopi*, he directed on Broadway in 1984. *(DMI/The* LIFE *Picture Collection/Getty Images)*

Mike directed Steve Martin and Robin Williams in Samuel Beckett's absurdist classic, *Waiting for Godot*, in 1988. Mike once played Lucky in the play, while a student at the University of Chicago. *(© Brigitte Lacombe)*

Mike with his fourth wife and widow, journalist Diane Sawyer, leaving the 1992 Hampton Classic horse show in Bridgehampton, New York. "He just strove to be better, to equal her," Candice Bergen said. *(Kimberly Butler/The* LIFE *Images Collection/ Getty Images)*

Al Pacino, Meryl Streep, and Mike receiving Emmy Awards for the HBO adaptation of Tony Kushner's Pulitzer Prize–winning drama, *Angels in America*, 2003. Mike was among the first A-list directors to embrace the possibilities of television in the twenty-first century. *(Carlo Allergi/Getty Images)*

Mike on location in Morocco for *Charlie Wilson's War* with Julia Roberts, Tom Hanks, and Philip Seymour Hoffman. It would be Mike's eighteenth and final film. *(© Brigitte Lacombe)*

Mike with Diane Sawyer and his son, Max, at his American Film Institute lifetime achievement tribute at Lincoln Center. Mike was ambivalent about tributes, awards, and retrospectives, which he referred to as "ratfucks." *(Frazer Harrison/Getty Images)*

Philip Seymour Hoffman in Mike's 2012 revival of Arthur Miller's *Death of a Salesman*. Mike saw the original 1949 production, directed by Elia Kazan, when he was a teenager, an experience that changed him forever. *(© Brigitte Lacombe)*

Mike directing Daniel Craig in a revival of Harold Pinter's *Betrayal*, with Rachel Weisz and Rafe Spall. Right up to the end, he was still "bursting with ideas about truth and life," Tom Fontana said. *(© Brigitte Lacombe)*

SUSAN FORRISTAL: I know he always says Quincy Jones told him. Quincy may have backed it up, but he and I had the first conversation about it. But you always go with the bigger name when you're telling a story.

ROSE STYRON: It happened to Bill Styron before it happened to Mike. When Bill was having trouble sleeping, a doctor on the Vineyard—terrible man—gave him Halcion, and said, "You can take as much as you want for as long as you want." A year later, he was still taking it.

JAMIE BERNSTEIN: All our parents' contemporaries were drug abusers, because that's what everybody did back in the '60s. My parents were no exception. My father was such a terrible insomniac that he really needed sleep aids, and then, of course, he needed wake-up aids, and Mike was the same.

SUSAN FORRISTAL: A month later I got a phone call. He asked me to come over. So I get there, and he asked me, very matter-of-fact, he said, "How did your sister kill herself? Because I think about it a lot." And I went, *Shit, this is serious now.*

CARLY SIMON (*musician*): Annabel asked me to intervene. He was so vulnerable, trying to intellectualize all of what was going on. I really think it was the drugs, but he dragged out every possible explanation there could possibly be.

SUSAN FORRISTAL: Carly arrived with big hair and smiles. We sat down for a few minutes and decided it was time to go to the hospital. I don't know how, but we talked him into it. We went downstairs and got a taxi. It was during the marathon. We were going to Presbyterian–Columbia, and it was just a nightmare—it took us an hour. He admitted himself, and it got better after that, but it was terrible.

TONY WALTON: He was sure he had lost everything, which John Calley was gradually educating him out of, plus the removal of Halcion from his diet.

PETER DAVIS: He called up Candy [Bergen] and me, probably on the same day, and he said, "I'm back," and I kind of knew what he meant.

GREGORY MOSHER[3]: Mike finally pulls out of his depression right before Christmas. Some clever-enough doctor says it's the Halcion. At the end of this phase, we were having dinner, and I said, "I'm glad you're feeling better, because Lenny [Bernstein]'s not doing well at all." I said, "I'm ending the evenings with you, and I'm beginning the days with him. As you're coming up, Lenny's going down." And Mike said, "Hang on." He went into the next room and called Lenny, and he said, "We're having dinner tonight." And he said to Lenny, "You're taking Halcion, aren't you?" And Lenny said, "How the fuck did you know that?" Mike explained what he had just gone through, and Lenny got into the hospital and off of Halcion. Mike saved him months of agony.

ALEXANDRA STYRON: My father had a bunch of friends who had massive depression in middle age and were able to support each other and also make dark humor out of it. He and Mike had that in common. They compared notes: *Yes, of course it's the fucking drug.* The combination of his incredible sense of humor and his artistry allowed him to be wonderfully honest about having been to the dark side.

Mike was the first of my parents' friends whom I gave the manuscript of my memoir to, with my heart in my throat. Maybe three days later, he called me and he began to cry. He said, "It was exactly that way."

JOHN LAHR: At the end of my final interview with him for the *New Yorker* profile, I remember he was lying on his bed, and I was sitting on the chaise longue. Mike said, "I've really enjoyed this," and I said

---

3. Courtesy of the John Lahr collection at the Howard Gotlieb Archival Research Center, Boston University.

quite spontaneously, "I do well with the fundamentally inconsolable," and his eyes fluttered—he took a beat—and he said, "We get a lot done, you know." My father was inconsolable, and I'm sort of drawn to those kinds of people. The thing that's great about Mike is he didn't deny it. He took it forward. He fielded the ball and threw it back in an interesting way.

RENATA ADLER: I don't think this particular blue period was brought on by any particular thing or medication. There are times when everything seems to be closing in and the only way out seems to be *out.* When it passes, one tends to look for a single, simple thing to have been the cause.

JUDE LAW (*actor*): Several years after we worked together on *Closer*, we went to lunch. He talked about having faith that if your pendulum is taking you into an area of darkness or of drought, whatever it may be, that it can only get so bad before it has to go the other way. That kind of insight can only come from experience.

DAVID HARE: When I first knew him, he had a slightly terrifying melancholy late at night that I would describe as European. There was a sort of pessimism that could overwhelm him. He didn't really like alcohol. He once said to me, "If I have a glass of wine, I forget to drink it." It just sort of didn't interest him at all. But he could by two or three in the morning be quite existentially gloomy about, *What the fuck am I trying to do?* That was when I first knew him, and the depth of his gloom frightened me. It really did frighten me, his sense of meaninglessness. That was part of his sensibility that could slightly overwhelm you and make you feel like, *I want to get away from this man.* He never lost his sensitivity to other people's unhappiness, but I do think that he found happiness with Diane. He just was anchored with Diane in a way that I don't think he was anchored before.

TOM STYRON: One Sunday evening in my family's living room in Roxbury, around seven, Mike, who had recently separated or divorced from Annabel, and my dad and me were watching *60 Minutes*. Suddenly Mike said, "Oh my God, that's the most beautiful woman I've ever seen," referring to Diane [Sawyer]. Two or three years later, they were dating.

EMANUEL AZENBERG: He was always in love with Diane Sawyer, even before he met her. We talked about it. In Washington, when we were doing *Social Security*, we were staying at a kind of boutique hotel. I went downstairs, and *guess who* was checking in. I called Mike. One assumes he found some way to go, "Oh, hi!"

DAVID GEFFEN: Warren Beatty told me he was talking to Diane— this is many years before she got together with Mike—and she said to Warren that he knew everybody and there were a couple of people whom she'd love to meet: Stephen Sondheim and Mike Nichols. This is years before they got together.

ROBERT GREENHUT: We were watching *60 Minutes* together. He says, "You see that girl?" I said, "Yeah." He says, "I'm going to get a date with that girl. You watch." Six months later, he said, "Remember Diane Sawyer?" I said, "Yeah." He said, "I've gone out with her a couple of times." I said, "Good for you. You get any?"

TOM HANKS: They met in the Concorde lounge. That's like meeting on the *Queen Mary* in the old days.

MARIE BRENNER: He went over to her, smiling, and said, "You're my hero." And she looked up with that beautiful smile of hers and said, "And you're mine."

LIZ SMITH: Diane was living with Richard Holbrooke. Holbrooke didn't like me and I didn't like him. So when I found out she was seeing Mike, I did everything I could to get her to dump Mr. Holbrooke because Diane was too nice. Mike never forgot that.

DOUGLAS WICK: While we were shooting *Working Girl*, Mike was courting Diane Sawyer. One of the many things I admired about

Mike was his self-awareness. He was a big deal in New York, and he had a lot of courtesans who were chasing him, but he said, "If I don't get a woman who will kick my ass when I'm rude to a cabdriver, I'm over as a human."

JACK O'BRIEN: I remember going to see *Juan Darién*, the Julie Taymor piece, and sitting two seats away from me were Diane and Mike and they were all in leather. And they were making out and necking the entire show. After, I said to him, "What the fuck was that?" Of course, he didn't remember it.

SIGOURNEY WEAVER: He was so happy during *Working Girl* because he and Diane had just met and fallen in love. And because I had been engaged during *Hurlyburly*, he would talk about how happy he was, and how great Diane was, and how they weren't going to have kids, they were just going to have this time to themselves.

MIKE HALEY: One day during *Biloxi Blues*, we were driving, and he says, "I met a woman." I said, "Oh, good." He says, "Diane Sawyer!" I said, "That's great." "I'm going to marry her." And he looked out the window with this half-smile on his face. And it wasn't like, *This is my next conquest.* It was more like, *There's something about her.* It was magical.

RENATA ADLER: Before they married, Mike told me, he had a conversation with Diane in which he said, "You know what they'll say—'His fourth marriage, her first.'" And Diane said, "No. 'His fourth, her only.'" And she was right.

JOHN CALLEY[4]**:** Mike's marriage to Diane changed his life. How it works for the individual is so private and so personal that I don't know. I just know he's a different person.

---

4. Courtesy of the John Lahr collection at the Howard Gotlieb Archival Research Center, Boston University.

LIZ SMITH: I think after he married her, he felt, *No new worlds to conquer, except to just keep doing plays that I like.*

JACK O'BRIEN: When he would talk about Diane, and you'd make a compliment—because she was Diane, and she was beautiful, the shiksa goddess of all time—his answer was always, "I *know!*" I loved that.

TOM FONTANA: He was like a high school kid in love with the prom queen.

HANNAH ROTH SORKIN: He'd say, "I'll have to check with the ball and chain." But he could say that because he was madly, madly in love.

MAUREEN DOWD: When I was promoting my second book, Chris Cuomo was going to interview me at ABC, and I'm deathly afraid of television. I walk into the studio and the producer says, "Here, this is where you'll be sitting," and I go, "Oh, no, I'm not going on TV without makeup." And they go, "Trust us. This is Diane Sawyer's lighting." So I did the interview, and I never look at myself on TV, but just out of curiosity I looked at this, and I was honestly dumbfounded, because it looked like I had on full glowing makeup with false eyelashes. Everything looked gorgeous. I called a friend of mine at ABC and asked, "How is that possible?" And he said, "Mike Nichols designed her lighting for her show."

CHLOE MALLE (*goddaughter*): Mike felt that no one should ever talk for more than eleven seconds straight. Any story that goes beyond eleven seconds is just too long. He said, "I go to dinners with Diane constantly—she's just been to Afghanistan, she's just interviewed Malala—and no one wants to ask her anything, no one cares, they just want to talk about themselves, their dental problem, their most recent movie." He felt very strongly that that should not be the case.

MARIE BRENNER: I ran into Mike at the theater, and he was just glowing that Diane was off doing some incredible story. All he wanted to do was live her triumph. And that's how Diane would talk about Mike.

TOM HANKS: I can only imagine the conversations those two had over coffee and pancakes in the morning.

JULIA ROBERTS: I've had dinner with him at his house, just the two of us, and he'll suddenly say, "Oh, it's time. Come on," and we'll get up from the table and go sit on the couch and turn on the evening news. We'd sit and watch Diane, and then when it was over, we'd go back. I could completely relate to him in that way—how totally in love and besotted he was all the time with his beautiful wife. Look at how long they were together, and he was still smitten—she would take his breath away. And the way she would sit and listen to his stories. It was just this mutual, active love affair.

CYNTHIA O'NEAL: We'd be going to the theater and afterward and he'd say, "Dinner's going to have to be quick because Diane's getting back" from wherever and "I want to be there when she gets home."

DOUGLAS WICK: Mike told me that Diane had a rule for him, that he wasn't supposed to tell stories about the past, because it's so easy to be in a conversation where you fall into just reminiscing as opposed to engaging fully in the present. He was as good as anyone I've ever met at recalibrating when he was off course.

LORNE MICHAELS: Mike was just always in the present. It's a really hard thing to do because to lapse into stories about your hits is the easiest thing in the world.

CHRISTINE BARANSKI: He was completely up on *The Good Wife* and every other show on television. It was his and Diane's favorite thing to just stay home and read or watch great television, because the last thing she wanted to do was get dressed up and have to schmooze. They loved their cozy life. And who wouldn't want to snuggle up with Diane Sawyer? I mean, my God, nice work.

ROBERT GREENHUT: The week before he died, I was having lunch with him, and the whole lunch pretty much was, "I'm so lucky to have been married to this girl. Best thing that ever happened in my life, our romance," and on and on. All he did was talk about her. It's rare for guys having a guy lunch together and one guy's just talking about how much he loves his wife.

JOHN CALLEY[5]: There were dark years. Things weren't quite working. His relationships weren't giving him a lot of joy. I think now—I know it, because it happened to me too—it finally comes together after years of believing it won't. It comes together late, but thank God. Mike found that the fantasies weren't merely fantasies, that there was a Diane, that Diane made him the man he wanted to be. They're equals. I don't mean to say that the predecessors weren't; it's just that he doesn't have to pretend not to be who he is to make a partner comfortable.

CANDICE BERGEN: Mike got better and better, and this was because of Diane, the influence of Diane, of wanting to be a better person, to justify living with this extraordinary woman. He would say, "When she goes to a ball, all she does is just run a brush through her hair." He just couldn't get over her lack of vanity and her intellect. He described himself as Pinocchio, who became a real boy. That's the Diane effect. He just strove to be better, to equal her.

EMMA THOMPSON (*actress*): He was always fond of saying that when he got to the gates, he wanted Saint Peter to say, "Hello, Mike and Diane."

PEGGY NOONAN (*columnist*): I said to Diane once—we were talking about marriage, and she had by that point been married long and happily—and I said, "Oh, Diane, don't you think you were made to be married?" And she said, "No. I don't think I would have ever been married if I hadn't met Mike."

---

5. Courtesy of the John Lahr collection at the Howard Gotlieb Archival Research Center, Boston University.

Mike with Melanie Griffith and Harrison Ford on location for *Working Girl*. He passed over a number of better-known actresses before deciding on Griffith. His longtime editor Sam O'Steen said, "I think Melanie just walked in and Nichols knew, boy, that was it." *(Picture Lux/The Hollywood Archive/Alamy)*

CHAPTER 10

Can I Get a Wild Take?

DOUGLAS WICK: I was in Lower Manhattan, and I saw a really attractive girl who, from the ankles up, looked really fancy, and from the ankles down was wearing tennis shoes. In those days, that was completely a badge of class. It was not yet fashionable. That meant bridge and tunnel. I talked to Kevin Wade about doing a story about her, and we developed the script that was *Working Girl*, and I sent it to Mike Nichols.

I got a message that he was interested and that I should come to Mississippi where he was shooting *Biloxi Blues* and meet with him. Mike, at some point along the way, said, "If you ever want to make money, do *Cinderella*," but even more so there was a part of him that immediately connected with the sort of Charlie Chaplin figure of the Jew with their nose pressed against the window looking into the fancy party inside.

I went back to my hotel room very excited, and he called me in my hotel room and he said, "Turn on your TV. Madonna's on *The Tonight Show*. See what you think of her as a possible Tess." Suddenly I was in the Mike world where I was getting calls in my hotel room at night telling me to turn on my TV, like an old friend.

ROBERT GREENHUT: It was a nice, easy-to-do script. It wasn't anything that was intellectually challenging. It was like, hey, let's do a good job of telling this fable.

MELANIE GRIFFITH (*actress*): I got this call from my manager who said, "Mike Nichols is doing this movie called *Working Girl*, and it's the hottest thing. Every actress wants it. It's a long shot that you would ever get it." When I went in to read, there were twenty people in the room. You could pick three scenes to read, and I said, "I couldn't pick three scenes, because I love them all, so why don't we just read the whole thing?" So I read a bunch of different things, and then I went back to LA and waited. I heard that they were interested. Mike apparently was the one who was on my side, because the studio wanted a name, and I wasn't a big name yet, but he fought for me.

BOBBIE O'STEEN: The studio was nervous when Mike turned down Cher, Goldie Hawn, Shelley Long, and Natasha Richardson. But, as Sam said, "I think Melanie just walked in and Nichols knew, boy, that was it."

DOUGLAS WICK: Michelle Pfeiffer wanted to play Tess, and, of course, the fear with Michelle Pfeiffer was that if she was sitting at a desk, everyone in the building would be chasing her. We needed it to be, in that kind of old-fashioned movie sense, the girl who takes off the glasses and *then* she's a beauty. Mike and I sat in a room with Juliet Taylor and we heard a lot of different actors read. When Melanie read, immediately you both saw that she could be very underestimated, that she had a lot of native IQ, and that you could dress her up or dress her down. From the first reading, we all got a giant crush on Melanie's talent. It was like her skin was transparent, and you saw her inner life on her face. She incarnated Tess, and there was no great version of the movie without her. But it was challenging.

ROBERT GREENHUT: Melanie was good, but she was very unreliable. She was doing a lot of cocaine at the time, and you couldn't count on her to be in shape in the mornings. We always had our fingers crossed each day that she would have it together enough to perform.

JULIET TAYLOR: Mike wanted Alec Baldwin in the lead because he was new and we were all really excited about him, but the studio freaked out. Of course, Harrison Ford was great, and Alec played the other role.

DOUGLAS WICK: First we had the expensive version, which was Harrison Ford and Sigourney [Weaver], and then what happened was Fox said it was too expensive, so we suddenly were looking to do a version where Alec Baldwin was told he would get the male lead, and one of the Richardsons was going to get the Sigourney part. Then Fox relented, because obviously it was such an extraordinary cast. Mike had to call Alec and say instead of playing the lead, here's a great character actor part, which Alec was a really good sport about doing.

ALEC BALDWIN (*actor*): Mike told me that they said to him, if you make it with these people we'll give you $15 million, and if you make it with these other people we'll give you $50 million. He was very straightforward, as he always was, about what those realities were. So he asked me, "Would you want to play this other part?" I just wanted to work with him. I did a bit of that back then. There were people I wanted to work with, so I did small roles just to be around them, like *Married to the Mob*, and *Great Balls of Fire*, and *Beetlejuice*.

JULIET TAYLOR: Kevin Spacey was an understudy in *Hurlyburly*, which Mike had directed off-Broadway. And Mike said, "There's this kid out of Juilliard, he's really good, and I think we should have him in for this part."

SIGOURNEY WEAVER: Mike really did his homework for *Working Girl*. We started out with a two-week rehearsal period. The script is okay, but he made it so much better by telling the story physically through Tess's costumes and everything else. That transformation from Staten Island girl to Grace Kelly was something they really worked hard on. He had us all watch *Pygmalion*. I don't know if he felt that that kind of transformation was something he'd experienced, coming here as an immigrant kid and then becoming a member of the ruling class. I always felt that they were both there: the breezy guy who would take care of everything, but also the person who hadn't always been in that position, and I think that goes through all his films.

MELANIE GRIFFITH: Mike created a space for us so that we had our own little language. I could just look at him, and I would know if he liked what I did or if he didn't. He was very thorough and very clear in what he wanted, and he made you work. It was serious. There was no fucking around.

DOUGLAS WICK: Every day at lunch, often a few of us would go to lunch—Mike, me, maybe Harrison Ford—at some really cool Manhattan restaurant during the break.

HARRISON FORD: Mike liked to get away from the set for lunch. It was always a great break in the day. He was a great storyteller, and he had a great mind for connecting the social and intellectual world with a current topic. He knew everyone and had read everything, and actually retained it, unlike others of us.

ALEC BALDWIN: On the set of that film, I was dating a woman and I was very unhappy. Sometimes I'd sit in Mike's trailer and talk about relationships, and he said, "If, when the two of you are alone together, there aren't enough people in the room, that's when you know it's over." Years later, he wanted me to do *Postcards from the Edge*, and I told him I couldn't do it, because I was having a lot of problems with my girlfriend—same situation. He said, "Well, we're not shooting the movie until May." He was calling in January. And I said, "I can't really say where I'm going to be at." There was a long pause, and he says, "What kind of problems could you possibly have that couldn't be solved by *May*?"

SIGOURNEY WEAVER: In *Working Girl*, I had to speak in German to the innkeeper in Gstaad or something, and I said, "Mike, they want me to work with a dialect coach to do this German stuff." He just smiled and said, "I'll do it." He made me a little tape, and his

German was so beautiful. Not that I know anything about German, but it was so *saucy.* I realized what a cultured man he is.

DOUGLAS WICK: I remember him saying that he didn't like actors doing accents, because he thought it was a ten-thousandth-of-a-second filter in terms of pure behavior and performance—that some part of their brain having to remember to translate their impulse was a filter from the more pure reaction. Needless to say, drugs were an even bigger filter.

MELANIE GRIFFITH: There were a lot of things that happened on *Working Girl* that I did that were not right. It was the late '80s. There was a lot going on party-wise in New York. There was a lot of cocaine. There was a lot of temptation.

DOUGLAS WICK: As we were shooting, Melanie was a little bit erratic, and Mike was getting very upset. I remember being surprised by how troubled he was, basically because the instrument he played so well was somehow impaired. It was the mid-'80s, and drugs were everywhere. No one had any judgment about drugs. It was just that if you were an actor and doing them during the workday, it hurt the performance. Melanie told me she wasn't doing them, and said, "I thought you were one of the few producers who understood creative people."

MELANIE GRIFFITH: It was probably three days before we finished shooting. Alec Baldwin and I were shooting on Staten Island. We had eight hours to wait until it got dark so we could shoot, and Alec said, "Come on, let's go play pool." Alec was sober at the time, and I was *kind of* sober, but not really—trying to be—and so when I went to the bartender at the pool hall, I said, "Whenever he orders a Coke, bring me a rum and Coke." I could really hold my liquor, but I got pretty drunk. When we got back to the set, I had vodka in my motor home, so I had a slug of vodka, and it mixed and made me so drunk, which I thought was really funny. But it wasn't, and it was cold, and I had to walk down the stairs with Alec, and I couldn't do it.

DOUGLAS WICK: I got a call from Mike. We were shooting in Staten Island, and Melanie was clearly high, and it was hurting the work, and he was really distressed, because he literally couldn't do his job. For him there was no approximation of performance. There was no *good enough*. I talked to some of the PAs, because I was young and knew them all and found out that she had been getting deliveries. Someone was picking up drugs. It was clear that she had a little coke problem, so we confronted her, and we had to stop shooting that night.

I asked Michael Black, the agent, "How do I handle this?" And, by the way, I loved Melanie, she had such a great heart. He said, "You've got to give her cause and effect. There has to be a consequence, or it's too easy for the person to remain in denial." So we told Melanie that we were going to withhold from her salary the fifty-three hours that it cost us to shut down, and that we were going to have a nurse on the set for the rest of the shooting. There was enough mutual goodwill that somehow it all stayed friendly and constructive.

MELANIE GRIFFITH: Mike got so mad at me, he wouldn't talk to me. Mike Haley, the first AD, just came up and said, "We're shutting down. Go home," and I knew I was in so much trouble. The next morning he took me to breakfast and said, "Here's what's going to happen. You're going to pay for last night out of your pocket. We're not going to report you to the studio, but you have to pay for what it cost," and it was $80,000. They wanted to get my attention and they really did. It was a very humbling, embarrassing experience, but I learned a lot from it.

BARRY DILLER: We knew, at the studio, what was taking place. But look, I've had so many worse situations on movies. This was not some cataclysmic nightmare, it was just a somewhat troubled situation that was managed. Mike managed through it. He got the performance out of her that he needed.

DOUGLAS WICK: The thing that surprised me—because Mike was so sophisticated, he'd seen it all—I was surprised how genuinely distressed he was, how in pain about it he was, how much he was traumatized by it, and I think the reason is that it made great work impossible.

CARLY SIMON: I first met Mike with Lillian Hellman in front of the drugstore on Main Street in Vineyard Haven. You had to fall in love with Mike the first time you met him—that first blaze of attraction that lasts a lifetime.

When *Working Girl* was written, Mike asked me to do it. As soon as I saw a script—I didn't have to see any footage—I knew it was going to open to a tribal-y, gospel-y feel, I was going to mix the two. It was going to be like African drums in a Southern church. So I went on and wrote the song. And I remember Mike and Diane coming to dinner and my playing it for them. They just said, "Wow, it's just absolutely perfect, we couldn't ask for anything better."

And then, as so often happens, somebody puts doubt into your head. After the song was written, the demo was made, it was all lovey-dovey, everybody just adored the way it worked against the opening footage of Melanie coming over on the ferry. Then, I don't know, four months into shooting I got a call from Mike saying, "We tried another song over the beginning and we really think we like that better." It was the Eagles' "Witchy Woman." I screamed and said, "No! No, you can't do that!" I don't know what made the tide turn again, but they went back to using "Let the River Run."

DOUGLAS WICK: We got Carly Simon's first songs for the movie. They were all cut in, and it really didn't work. They were good songs, but she sort of told you what you were seeing. They didn't add a level. Then I remember Mike talking to Carly about what the movie was about, and about the Tower of Babel where people converged with all different languages, and about the journey of all these immigrants into the dream Manhattan. Out of that strong push came "Let the River Run." Mike was like a geologist looking for oil, where he would always find the deepest part of it. You'd constantly see his brain going, *What's this really about?*

HANK AZARIA: There's a reason why the beginning of *Birdcage* is "We Are Family." It's not about a gay family; that's just a metaphor for all dysfunctional, crazy families.

ROBIN WILLIAMS[1]: Just knowing Mike—the reason I wanted to do *The Birdcage* was to do a comedy with him. He would let us try things. I miss some of the more outrageous things, but it was an elegant highbrow-lowbrow. Somehow he pulls it all together. Elaine, too—they both do it.

NATHAN LANE (*actor*): The first time I met him, he was standing in the doorway of my rehearsal room, talking to either the director or someone he knew in the room, and I was introduced to him. It was like meeting the president, or God, if you believe in a supreme being. His name was like a brand name that represented class and sophistication and wit and intelligence and a sort of guarantee of superior goods. He was very charming, very nice, although he seemed to know something I didn't know. I later found out it was a lot.

The next time I saw him I was doing a Neil Simon play on Broadway called *Laughter on the 23rd Floor*. I had been filming a movie during the day, so I got to the theater a little late, and I quickly raced in and got dressed. As I was waiting to go on, the stage manager said to me, "Mike Nichols is here with Diane Sawyer." I was feeling a little tired, but I thought, *Oh, I better be good tonight*.

He came backstage afterward. That was unusual. I know he had seen me in things before, but he had never come backstage. Again, he was charming and very complimentary and then he said, "I would like to talk to you about a movie. Would you call me tomorrow?" The next day I called him, and he said he was working on a remake of the French film *La Cage aux Folles*, that Elaine May would do the adaptation, and Robin Williams would play opposite me. And I said, "Which part would I be playing?" And he said, "Well, the drag queen." And I said, "Oh, well, that's a very good part." He said, "Yes, it is." Originally,

---

1. "Nichols & May—Take Two," *American Masters*, directed by Phillip Schopper, produced by Julian Schlossberg, season 10, episode 5, aired May 22, 1996, on PBS.

it was supposed to be Steve Martin and Robin, and Steve was going to play the husband and Robin was going to play the drag queen, and then Robin sort of rethought it after Steve Martin couldn't do the movie. Robin felt he had just done *Mrs. Doubtfire* and maybe following that with another role in drag wasn't the greatest idea, so he decided he wanted to play the other part.

At one point, it seemed like maybe Robin wasn't going to do the film and Mike would call and say, "What do you think of Billy Crystal?" I said I love Billy Crystal. Then I ran into Mike at a benefit, and during the cocktail hour—what he used to call a "ratfuck"—he said, "What do you think of Robert Redford as your husband?" And I said, "Well, I've been thinking about *that* for years, but, really, if you could make that happen, this is more than a movie." Finally and fortunately, it all worked out with Robin.

JULIET TAYLOR: When we did the first table reading, Robin had never met Nathan, but he went so nuts over him—he thought Nathan Lane was the funniest person he had ever heard in his life. He just went crazy. He got more and more off-script because he was laughing so hard.

HANK AZARIA: Mike had seen *Quiz Show*, and I guess he had liked me in it. He called my manager and said to pick a small role in *Birdcage*. I told Mike I'd like to do the Latin dresser, who was originally only in one scene—the maid was a whole different character. Mike was surprised, but then I did a table reading with Robin and Gene [Hackman] and, as I do on *The Simpsons*, I read six or seven roles, including Agador, and he said, "Okay, I get it." About a month later, I got a call that they had combined those two roles, which I heard was Robin's idea.

NATHAN LANE: Mike was always saying, "Nathan, I only want nice people on this movie. It's very important we have only nice people." And I'd say, "Oh, sure, good idea. Nice *and* talented, that's always a wonderful combination." But his experience on *Wolf*, the previous film, had been a difficult one, and I think that's how he and Elaine were reunited. He called her to help with the script, and he was very, very grateful to her for that.

DOUGLAS WICK: Mike was very hurt during the shooting [of *Wolf*], because Jack [Nicholson]—I'm giving him the benefit of the doubt—but possibly he felt a little bit creatively at a loss, and he would occasionally act rude or dismissive to Mike. I remember that really hurting Mike's feelings, because of their history.

ROBIN WILLIAMS[2]: I worked with Mike on *Waiting for Godot*, and then met Elaine. On *Birdcage* is where you really see how they work together. They have this amazing timing where they remember old bits, and you'll see this incredible thing. They bounce off each other, amazingly so. She'll kind of go out and Mike will be able to ground it. To see the dynamic of the two—I first saw it in the rehearsal for *Birdcage*, which we rehearsed like a play.

HANK AZARIA: We were in a soundstage at Paramount, and Mike taped out on the ground where all the furniture would be, which is a rehearsal-hall thing to do. He wanted it to play like a farce, without a lot of cutting. He said, "I want it to feel like a train that keeps moving." Because he knew, I think, that Robin and Nathan are so given to ad-libbing and improvising, he said, "Get it all out in rehearsal. We're going to take what we feel are the best lines you come up with, then I want to lock it." It was a true meritocracy. Best idea, funniest idea, whatever works best. It doesn't matter who it comes from—he was blind that way.

ROBIN WILLIAMS[3]: Elaine wrote *The Birdcage*—even though it's based on a French movie, she orchestrates it, like a concerto. A four-seat—actually a six-seat, because everyone seems to play off their solos, and you play background. Mike said a wonderful thing about her writing: "She's worked very hard to condense it, so every word counts." It's like every note in a piece of music. The timing, you know—they have that together.

---

2. "Nichols & May—Take Two," *American Masters*, PBS.
3. Ibid.

HANK AZARIA: That was the only job that after I'd wrapped for the day, I would stay, (a) because I was just enjoying watching it all happen, and (b) I would literally sit on the floor between Mike's and Elaine's chairs to listen to their stories about the old days. They'd make each other cry laughing.

EMMA THOMPSON: They had a shorthand that was shorter than shorthand. It was really a kind of telepathy. Elaine is very shy—she's not a gregarious person, so to be with her and Mike together was something you hoped and prayed for. It didn't happen very often, but when it did, it was just fabulous.

NATHAN LANE: It was wonderful to see Mike and Elaine together, not only because it was their reunion, but they had this wonderful relationship, and he was so tickled by her sense of humor. It was a kind of brother-and-sister relationship, and he was very protective of her. She's so fiercely intelligent—she hardly needs protection—but she'd be eating at a catering table, and he would sometimes go over and just brush away a few crumbs. He was very protective of her script too. Although he would allow Robin and myself to have one take where we could improvise a bit, which was just a wonderful luxury, he wanted what was written.

HANK AZARIA: We didn't do much coverage, so when there was coverage, Robin would—he'd call them "wild takes": "Can I get a wild take?"—where he could just jam however he wanted. Not a lot of people know this, but Nathan is insanely quick, one of the masters at improvisation. I think sometimes the two of them felt that their spontaneity was being taken away, and I could tell they felt frustrated by that sometimes, but things never got weird or unpleasant—it was too tight a ship.

Mike would say, "No, no, dear boy"—by the way, he's the only person I know who could get away with calling me "dear boy." "Dear boy, here's how we're going to do it." And he always had a good reason. He could tell you very eloquently why it should be that way, how it serves the piece psychologically, or just why it was funny. But everybody got their day in court. Robin was always saying, "Please, boss, please, boss, I have an idea."

Within the structure we had, there was plenty of room for surprises. There were mistakes that are in the movie. At one point, I'm carrying around shrimp in the kitchen and they're dripping and making the floor slick, and Robin falls down, and he wasn't supposed to. If you look at it again, I bury my head as if I'm crying, but I'm actually laughing. Mike loved that kind of improvisation.

NATHAN LANE: Very often takes would be ruined because Mike was laughing so hard in the video village watching. You would hear him roaring with laughter.

HANK AZARIA: You'd have to cover him with a blanket and move him farther and farther from the set because he would laugh out loud. It's like, "Mike, what's the matter with you? We're never going to do it that well again!"

CHRISTINE BARANSKI: That scene between Robin and I, I think that's my favorite scene on film that I've ever done. Ann Roth had put me in the sexiest, most wonderful Pucci pink silk Capri pants. Yet in rehearsal, I wore a short, rather inexpensive skirt. And when I was sitting on the desk with my legs crossed, Mike said, "That's what you're wearing, right?" And I said, "Oh, no. This is mine. Just a cheap skirt." And he said, "Nope, you're wearing that. I want your legs to show." It's a kind of Mrs. Robinson moment. Mike did have a ferocious appreciation of women. It was wonderful to be seen by him if you were a woman.

HANK AZARIA: I was having trouble in one scene with Nathan, where I'm getting him ready for the show and he's refusing to go on. I said, "Mike, I don't know how to play this scene because it's very obvious that this dynamic happens every time, but they're treating it as if it's a disaster." And Mike said, "Your character is partially based on Judy Garland's dresser. Judy would panic before every performance, and her dresser would panic with her, and he would panic more than her so that she'd have to be the one to tell him to calm down, and that was the ritual they had." And I was like, *Brilliant!* No other directors say things like that to you, at least in my experience.

NATHAN LANE: Mike invited me to his home on Martha's Vineyard and he showed me the first cut of the film. As usual, the first time you see something, you're disappointed. You think, *Why did they use this instead of that?* Mike looked at me and said, "You're disappointed," and I said, "No, I think it's terrific, I think it's very funny." He said, "I know why you're disappointed."

He had let Robin and me do an improvisational take of the scene just before we decide we're gonna try to make this work, and he's gonna teach me to be a little butcher—the scene of me leaving the apartment and walking down the street and him trying to comfort me. I had gotten much more hysterical in this take, talking to people on the street, telling them I was being abandoned. And then I really fainted—I fainted to the ground—and Robin had to pick me up and carry me in. And when we finished, all of the extras applauded. Mike said, "You're disappointed because we didn't use that take," and I said, "A little bit." He said, "The problem was, it was funnier than the scene that followed it." I said, "Okay, I understand."

LORNE MICHAELS: I went to a preview of *The Birdcage* with him and it destroyed, as we say in comedy. He was so happy because—it happens to all of us—you go in for a meeting at the studio and the implication is: *Why are you here? We grew up on your stuff. You're already in the Hall of Fame.* There's a generation for whom *Animal House* is *Birth of a Nation*, and it's the same with *The Graduate*. You're being treated politely, but you're no longer in the game. You can be an icon and treated badly. Steve has this great joke about how after you have a flop, you call your favorite restaurant and they go, "Absolutely, Mr. Martin. How's 5:45?" But after the first preview, Mike knew, *It's going to work.* And then suddenly the entire attitude at the studio changed.

ERIC IDLE: When Python did City Center in '75 or '76, I went to a party at Paul Simon's apartment. I met this guy, and we immediately hit it off, and we talked for two hours. I asked Paul, "Who was that?" He said "Mike Nichols," and I went, *Oh, duh*. So we were friends for about almost thirty years before we worked together. Working together was sticky and then fabulous, because we both had to establish where we were.

Bill Haber, who was involved in *Annie*, asked me who I wanted to direct *Spamalot*, and I said Mike. He said, "Good luck. He takes three years to get back to you, but I'll give it to him anyway." Three days later, the phone rang, and it was Mike, and he said, "Yes, yes, yes." It reassured the Pythons that their work wasn't going to be just left to the mercy of me, God forbid.

JEFFREY SWEET: The significance of *Spamalot* was that it was the first time you had the American improv school, represented by Mike, working with the English satiric school, represented by the Pythons.

JON ROBIN BAITZ: Mike said he almost never had so much fun as he did on *Spamalot*.

MARTIN SHORT: He said, I'm going to do *Spamalot* and you're the perfect person to play almost every role, but we can't afford you. I never got to work with him. It's one of my great regrets. But I had a lot of hangs with him, and if I had to chose between the two, I'd go with hanging.

TIM CURRY (*actor*): There was this planeload of Californians who went to New York to be part of the casting of the play.

ERIC IDLE: Somebody would come in, sometimes quite a famous star. They'd do their bit, and Mike would say, "That was absolutely brilliant. Thank you so much," and then to me, "Take them off the list." Some actors he just hated. Not many, but a few. I'd say, "What about so-and-so?" and he'd say, "I hate him." "But he won an Oscar." "Yeah, yeah. I hate him." You never quite got the idea whether it was something personal or just a taste thing—they were doing something he didn't like in acting, which he found dishonest. Because honesty was the thing about it all. Honesty is what he liked most in an actor.

HANK AZARIA: I got a famous Mike phone call: "Hello, dear boy." "Hey, Mike, how are you?" "Good, good. We must eat something together soon. Now, I'm doing a musical version of *Monty Python's Holy Grail* called *Spamalot*"—a big Mike laugh just at the name of it—"and you must play the [John] Cleese role. So, are you available?" It's like, Mike, if I'm not, I'll make myself available.

When he did that movie with Garry Shandling about the guy with the talking penis, he offered me the role that Greg Kinnear ended up playing. At that time, I was very busy, career-wise, and I wasn't so sure I wanted to play it, so I said, "Okay, send me the script," and he laughed. I remember thinking, *Why is he laughing?* I realized years later that he knew that was actor-speak for, *I'm not so sure I want to do this, let me think about it.* And I think partly it was because he might have been thinking, not, *I made you,* but *I don't think you'd be in the position to turn down this role if I hadn't given you the last one.* So on the set of *Spamalot*, I told him I was sorry for the times I said no, and from here on in, anything you'd like me to do, big or small, I'm in. And he said, "No, dear boy. Things have to be right for both parties. If you don't want to do it, for whatever reason, you shouldn't do it." And he really meant it.

CASEY NICHOLAW (*choreographer*): I met him at his apartment. I had my choreographer's reel and my bag and my résumé, I was all prepared, but we just talked for an hour and he said, "Well, do you want the job?" That was it. He'd never seen my work, he'd never heard of me except for being recommended. But we hit it off right away, and he always said, Put your trust in the people whom you work with.

DAVID HYDE PIERCE: One of the reasons *Spamalot* was so successful is that Mike hates musicals, and so he had no interest in the stereotypical musical comedy performance. He was interested in real people telling a real story no matter how exaggerated the circumstances, which is also the essence of Monty Python: doing the most absurd thing in the straightest way possible.

HANK AZARIA: I played Lancelot. There is a beginning, middle, and end to that character. He wants to kill everyone; he's overcompensating for the fact that he's a closeted homosexual; once he makes peace with that, he's happy again; he falls in love with Herbert and they live happily ever after. It's ridiculous, but it is a throughline. That silly little thing I just laid out, I can't tell you how Mike wouldn't let it go. "No, there has to be a *reason* why he's in every one of his scenes. It has to make sense." And every character has that.

CASEY NICHOLAW: Anytime something's not truthful, it takes you out of the show, and therefore you're not invested as an audience member. Mike would always cut right to it and say, "All right, now do it again without all the bullshit." Or he would say, "That was wonderful, now do it as you." He knew that when someone's going out there saying "I'm funny!" they're not funny.

TIM CURRY: He wanted us to sing from the heart. Laughs had to be generated from something true. That was his great lesson, I think. Don't try to be funny. Just be funny from the situation.

DAVID HYDE PIERCE: He gave us a few great pieces of advice on *Spamalot*. I remember one was, "Everything that's funny goes; we only want what's *really* funny." He was ruthless about that. He would also say, "Once you have figured out exactly how to get your laugh, don't do that." It's the greatest gift you can ever give an actor because it frees you from ever saying, "Oh, I didn't get my laugh there." Sometimes you discover there's a huge laugh two lines later that never would've happened.

ERIC IDLE: An actor will get hold of something, and the next night he does it again, and the next night, and now this becomes part of the schtick. Mike wanted all of those gone. He would make them lie on the floor and just say the words without any inflections. He would say to the actors, "You've got to take this seriously. If you don't believe in it, why should the audience?" And I'm sitting here going, yeah, that makes a lot of sense, except he's giving notes on the Knights Who Say "Ni!"

PETER LAWRENCE: His note sessions were famous. He said during *Spamalot*, "If you truly enjoy what you're doing onstage without a purpose, then you will be in hell wandering forever amongst the Broadway undead." *Wandering forever amongst the Broadway undead.* Who says stuff like that at a note session? Stagehands would come out and listen to Mike's notes.

TIM CURRY: Because he was so smart, early in rehearsals I was trying to be Mr. Smart, until he made me realize that I had to play it true—that there was nothing wrong with King Arthur not being very bright—which was actually a lot more exciting to do. I remember him asking how I felt about the show—this was maybe a week into playing out of town in Chicago, and I said, "Like I'm driving a Porsche." It was magnificent engineering.

HANK AZARIA: I was so blinded by my love for Mike, and for Eric, and for Python, but the truth was, it needed a lot of work.

CASEY NICHOLAW: Halfway through rehearsals, we completely scrapped act 2.

HANK AZARIA: He said, "You have to deliver the thing you're making fun of. You can't just be saying, 'Oh, isn't it silly how musicals do these things.' You have to also deliver those things." And he spent pretty much all his time figuring out how to do that.

ERIC IDLE: Mike would say, "How am I going to do the Black Knight? How am I going to make the legs and all that come off?" I'd say, "You're the director. I'm just the writer." We spent hours working on that, and then on the killer rabbit. In the end, I said, Let's just use a hand puppet.

CASEY NICHOLAW: Trying to get the killer rabbit right, we went through so many different versions—strings, bunnies on slingshots—all kinds of stuff. It ended up being just a fucking puppet that somebody put on their hand and screamed. And it worked! What made us laugh was always the guiding principle.

ERIC IDLE: Mike was a comedian first and foremost. That's why I loved him. He was always very forthright about things he'd been through. That's a comedian thing; you never try and conceal what may be used against you. It's a disarming dishonesty.

He could be brutally frank. We had one actor, we had to cut his big scene, and he went around moaning and pissing and grumbling. Mike said, "I see I have to give you my asshole speech." He said, "Look, you can either be an asshole and leave or you can get with the team and understand that this is not about you. This is about making the show better." And the guy was lovely and adorable ever after.

HANK AZARIA: A dresser was once, twice, three times not where they were supposed to be, and the actor wasn't ready with his entrance. We were about to perform for a live audience in a day or two. Mike stopped—he's on his God mic—and he said: "Steve, why are you not out?" Steve truthfully said his clothes weren't ready. "Who's your dresser?" Out comes the dresser. "What's your name?" Rather defiantly, he said, "My name is Virgil!" Mike said, "Well, Virgil, we are no longer going to need your services, thank you very much." And I'll tell you something: everyone snapped to. The crew was a lot more alert after that.

DAVID HYDE PIERCE: I never saw Mike raise his voice to an actor, and he didn't raise his voice to this dresser either. It was very quiet, but extremely lethal.

HANK AZARIA: He had a love and joy for what he was doing, and he knew that a loving, happy environment was the best for everybody. Anybody getting in the way of that, he had no tolerance for.

ERIC IDLE: Mike had several slight episodes during the making of *Spamalot* where he'd disappear for some medical thing, but because Casey was such a genius, he never worried.

CASEY NICHOLAW: When we were out of town in Chicago, we got good reviews. And then we just kept working for another month. We cut another thirty minutes. Mike's favorite number in the whole show was "The Cow Song," but he ended up cutting it because it didn't keep the momentum going. *Yes, it's wonderful, but it must go.*

PETER LAWRENCE: Sara Ramirez would appear dressed as a cow and sing a torch song à la Marlene Dietrich under a streetlamp. It brought the house down. Everybody was devastated and couldn't understand why Mike would cut what we thought was the best number in the show, until we saw the effect it had: it streamlined the show. Suddenly, there was more of a plot. I think the show was a success because of all the trims, cuts, and rewrites that Mike did.

ERIC IDLE: The cow had a song just before it's thrown over the battlements. She's going to sacrifice her life—*au revoir, ciao.* Two French guards just lean against the wall as she sang this farewell. It was fabulous. But when the cow landed on Patsy, nobody laughed, because now we knew who the cow was, and we sympathized with the cow.

DAVID HYDE PIERCE: We didn't know until our first audience of *Spamalot* that it would be successful. In Chicago, I had a big number about "You won't succeed on Broadway if you don't have any Jews." We didn't know if the audience was going to stone us when we sang it, and Mike didn't know either. That was a big risk.

ERIC IDLE: It went off like gangbusters from the first preview. And even then, he cut two numbers. He'd still be giving notes after four years on Broadway: *Get the cast in.*

We got about thirteen nominations, but we kept getting *no, no, no, no.* He said, "Look, I think they're gonna stiff us, so you have to prepare something funny to say." I said okay. I'm sitting there, starting to write, and he goes back to his seat. "And now for best director. The winner is: Mike Nichols!" *Thanks a lot.* But then we won the Tony for best play. I think working with him for those four or five years was the most fun I've ever had in any form of show business.

Mike in the film version of Wallace Shawn's play *The Designated Mourner*. Meryl Streep called his performance "some of the best acting I've ever seen any man do." *(First Look International/Photofest)*

CHAPTER 11

Caviar for the General

WALLACE SHAWN: When I was writing *The Designated Mourner*, I heard his voice in my head. It helped me to write the play.

DEBORAH EISENBERG: When Wally finished the play and gave it to me to read, he said, "Whose voice do you hear in that part?" I said, "Mike's." And Wally said, "So do I."

JOHN LAHR: Mike was who Wally had in mind when he wrote the play: his voice, the inimitable whiff of superiority that he had, which was not quite hauteur—okay, let's call it hauteur. Wally does the reverse thing when he plays it, because he plays it like a schlub, so the arrogance is mitigated by his physical presence.

WALLACE SHAWN: David Hare was going to direct the play at the National [Theatre]. This was during the reign of Richard Eyre. I wanted to do a reading of the play for him, so I thought, *What the hell, I'll write Mike and ask him if he'd be in the reading. I would enjoy hearing him just read these words.* So I wrote to him, maybe I called him, and he said, "Sure, I'll do it." And then I think he must have asked Avedon, "Could we do the reading over at your studio?" There were maybe ten or twelve people there to listen. Mark Strand read the part of Howard and Julianne Moore read the part of Judy. The reading must have lasted two and a half hours. Not only was it sort of astounding, but

Mike himself seemed incredibly caught up and affected by it, if I may presume to say that. David and I looked at each other.

DAVID HARE: I was one of the early enthusiasts for Wally's plays—I was responsible for one of his plays being put on in the 1970s in England—so he wanted me to premiere *The Designated Mourner* in London rather than have it done in New York, where I think Wally probably felt he wasn't terribly well understood at the time. He also had this idea that Mike should play the part. I knew Mike, and I knew his work as a director, but I didn't know Mike acted, though I'd heard he'd done *Who's Afraid of Virginia Woolf?* at Long Wharf.

We went to Richard Avedon's with Julianne Moore, and we just read it at the kitchen table, and Mike's reading of the part was electric. I immediately said, "Will you come to London and do this?"

WALLACE SHAWN: I think maybe my girlfriend, Deborah Eisenberg, went up to Mike immediately and said, "You have to do this for real." David and I said, well, let's see if he's free. He's a very busy guy. So we asked him, "What about actually being in the play?" which I have to say, had not crossed my mind before that. But of course, I had been watching Mike and Elaine since I was very young, and I was fully aware that the man was a great performer.

DEBORAH EISENBERG: I sort of remember very gauchely afterward saying to Mike, "Well, don't you see that you have to do it?" Which is a terrible thing to do, really. Really unconscionable. At any rate, Mike told Wally or whomever that he would give it some thought, and he wanted a week, or two weeks, to think about it. I, at least, was pretty sure that he wasn't going to do it. How could he? It's a mammoth part. He had all his own projects, of course, and it was in London, which meant that he'd have to be separated from Diane for long periods, which he certainly wouldn't be pleased about. It just seemed incredibly unlikely. The period that he asked for went by, and we were waiting with sinking hearts, almost certain that he would say no. Then he asked for a little more time. Eventually, he astonishingly said yes. And once he committed, it was complete commitment.

WALLACE SHAWN: He was shocked by the suggestion, but he said, "Give me two weeks to think about it." Rather than just saying, *Well, come on, I'm not an actor.* By the way, Mike was not really a card-carrying member of the avant-garde. If he was going to be in a play, you wouldn't necessarily have thought he was going to be in *this* play. He took the full two weeks, and then to our absolute amazement, he said yes. Within a very short time, he was in London.

DAVID HARE: I think the appeal of it was that it was in London. I think he thought, if I'm going to act in a play, I want to do it in a place where I'm not exposed. As the uncrowned king of Broadway, he certainly didn't want to do it in New York.

DEBORAH EISENBERG: In a way, I feel that Mike exposed himself more doing that than he did with most or maybe even any of the movies he made. This character is charming, but monstrous, and Mike, who was a total delight and the most charming person really ever born, committed utterly to the horrifying aspects of the character. Sometimes an actor who is required to play a distasteful character manages to slither around so that there's some disclaimer in the performance, and Mike definitely did not do that. He did not pull back at all. Also, he had not acted for many, many years, and just to get out on a stage takes a lot of nerve, particularly if you already have an immense reputation in place.

DAVID HARE: The character is someone who is left to mourn the passing of culture, who is himself one of the most doubtful and morally queasy people you could possibly meet. Part of Mike identified with human weakness and frailty and vulnerability and unpleasantness. Mike wasn't frightened of the idea that human beings have very, very ugly feelings as well as very noble feelings, and I think from his past, he knew a lot about that.

JOHN LAHR: There will never be an actor in the universe who can embody the idea of the play in a more performed experience, because he was that culture. He was that snobbishness. He exuded the world of accomplishment and the patrician disdain for the hoi polloi. Not that Mike didn't have a social conscience; he was a meritocrat. I can't imagine there's an actor in the world who could play that. He just was it.

MIRANDA RICHARDSON (*actress*): I felt rather privileged to be in this four-hander, little jewel case of a piece. But it's an alarming piece of work. All Wally's works are alarming. They're also funny. All the things which drew Mike, against his wishes, to want to be part of it. I think it was one of the most frightening things that he probably ever had taken on. He was sort of perfect in a way. I just remember his death-calm face, exacerbated by the setting and the lighting. That line from the Wilfred Owen poem comes to me: "His hanging face, like a devil's sick of sin." It's a dark thing to say, but then the play is dark. The character is dark. Mike was in touch with that. He was sometimes quite emotional in the rehearsal room. It was never articulated, but I think it was the guilt of when he got out. Because he and his family could have gone to the death camps.

DAVID HARE: There was a moment when Mike said to me, "You obviously feel I'm not doing this right. Why don't you come here and show me what you want?" From any professional actor, this is a complete no-no. The unbreakable golden rule of directing is you do not demonstrate to the actor what you want. You let the actor find it. Wally always says the ten seconds when I walked onto the rehearsal room floor and Mike walked back to the director's chair were the longest ten seconds of his life. But I acted the scene with Miranda Richardson, and Mike said, "Oh, I can do that." There was no vanity. There was no ego. Mike was like a sort of garage mechanic. Any note you gave, he'd just say, "Great, that'll help." For him it was a completely practical business.

WALLACE SHAWN: He not only never missed a rehearsal, but he was never late. He never said once, *Today I have to leave half an hour early because I'm promoting my film,* or *I have to make decisions,* or *I have an impor-*

tant phone call. He just was a completely cooperative actor. And he loved David Hare. We might have thought, *Well, he's a director. What is he going to be like with a director directing him?* But he was just an utterly adorable lamb. He loved being directed. I think he really enjoyed the process of a director giving you a suggestion and you try it out and, wow, your performance suddenly is better in that passage or that moment. That's quite thrilling. David is a wonderful director and Mike dug it. And never, not ever, did he say, well, that's wrong, or try to direct it himself.

DAVID HARE: Mike always had that joke about directing, that it's like sex because you never see how other people do it. He was sort of riveted by what I was doing, because he'd never really observed another director at close quarters, except when Orson Welles was in *Catch-22* and tried to take over the film.

CYNTHIA O'NEAL: Mike walked out on the stage and started talking. I thought he was just making an announcement or something. I had no idea the play had started because it was so real.

WALLACE SHAWN: He was absolutely amazing at playing with the audience. He gave the impression that he was just improvising, that he was making up the whole thing on the spot. If someone would cough in the audience, he would turn right to that person and make a gesture as if they were agreeing with him, as if they had just said, "Oh, that happened to me too," and then he would go on with what he was saying. I think everybody in the audience thought that he was talking to them. Of course, he was not improvising, but having devoted many years of his life to improvisation, is that related to what he did? It must be somehow, because it had a kind of spontaneity that went very far in the direction of pretending that he couldn't think of the right word, and finally finding it. Yet it was all moving along at an incredible speed, which the ordinary actor couldn't possibly do. He would toss off things very casually that anybody else would be struggling to explain, and somehow the audience understood it.

DAVID HARE: There was absolutely no sense of it ever having been on the page. It simply was what Mike himself appeared to be thinking, and therefore saying. And yet a less Method actor I have never worked with in my life. It was an act of technique and concentration. And it's one of the most remarkable performances I've ever directed. When I asked him, "How do you do that?" he said, "All the time I'm directing, I'm thinking, *Surely you can make it seem a little bit more as if it's you that's thinking this, not the author.* Everything I do as a director is to try and make you believe that it's the character who's saying the thing, not the actor saying something that they've been given to say by somebody else."

I've tried, as it were, to suggest the same effect with other actors, and it's been almost impossible. It just doesn't work when anyone else does it, except Mike. Mike was a brilliant anecdotalist. I believe his stage manager would pick up a sign saying, "No anecdotes," because if Mike got off on anecdotes . . . And so, because *The Designated Mourner* is essentially an anecdote, he's like the ancient mariner. He just draws you in and says, *Come on, I'll tell you something that happened to me,* and the minute Mike Nichols says, *Come on, I'll tell you something that happened to me,* you want to know what it is. I've never been bored by a Mike Nichols story.

JOHN LAHR: He couldn't remember the lines. The way they built the set, you couldn't see it, but he had a monitor. There was not a whole lot of set design, but what was there was designed to mask the monitor he was reading from.

WALLACE SHAWN: Bob Crowley saw the reading at Dick Avedon's apartment and loved the three actors sitting behind the long table, and he immediately said, "That's the set!" So in the final set there was indeed a monitor, and it was concealed, but this was not why we had that particular set. Mike knew his lines, but he was terrified that he might forget them or forget to deliver a whole speech, and the fact that he could glance at the monitor gave him confidence. He was not sitting there reading the script. For some reason, performing bothered him. I think it's a tragedy, because he could have done amazing things in film and onstage. I don't know what it was. But something about being seen, being watched, it upset him. After some of the performances, he would sometimes say, "Oh, I was terrible."

DAVID HARE: A lot of American actors came to see it: Meryl Streep, Harrison Ford. Every night there were famous people, because it was caviar for the general—that's the phrase we use in England—meaning it was so good that it was almost only for connoisseurs. Any connoisseur of acting wanted to see Mike Nichols act, because it was at a level of technical spontaneity that I have never seen in any other actor. Sydney Pollack has something of the same quality, actually. It was a collector's item, I suppose, this performance, and it was very widely admired.

MIRANDA RICHARDSON: I think everybody felt the need to record this particular production in some way.

WALLACE SHAWN: Filming it was just an idea that came up in the last weeks of the play. I think the idea of recording it was pleasing to Mike.

DAVID HARE: At the end of the run I said, "Let's go off to Pinewood. We can shoot a movie in three days," and we literally shot it in three days. We just fired off this movie as fast as we possibly could before he went home. He, of course, would not do the play in New York.

WALLACE SHAWN: Of course, we asked him to do the play in America. But he really wouldn't hear of it, because being in England, he didn't know anybody there. I mean, he knew a few people. But it was like being on Mars in a certain way.

DAVID HARE: Mike was not so well known in London. In fact, during the run of the play, there was a memorial evening at the National Film Theatre for Louis Malle, who had been a great friend of both of ours. Mike was really shocked that when he was introduced as a speaker, there was almost no recognition from the audience. They clapped politely, but they had no sense that the name Mike Nichols meant anything at all. Whereas, when he was in his kingdom, in New York, you couldn't walk down the street without everybody coming up to him. He was shocked at how little prestige his name had in Europe. I'm not sure he was very comfortable with that. I said to him, "But, Mike, that's because you're so self-deprecating in interviews. You always say, 'I'm not an auteur. I'm not in competition with Bergman. I'm not pretending to be Fellini'"—because he had this horror of phoniness and pretension—"'I'm just a guy who directs films.' The thing is," I said, "people here believe you when you say that."

RICHARD AVEDON[1]: I talk very seriously about photography as an art. Very much at the beginning, he said, "It's so funny that you think of yourself as an artist." Not attacking me, but, *Who would ever call themselves an artist?* There's a deep—I don't know if the word is "sarcasm," about himself as an artist.

DAVID HARE: When the BBC wanted to distribute the film, he didn't want it to be distributed, and most of all, he didn't want it to be distributed in America. It had already been sold to America, but he did absolutely nothing to support it, and wouldn't, whereas when it was a play in London, he supported it 100 percent. He wanted it to remain an experiment that he had conducted in London.

Later, Mike was being honored by the American Film Institute, and he asked me to go. I didn't say anything to him, but I thought, *You've shown clips of all of your movies, and yet you won't show a clip of one of the greatest acting performances I've ever seen.* He didn't want to own it as part of his legacy. What that was about, I have absolutely no idea, but obviously it was incredibly hurtful to me and to Wally. He was never anything but completely congenial and friendly and loving and sweet and charming to us, but he just didn't want to be seen in that work on his home turf. He was a complex man.

Other actors—Christopher Walken, Meryl Streep—studied that film that we later made, because they say, *How the hell does he do it?*

---

1. Courtesy of the John Lahr collection at the Howard Gotlieb Archival Research Center, Boston University.

CHRISTOPHER WALKEN: I don't know how many people know it—actors know it—but Mike Nichols was a great actor. If he had been an actor, he could have done anything he wanted. He could have excelled in any of the plays and movies that he directed. Watching him in the film of *The Designated Mourner*—the nuance, the continuity—really was a lesson, a master class in acting—now, always.

MERYL STREEP: There is a piece of film of him performing in *The Designated Mourner*, Wally Shawn's terrific play. Mike suppressed it for years, went to great lengths to keep it out of circulation here in the United States. I don't know why, maybe because he just didn't like to look at himself. A lot of actors share this reluctance. It was so naked, absolutely riveting and upsetting and funny and, well, just like life. Mike in that just blew me away. It's some of the best acting I've ever seen any man do. And he barely moves. But it's so lived-in and naked and canny. It really made me understand something about him.

Mike with one of his Arabian horses in 1971. "The reason people want to have money is to surround themselves with things, because it's a barrier against the world," Mike told stage manager Peter Lawrence. "It gives you thinking time." *(© Mary Ellen Mark)*

CHAPTER 12

A Means to Egress

CANDICE BERGEN: He always lived like a prince. I don't know where that came from. But he was more princely than anyone I ever knew.

MIKE HALEY: We were in his office and he's trying to explain an idea of what something should look like, a color palette, and he says, "No, it's like . . . bring in the small Matisse." Somebody brings in a Matisse, and he says, "You see?"

HANNAH ROTH SORKIN: Some people know everyone in show business, but Mike had a much bigger reach than show business. One day Mrs. [Katharine] Graham calls. There were certain people who got treated with extra care, and she was one of them. It was the most coy phone call in the world: There's this property, Chip Chop, [in Martha's Vineyard] that will be coming up." Basically, she was saying, *This is going to be sold, and I want it to be sold to you.* And he knew how to make her feel like she hasn't said anything commercial.

NATHAN LANE: You know you got a fancy house when it has a name. I stayed in the Noel Coward cottage.

JACK O'BRIEN: You go down in the morning to the kitchen and there's a *New York Times* for every person in residence in case you want your crossword. You look in the bathroom and everything you could ask for except a hypodermic needle is there for you. It's unbelievable.

EMMA THOMPSON: He was always offering me, as a guest, just the best of everything. And sometimes I'd say to him, "For God's sake, let's just have baked beans!"

I remember hanging my coat up in the big wardrobe in the hall of their apartment, and there were about sixty-five really nice coats in there, all of them black in different kinds of styles, and I thought, *Does he have some sort of retail outlet here on the side?* I said, "Why have you got so many coats?" and he said, "Well, I like them all." I said, "You can't get much wear out of them," in very Northern tones, and he said, "It doesn't matter."

LOUISE GRUNWALD (*friend*): Mike lived big-time. I say this in an admiring way. He wanted to see how everybody grand lived, took it all in, and liked the big life. And given his druthers, he would've had an even bigger apartment.

MIKE HALEY: He used to say, "I always have to be kept at seventy-two degrees."

NEIL SIMON[1]: Mike got this big, beautiful apartment up in the Beresford, and I came up there to see him. It had been done by a really great decorator, and he was sitting there in a big chair—I don't think there were any people there besides us—and he looked at me and he said, "Citizen Hearst, right?" I just laughed, because I knew what the joke was, but I think there was maybe a little of the truth of what he was thinking: *I've isolated myself into this grandiose kind of life.*

JULIET TAYLOR: From the time he was very young, Mike was an enormously successful person. And as time went on he got more and more removed from the way other people live in this world. He would

---

1. Courtesy of the John Lahr collection at the Howard Gotlieb Archival Research Center, Boston University.

leave the Carlyle, and his foot would go into the limousine. He was a very empathic person, but he didn't walk the streets.

JON ROBIN BAITZ: Tina Brown had this *New Yorker* conference, and, for some reason, I had been invited. It was really awful. There were awful speeches and awful ideas and awful talks. I saw Mike was there, and he looked at me, and I just started stuttering, "I'm leaving, I'm leaving," and he said, "Yes, I think that's wise. Would you like a ride on my jet?" So I was sitting there in his plane, still sort of stunned, and he looked over at me and he said, "You're awfully blasé about my jet."

ROBERT NICHOLS: Mike loved what Diane called *Air Mike*. I did go to Martha's Vineyard on *Air Mike* once, and once you've done that, you don't want to sit in the back on United, that's for sure. Look, it's a funny thing about when you have seemingly everything you want. Mike said this himself. He said, "When you can have anything you want, it can actually wear away your patience." Diane is so different. She seems to care little or nothing about material things.

CANDICE BERGEN: She had more important, substantive pursuits, so she just left it all to Mike. And Mike would be going over fabrics and finishes with the decorator.

MARLO THOMAS (*actress*): He once said to me, "Phil [Donahue] is so lucky that you do all of this." He said, "Diane doesn't even know what a swatch is."

ANJELICA HUSTON: Mike lived large, but there was also something modest about it, too, a sort of jewel economics, if you know what I mean. It was on a modest scale, but incredibly precious. It wasn't enormous or garish or outsized—everything was just perfect, elegant.

TOM STOPPARD: He was a great artist, but he was also great at civilized living. He just thought we're all part of this marvelous civilization at its best, and he was sensitive to the fact that civilization at its worst was happening simultaneously just out of sight.

PETER LAWRENCE: Mike used to say the reason people want to have money is to surround themselves with things, because it's a barrier against the world. He said, "It gives you thinking time."

ROBERT NICHOLS: I do think that he had some resentment of my unspoken disapproval of some of the trappings of wealth and fame. He didn't act arrogantly, no. He didn't change in that regard. It's more of a reflection on me that I had these attitudes, and there is some hypocrisy there on my part. I kind of don't like the Yellow Brick Road, and yet I didn't hesitate to benefit from him being on it. To me, it was a wonderful bonus in my life to have Mike be rich and famous. I met all kinds of interesting people through him. I went to restaurants I never could have afforded. He was very generous with me. Mike subsidized me when I was at the Mayo Clinic and he was getting really successful on Broadway. Medical trainees were paid peanuts then. I made $300 a month, believe it or not, and we had three children. We sometimes ate horsemeat. He sent me $200, $300 a month, and it made a big difference. He also bought small shares for me in *The Odd Couple* and *Barefoot in the Park*, and I started getting checks. They weren't very big, but they were something, and every bit helped.

DAVID HARE: There was an incredible moment when we all went out to dinner, Debbie Eisenberg, a short-story writer who really probably earns less than a burger flipper; and Wally [Shawn], whose plays do not command huge Broadway audiences; and me, who is a serious theater playwright; and Mike. And Mike suddenly sighed and said, "I would love to know what it's like to be rich," and the three of us just went, "What?" He said, "No, but I mean *really* rich. I've just got the money I've made in my lifetime, but that's *new* money. That's not interesting. What I would love is to be old money." This was a distinction that was sort of lost on us. We didn't think he was living too shabbily. He had that huge Katharine Cornell house out at the Vineyard, and he had a house in Connecticut. He was certainly living higher than anyone else I knew in show business.

EMMA THOMPSON: The fabulousness of his life was always a compensatory thing for everything he'd lost, and a lot of the time he couldn't quite credit that he actually had it.

JON ROBIN BAITZ: He was utterly a refugee to the very end, a construct out of *Mitteleuropa*, an exile. He figured out that surviving meant becoming vaguely horsey and WASP-y, with a Balthus on the wall.

RICHARD AVEDON[2]: He said, "I bought a beautiful horse. It's in New Jersey. We've got to go out and see it." So Evelyn and I drove out, and I even took a picture of the horse. It was a beautiful animal, cantering across a field. He has this thing for collecting beauty, including the wives.

CANDICE BERGEN: The barn was happening. It was fourteen horses in Bridgewater, Connecticut. Then he bought an old Spanish ranch above Santa Barbara just before the market started to cave in. It was a lot of beautiful land, with cranes nesting in the trees. I don't know why he thought he could manage two ranches.

ROBERT NICHOLS: Santa Barbara is a lovely and picturesque small city near the central coast, and there's the Santa Ynez Mountains behind it, and a road going up, the San Marcos Pass, which takes you to the valley beyond the mountains, and that's the Santa Ynez Valley. Mike had a horse ranch there with a guy named Don DeLongpre where they raised Arabians. Mike had some national champions.

CANDICE BERGEN: He was phenomenally savvy and knowledgeable about it. He flew to obscure breeders in Poland and New Mexico.

ROBERT NICHOLS: I asked Mike, "How is Poland?" and he said, "Cold and weird."

---

2. Courtesy of the John Lahr collection at the Howard Gotlieb Archival Research Center, Boston University.

TOM STOPPARD: I remember going to one of his horse sales once, and it was like a theater production, absolutely breathtaking. At the back of this large arena where we were all sitting, a herd of horses galloped past our eyes in what I now remember as moonlight. It was just extraordinary. He made something utterly memorable out of the buying and selling of horseflesh.

ROBERT NICHOLS: The one I remember best, there was a stage, and the curtain parted, and there was this magnificent scene of a lush green hill, with a magnificent stallion galloping across it. It looked like a movie in Cinerama, but it was real. It drew gasps from everybody. I remember another where the horses appeared in a cloud of dry-ice smoke. They were first-class, Broadway-level stage productions.

CANDICE BERGEN: It was a tented auction, it was at night, and he lit it—he had the best lighting people do it. And the sawdust was colored and had sparkles mixed in so that when the horses were led out at a canter, smoke coming out of their nostrils, it was like a locomotive coming onto the stage. There was a little three-person orchestra, and when the mare was brought out they played "The Most Beautiful Girl in the World," and she came out throwing sparkles. He brought all of his showmanship to it because he was the great showman.

ANJELICA HUSTON: Oh my God, there were emirs and sultans, all sorts of Arabian dignitaries. At the end of this horse sale, in which some animals were going for millions, a whole backdrop opened up and the horses galloped off over the fields.

PAUL SIMON: We were standing together after the sale, and he said, "Not bad for a little boy from Berlin, huh?"

HANNAH ROTH SORKIN: He wasn't sybaritic, because he was so uncomfortable in his own body. But the horses were externalized.

JOHN CALLEY[3]: He really likes them. It's some displaced something, probably, just as my boats are. For somebody that works in incessant collaboration with people, it's great to have a horse. That's how I feel about boats.

JON ROBIN BAITZ: Ulu Grosbard, another member of Mike's club of refugees, once shared an apartment with him in the early '60s. He felt Mike was corrupt because he could not do *laundry*. He would buy like eight white dress shirts a week for his Village show with Elaine. Ulu told that story as though it illuminated everything. That story was true—Mike admitted it, and he howled in rage when I asked him about it: "I was young, I didn't know anything." No. He was young, but he was suddenly rich. And being rich was his way out. Each dollar was a means to egress, to exit banality.

SUSAN FORRISTAL: Mike, if he could, would always hire Cynthia O'Neal and me to help us keep up our SAG insurance. We weren't in all of his movies, but it was quite a few. On *Regarding Henry*, we were shooting a cocktail party in this very elegant town house, and my job was to be one of the elegant ladies eating caviar. So we start to shoot and Mike yells, "Cut! What kind of caviar is that?" And he comes up and he looks at it and he says, "This isn't good enough. I want big, bubbled beluga caviar." So they send this kid out to get caviar. It took an hour and a half. It wasn't lunch break—it wasn't anything. We're just standing around waiting. The kid comes back: wrong caviar. "That's not what I want! Someone go with him!"

ROBERT GREENHUT: We were all pissed off at him. *Mike, come on.* Even the prop man would tell me, "You can't tell the difference. You can put *shit* there and no one would know it wasn't caviar," but Mike wanted it. If you worked on a Mike movie, you knew you weren't going to be roughing it.

---

3. Courtesy of the John Lahr collection at the Howard Gotlieb Archival Research Center, Boston University.

GREGORY MOSHER: There are all these stories about how Mike would have meetings at his apartment and serve tea, and then bill the production for the tea. On movie sets, he'd invite everybody to lunch, twenty people, to an expensive restaurant, and they'd bring him the check, and he'd say, "Give it to Greenhut."

ANN ROTH (*costume designer*): If you said, "Mike, I really think we ought to have some obscure fish dried somewhere in Northern Scotland," you had it. I have seen planes arrive with Krispy Kreme donuts coming off of them and sent directly to us. Nora [Ephron] was very much the same.

JEREMY IRONS: I remember hearing that on one of the last plays he did, he'd insisted the management raise the stage by something like five inches all the way through, which is immensely costly to them, but because it was Mike, they did.

ROBERT GREENHUT: With Woody, we worked our way from *Annie Hall*, $3 million, up to $15 million, but we were working on a much lower price range than Mike. Mike didn't want to work unless everything was first-class.

EMANUEL AZENBERG: Mike liked money. He always asked for a lot. Sometimes he got it. In the case of *The Real Thing*, everybody including Mike asked for everything, except for Stoppard. And we came up with a way of dealing with it, and the one who gave up the most was Stoppard. He didn't care.

In one sense, did Mike deserve more? Yeah. But money was an issue for Mike.

PETER LAWRENCE: Money meant something else to Mike, other than just its buying power. I was never quite sure what it was, what it meant to him, but he needed it. He was always very generous artistically, ethically, personally, with everybody he considered to be an artist or a craftsman. But he was very rough on the business side. Mike was the first guy who ever had a 5 percent deal in the theater, on *The Odd Couple*. He got 5 percent of the gross. No director had ever gotten that before.

NEIL SIMON[4]**:** I was very pragmatic about it. I said, okay. I could win the battle and say, *No, I'm not going to give you my points*, and get a director not as good. I would rather have him do it and have the play great. It's not about money, because he obviously has all the money he could use. I think it was to show him the respect that he feels he should be getting. I wasn't pleased with giving it to him, but I can't argue with it. I can't find anybody as good as he is, I never will, so . . . I thought it was, I wouldn't say outrageous but I thought it was a lot to ask. My wife then, Joan, who is an extremely smart woman, said, "Give it to him. You don't want to lose him, do you? He's worth it." And we both felt that.

ROBBIE LANTZ[5]**:** He was the first director who got a million dollars. It was front-page news in *Variety*.

JON ROBIN BAITZ: He liked to be very comfortable, and if you like to be comfortable, sometimes you do things that you might not otherwise do.

CANDICE BERGEN: Mike and [Louis Malle] met at a very glamorous lunch on the lawn at Diane von Furstenberg's house in Connecticut. We were sitting uncomfortably on the grass, introducing ourselves, and Louis said, "I'm Louis Malle," and Mike went, "You are?" He was just so shocked by this normal-looking man, because Mike was a great admirer of Louis's work. They had great respect for each other. Louis always wondered about the importance of money in Mike's work, and if that didn't compromise him in some

4. Courtesy of the John Lahr collection at the Howard Gotlieb Archival Research Center, Boston University.

5. Ibid.

way. Louis had been born wealthy, so he could afford not to care about it.

EMANUEL AZENBERG: There are half a dozen films he did that are artistically inexplicable. You look at them and say, *Why the hell did you do that?* Because they're paying him a lot of money.

PETER LAWRENCE: Look, sometimes Mike did pick things for the money, which didn't work out well. That was Mike's Achilles' heel, I always felt.

DAVID HARE: He'd just seen some British film, maybe *My Beautiful Laundrette*, and he said, "How is it possible to make films like that? How do they get made when they're so lively and original?" I wanted to say to him, *Because the director doesn't take $7 million.*

JOHN CALLEY[6]**:** We're sitting on a runway at Kennedy. At this point Mike is still going to direct *Remains of the Day*. We're getting ready to go to England to choose locations, we have a budget of like 25 million bucks, and it's approved by the studio—to my astonishment, because I would never approve $25 million. It was not that kind of movie. It seemed like a very tiny movie. We're meeting with [Harold] Pinter, who is doing the screenplay, finalizing locations, Mike is making his decisions about actors—I think at that point it was Jeremy Irons and Meryl Streep—and the plane starts to roll, and I say to him, "Let me ask you something: Aren't you at all nervous about *Remains of the Day*, $25 million?" He says, "It scares the shit out of me. I'm not sleeping at night." I say, "Well, then, why the fuck are we doing it?" He said, "What do you mean? We're so far into it." I said, "Listen, it's the easiest thing in the world. There are not many things that I'm absolutely certain about in life, but one of them is that if we offer Columbia an out, they don't want to do it at twenty-five." He said, "You really think that?" I said, "Yes, they'll want you to do *Wolf*."

---

6. Courtesy of the John Lahr collection at the Howard Gotlieb Archival Research Center, Boston University.

JACK O'BRIEN: I think money became much more an issue for him in the latter part of his life than he was willing to admit. He had to maintain a certain standard, and you can't do it in the theater.

EMANUEL AZENBERG: If not a flaw, a tragic something of Mike's was the need to do things for money. Because Mike was capable of creating a new theater. He knew the world of the not-for-profits didn't work because the artists can't make a living, and Broadway was becoming a theme park. Mike could have created—and it was discussed—an artistic national theater that actually paid a decent salary to everybody, but that meant giving up a lot. It came up in a serious way—a conversation we had with Mike and the Shuberts—but it never really got off the ground. He would have had to give up doing all those movies and the movies were where the money was. Doing the theater was chump change compared to the film world.

HANNAH ROTH SORKIN: I think there was a tension, because making big successful movies that made money, that's what got you access to the actors you wanted, the scripts you wanted, the schedule you wanted. It was not even the money at that point. It was, *I need final cut. I need to have endless rights,* so that when Sony bought Columbia and wanted to use *The Graduate* in advertising, he still retained the ability to say *never, never, never.* That ability comes from success.

DAVID HARE: I think that it's absolutely unbelievable given how high he was flying socially that he kept his artistic radar. Most people who ascend to what I call the higher show business lose their direction up there, and a lot of them go nuts and become puffed-up and vain, and Mike was never puffed-up or vain. He was grounded in the artistic process, which he adored, much more than he adored the rest of it. He seemed to me one of the people who best survived being offered the world, which he was. He was offered the world over and over and over again, and that drives a lot of people mad. Mike never lost his moral and artistic compass in the middle of that, I don't think. He made some films that were better than other films, but of whom is that not true?

LORNE MICHAELS: For those of us who came after, he defined how you could be successful and not lose touch with the thing you liked in the first place. Somehow he kept his balance. I think part of that was living in New York and not being in the industry, because the industry makes you always feel, *That was great, but now what?* And I think part of it was the theater—that he could go back to that rehearsal hall and a ghost light. To what Yeats called "the foul rag and bone shop of the heart." He always connected back to the core.

DOUGLAS McGRATH: Some people use the theater to get to the movies. Mike didn't. He loved both, and did both right to the end.

PETER LAWRENCE: The reason I think he liked the theater was because the economic pressures weren't like movies, and he could actually rattle around in a production and figure out what it meant to him and the people who were doing it with him. The thing he didn't like, I think, about movies is once it was done, it was done. He couldn't go back and re-edit a movie. But with a play, Mike could always change his mind and move things around. He wanted a living experience every night on the stage. Mike would say, "Just change it so that the actors have to deal with something new." It wouldn't neces- sarily end up in the show, but it taught us something. He liked blind alleys. I've always thought he was a much better theater director than he was a film director. You look at plays like *The Gin Game.* Or even a minor one like *Comedians*: Mike found anger in there—because he was a comedian, of course—that didn't exist in the play itself. He went in with an idea, but then he would rattle around and find new things that would just come to the surface, things that nobody else could find.

*

Mike with Emma Thompson at Silvercup Studios in Queens, filming *Angels in America*. "There were some others who might have been able to pull that off, but not many," says Jeffrey Wright. "And in this lifetime, it was him." *(HBO/Photofest)*

CHAPTER 13

Like Church, but a Fun Church

DAVID GEFFEN: One of the things Mike regretted the most was doing the movie with Garry Shandling, *What Planet Are You From?* He felt he got talked into it by John Calley. He wasn't right for it at all, and he took it out on Garry, which he regretted later. I mean, he didn't have to say yes. He was angry with himself more than anything, and the movie did not do well.

DOUGLAS WICK: When Mike was doing the Garry Shandling movie, I had an office on the Sony lot, where they were shooting. He was the most miserable I'd ever seen him.

Mike's cachet was slightly on the decline, and he was having some trouble getting his full price, whatever it was, at that point. So suddenly he read this Garry Shandling script, and John Calley was head of the studio and wanted him to do it, and they agreed to pay his full fee, so he said yes. He got sort of swept along. He didn't scrutinize it like he would under normal circumstances.

If you think of an actor as a piece of fruit, like an orange, one director could squeeze out of that orange a cupful, and Mike could squeeze a bathtub-ful. For Mike, Garry Shandling was a rock. Every day he tried to squeeze juice out of it, and he failed, so he felt terrible and he made Garry Shandling feel terrible.

Annette Bening was shooting a scene, and Mike had a microphone, and, because he had injured his ankle, he was working like *Chorus Line*, giving instructions through the megaphone, which was very loud on the soundstage. He was in a terrible mood. They were preparing a shot with Annette Bening, and hair and makeup comes into the shot to tune her up, and Mike suddenly booms on the megaphone, "Scat, dwarves!" Which was jaw-droppingly rude, and also sort of crazily witty.

It was so clear that his career had careened off course. And then he did *Wit*. He was the first really high-end director to do cable. He knew to return to the thing that actually nourished him, which was the work. When he got lost, he always found his way back.

RICHARD PLEPLER: Mike had just done this *fakakta* thing about somebody going into space, and he was depressed. Pete Peterson told me he had lunch with Mike and said to him, "You are not doing what you are meant to be doing. You are moving farther away from who you are, and that's why you're not happy with your art. You need to be at HBO." Mike would later say that was a very pivotal conversation.

When I came in the early '90s, the notion that we could be mentioned in the same breath as network television was almost unimaginable. That we could get a little halo for winning an Emmy Award for a movie was incredible. That we could work with the leading minds and talents in American culture? That didn't come until later. Remember, even David Chase and David Simon were not David Chase and David Simon when they came here.

I think it's fair to say that the experience Mike had at HBO with *Angels in America* created a very special new proselytizer in the creative community for HBO, and he was a great cheerleader not only for me but for the company in the years that followed.

COLIN CALLENDER (*producer*): I was president of HBO Films and we bought the film rights to a play by Margaret Edson called *Wit*. I approached Emma Thompson about playing the central role. I flew to London and met Emma at her house in Belsize Park, and right out of the gate she said, "You know, the director I would do this with is Mike Nichols."

EMMA THOMPSON: Mike had just come off a film that hadn't done well. Even though Mike had never done telly in that sense, I thought, *Well, maybe he's feeling a bit battered, and he might be interested in this material.* Because as soon as I read Margaret Edson's brilliant play, I thought, *God, there's only one person who can do this.* He said yes immediately.

COLIN CALLENDER: It was the first time he had directed anything for television, and it was a great experience. He and I were talking about what we could do next. I had been tracking *Angels in America*, which had been developed at New Line Cinema as two movies with Robert Altman, but they never got off the ground. So I said to Mike while we were in one of the breaks shooting *Wit*, "What about *Angels in America*?"

JEFFREY WRIGHT (*actor*): At one point, there were discussions about Robert Altman possibly doing it. I was attuned to these rumors. I'd made a personal pledge that if I were not included in the film adaptation, I would burn down any sets that had been built. So my antennae were up.

TONY KUSHNER[1]: Cary Brokaw, a film producer who had been working with me I think about ten years to try to figure out a way to bring *Angels* to the screen, called and said, "Mike Nichols is interested in talking to you about *Angels in America*." So we met at Trattoria Dell'Arte across from Carnegie Hall. I was very nervous about meeting him, because he was Mike Nichols. And I was also wary about anybody trying to make a movie of *Angels*. I had sort of given up on the idea. I'd worked for about two or three years with Robert Altman, and then Bob and I sort of decided at the same time that this is probably not going to happen.

So Mike and I sat down and he said, "It's lovely to meet you and I really love your play," or something like that. And I don't remember exactly how he got into it, but he immediately said, "I want to keep

---

1. "Mike Nichols," *American Masters*, directed by Elaine May, produced by Julian Schlossberg, season 30, episode 1, aired January 29, 2016, on PBS.

all of the doubling of characters." Which was a shock to me because I thought, of course, that would have to go. And I said, "I'm surprised, but that's very intriguing. Why?" And he said, "Because I want to see Meryl play all of these different parts."

So he had done two things instantly that were sure to hook me. One was letting me know that if I said yes to working with him, I would maybe get a chance to work with Meryl Streep, which was one of my dreams. And also, I thought, this is a guy who's not only a great filmmaker, he's a great theater director, and he gets the essentially theatrical nature of the script. He's going to find ways—as he had done with *Wit*, and way back with *Who's Afraid of Virginia Woolf?*—to make a film out of it, but still keeping it a little bit in the world of theater.

Immediately, I thought, *This is the guy*. It felt like I had been waiting for that.

COLIN CALLENDER: Al Pacino had known about Robert Altman's attempt to do it, and was very keen to play Roy Cohn. He was nervous about the idea of doing it as two separate movies and not convinced that would work. When he heard that we at HBO were interested in making it and had Mike Nichols attached to direct, he came onboard immediately. It's sort of commonplace now, but back then, movie stars never did television. Agents would protect their clients from doing television because somehow it would signal that their movie career was in trouble. So, Al Pacino committing to this was a really bold move on his part. It was an inflection point at HBO, absolutely.

AL PACINO (*actor*): I saw the two great performances, one with F. Murray Abraham and another with Ron Leibman on Broadway, and I was extremely impressed. The whole evening was spectacular, but I never had any interest in playing the role whatsoever until Robert Altman came to me with the film version. Somehow it fell apart. Then a few years later, Mike Nichols was involved and he wanted me. I knew Mike socially, and loved him also as one of the great directors. I was thrilled to have the opportunity to work with him.

PATRICK WILSON (*actor*): It was such a different time. The first reaction from people was: *Al Pacino and Meryl Streep are doing TV?*

BEN SHENKMAN (*actor*): When HBO made the announcement, I remember thinking, *Of course, that is the perfect thing.* Nichols doing it with these people on HBO. It can be as long as it needs to be, and HBO has already identified the audience that is ready for this.

COLIN CALLENDER: I think Mike's initial reaction was, *Is there a way to do this properly, and will HBO support me to do it properly?* It was a $60 million budget, which was $10 million an hour. That was a hell of a lot of money back then.

RICHARD PLEPLER: Mike's fee? Top of show for directing an HBO movie in 2001, it absolutely wouldn't be more than $1 million— probably less. I can assure you this: Mike was not working at HBO in the early 2000s because he could make the most money there. In those years we weren't paying the kind of money to big directors that they could get elsewhere in the business.

TONY KUSHNER[2]**:** Once I said yes to Mike, the deal with HBO happened very quickly, and I was then expected to produce the first hourlong episode. I'd never worked on anything, so I sat down and started writing what I thought was a screenplay. Bob Altman and I never really got past a lot of wild talking. That was a lot of fun, but we never got close to a script.

I sent Mike the first sixty pages, and then we met at his apartment for lunch. He looked at me and—he has a sort of smile where his eyebrows go up, and you couldn't tell whether you were seeing somebody who was really delighted or who was about to tell you something that he knew you weren't going to want to hear—and he said, "So, have you ever been on a film set?" And I said, "No." He said, "I can tell." And he said, "I have." Then he took out the script and said, "Now these things," and he pointed to the "POV," "CUT TO," and all that

2. "Mike Nichols," *American Masters*, PBS.

stuff, he said, "I don't need that from you. Just tell me what you want the audience to hear and see. Everything else I can supply." It was the only screenwriting lesson I'd ever had, and it was exactly the right one to get started. After that, everything was easy.

COLIN CALLENDER: Mike really wanted to find exciting, young, new talent. And of course, that's exactly what he did.

MERYL STREEP[3]**:** He put together a group—some of his favorite people, some people he'd never worked with, some unknown people— he made this combination of characters adhere in a very beautiful, seamless way. I'm not sure what that particular alchemy is. I don't quite understand how he achieved it.

BEN SHENKMAN: Most directors are terrified and want to be reassured every minute, every take, every second by the actor that they've made the right decision in casting that person. Mike, on the other hand, not only had the vision to imagine these not-very-experienced actors in these incredibly demanding roles, but also the clout to sell that to HBO, and as a director, the courage and the largesse to take on the inevitable anxieties of the nobodies he was determined to cast— which is really, really rare.

JULIET TAYLOR: You start thinking of all the well-known guys, but they really couldn't do the words. Some of the monologues go on for two pages, and people who haven't been trained in the theater can't do it. So it ended up being a cast of real New York theater actors. Mike would almost always go for a better-known person over an unknown— that would be the inclination. But not at the expense of being good.

There was one pretty well-known actor who said he'd only do it if he didn't have to kiss a guy. And we said, "Sorry, bye-bye."

MARY-LOUISE PARKER (*actress*)**:** I think I was the first one who auditioned. Al and Meryl weren't auditioning, obviously.

---

3. "Mike Nichols," *American Masters*, PBS.

JEFFREY WRIGHT: I think my year and a half on Broadway in a seven-hour play was my audition. Mike, from what I understand, he wanted to start fresh—with a fresh cast. But he happened to come see *Topdog/Underdog*, a play that I was doing at the Public, and I think that changed his mind about my being a part of it. Here he was down at the Public Theater watching Suzan-Lori Parks's latest play before it hit Broadway. He was as vital and curious as any twenty-one-year-old.

He had seen me in the original production of *Angels*, maybe more than once. I certainly remember him coming backstage, welled up with emotion. I knew him because I had gone through a fairly long audition to play Henry in *Primary Colors*, which if I hadn't learned over the years to think differently, I might look back on with some bitterness.

MERYL STREEP[4]**:** I was supposed to play three roles: the Mormon mother, Ethel Rosenberg, and an angel at the end. Then he said, "Would you want to play the rabbi, too?" And I said, "Well, would I get paid more?" He said, "No." I couldn't believe he was asking me. But I was already preparing for the other three, so I thought, *Why not?*

Maurice Sendak, who played one of the other rabbis, and I spent the whole day together. We had lunch. And he said to Tony Kushner, "When is Meryl Streep coming?" Tony said, "Schmuck! That's her."

JUSTIN KIRK (*actor*): I read in a room with Mike and Tony Kushner and Juliet Taylor and at the end of the day my agent was like, "It couldn't have gone better." I get a call a month or two later saying, "No one at HBO knows who you are. You have to go to LA and put it down on tape, so the executives can sign off." Then Mike called, which I suppose he probably did quite often, to freak a young actor out. Rather than hearing it from your agent driving around LA, probably stoned, you get a call from Mike Nichols saying, "Let's do this," in his inimitable voice. So off we went.

I have a bit of a history with Mike before that, as I would have to continuously remind him. They needed a picture of Michelle Pfeiffer's dead brother to use in *Wolf*. Ann Roth recommended me for it, so we

---

4. "Mike Nichols," *American Masters*, PBS.

shot this picture and it's in the movie. The second time was for *Birdcage*. I auditioned for the role of the son, and—I've heard that Mike could do this—he absolutely made me feel in the room as though I had gotten the part. By the time *Angels* rolled around, all was forgiven.

Early on, I was told to go to his office for lunch and he essentially said, "It's not working." And then on the very first day of shooting, he's like, "We're good. It's happening." Of course, I never lost that fear throughout the rest of the shooting.

PATRICK WILSON: I had recently left my agency, and I get this call from them saying, "Mike Nichols's office called. We told them you're no longer here." "*What?* For what?" So I called my new agent, who said, "They want you to audition for *Angels in America*." It was such a crazy long shot for me. This was not my world. I was a theater guy. But I really wasn't nervous, because there was literally no way. I heard through some friends that HBO wanted Matt Damon. So I thought, *I'll just go to have fun.* And I get to meet Mike Nichols.

I had never seen the show. I had just moved to New York when it was playing the first time, and I missed it. So while I knew of the material, this was all very fresh. It just became a very raw experience. I sat there, reading scene after scene with him. And then he goes, "I'd like you to do this."

My jaw dropped. But I had already agreed to do *Oklahoma!* on Broadway in the spring. So I had to come clean. He said, "Well, we'll work around that. I just did *Wit* for them, and they owe me one." For six months, I did double duty. I'd shoot during the day, and then go do the show at night.

BEN SHENKMAN: By the time I auditioned in 2001, I had this whole history with the play. I played Louis in a production at American Conservatory Theater from 1994 to 1995. Before that, I had played Roy Cohn in a workshop production that Tony himself had set up at NYU in 1993 when I was graduating from that program. So when I got the opportunity to meet with Mike, I found myself fantasizing about doing this amazing audition and having him say, "I'm so sorry. It's not going to work out for this one, but I'll keep you in mind for something else." I wanted to somehow not blow the audition, but also not actually *get* the role, because I just didn't feel up to it, frankly—not on the Meryl Streep level. But I went and had an amazing meeting with him, and left feeling like I am probably going to get this role, although I didn't actually get the callback until a few weeks after that.

I felt there's something intimate going on here, because of how raw and how emotional I was allowing myself to be in the performance of it, and how visibly emotional he was allowing himself to be in watching it. It made me feel like he and I are now in a dialogue about what it means to tackle this material. I had a connection with him in the audition room that already had me worrying, *How will I do that again when we're actually filming?*

I was meeting him in a kind of dramatic way—this incredible person who's part of why I'm even an actor in the first place, beginning with casting someone like Dustin Hoffman in *The Graduate*—and I was being received by him in a certain way, which I now know is the way he is with actors: how available he is, how emotional he is, what a good audience he is.

PATRICK WILSON: There's a picture that Richard Avedon took of the cast. You've got Al, Meryl, and Emma on one level. And then under them, you have Mary-Louise and Jeffrey Wright. And then on the bottom you've got me, Justin, and Ben. I remember seeing that picture and going, *Yeah, that's it right there. He's got the stars on top, he's got the medium stars on the second level, and he's got us down here.*

I remember watching Al and Mike greet each other for the first time. It was so cool watching the reverence that they had for each other, having never worked together. Mike said, "You know, I wanted you for *Catch-22.*" Then Al says, "Wait, where'd you shoot that— Mexico or something?" Mike said, "Yeah." And Al goes, "I remember the offer, because I was not in a great place. I knew that if I went to Mexico, I was going to come back in a pine box."

AL PACINO: I had my eyes on Milo Minderbinder, and he offered me another role. I would have loved to have played it, but I had another commitment.

JUSTIN KIRK: We had a couple months of rehearsal which were mostly sitting around a table and him telling great stories about Warren Beatty or Buck Henry.

MARY-LOUISE PARKER: He did a lot of his directing in the rehearsal hall speaking through anecdotes and getting people tonally in the same range. We would agree on the event that took place in a scene, and the relationships, things like that. Then he would be open to what happened on the day. He wanted to see what people would bring to it and didn't want to get in the way of that. He knew when to jump in and say the right thing at the right moment, and when not to say anything. He was really *with* what was in front of him. That's what made him feel so youthful even into his eighties.

He treated one talented person like another talented person, if they were nice. Hierarchy really isn't useful in a rehearsal hall. I said to somebody recently that it was good that it wasn't my first job, because I might have thought that that's how all jobs were. It would have ruined me forever.

PATRICK WILSON: Every actor, every creative person on that set was of equal value. That's how Mike treated his actors. He knew that the best performance that an actor's going to give is going to come from their heart, and it's his job to guide that. We got Mike at a very creative and happy time in his life, I believe.

JEFFREY WRIGHT: We spent days, weeks perhaps, just around the table, a wonderfully inordinate amount of time, reading through the script and talking about it and trying to mine down, through all of its complexity and layers and nuance, to understand what these stories were that we were telling. It's to Mike's credit that he recognized that had to be done, and that he was able to ensure that the production accommodated that. Material like this lends itself to all manner of tangential conversations about politics and society, and he was the orchestrator and conductor of those conversations.

TONY KUSHNER[5]**:** There's no such thing as an unpressured rehearsal, because there's never enough time to rehearse. But Mike could make you feel like there would always be enough time to get done what needed to get done.

I certainly saw Mike give exquisite bits of direction. But you don't want to burden them with nine hundred things they have to remember while they're pretending to be somebody they're not and a giant machine is pushing in on their face to record them, and people are in the background drinking coffee. Mike was Prospero. He's constantly saying to the actors, "I want you to do this little thing but then you're going to be free," reminding them that ultimately it was theirs, it belonged to them. His method was very much one of freeing people.

BEN SHENKMAN: When he directs you, he tells stories about himself—not in an indulgent way, but in a creative way—to blur the line between the performer as a human being and the performer as a trained professional, which is something I know he borrowed from Kazan. Kazan was a hero of his, and like Kazan, Mike invited actors to become more personal by volunteering personal things himself. Also, Mike's history of translating plays to film, that was very alive in him.

He'd met everyone. He had a front-row seat in media and entertainment and culture and politics for about four decades. So there was no one you could think of—*Jackie Onassis? Kissinger?* You could go on and on. *Paul McCartney?* And he'd have some delicious nugget of a story. It was impossible not to just sit there asking, "What about this person? What about that person?" I had to constantly restrain myself.

I'm a mimic by nature, but he is someone you cannot be around without wanting to sound like. He is a performer from way back and he knows how what he is saying lands, even if he's not doing it consciously anymore. The way he talks is just perfectly musically calibrated to deliver the idea with the maximum amount of delightfulness—that's why you remember things he said verbatim.

---

5. "Mike Nichols," *American Masters*, PBS.

EMMA THOMPSON: Ben Shenkman does the best Mike imitation.

JUSTIN KIRK: If you watch the scene at the end where I go up to heaven, the big council of all the angels, Ben's doing Mike as the angel.

MARY-LOUISE PARKER: I remember walking onto the set the first day, wondering if something was wrong, because it was so quiet. I've never been on a set that was that quiet. And then I realized, *Oh my God, it's just that no one is in a hurry. No one is anxious.* It was like being in church, but a fun church.

MIKE HALEY: *Angels in America* was a 183-day shooting schedule. We came in at 182.

BEN SHENKMAN: We shot April through late September, including all of Pacino's work in both parts, because that's when they had him, and then a break for about a month; then October through December for part two, and then another break; and in January, we went to the Villa Adriana in Rome to film the heaven sequences. If you think of that as three or four feature films, which the running time is the equivalent of, it's a reasonably efficient shooting schedule. Though he never said, "We're running out of time." If you said, "Can I do another one?" the answer was always, "Of course."

It was a very un-Hollywood experience, making it. Even though it had these incredible Hollywood people involved, it felt very outside of that culture because of the nature of the material, and the fact that we were shooting it in New York, under the protective umbrella of Mike Nichols. One time when something had gone wrong involving catering, I remember a makeup artist saying, "Isn't this a Mike Nichols set, where you walk on brie?"

PATRICK WILSON: He would get famous people to sing on your birthday. He got Barbara Cook to come sing for me. And then on Meryl's birthday he got Joshua Bell to come play violin. He got Nancy Sinatra for Al.

JUSTIN KIRK: I think Tony Bennett was for Al Pacino, if I remember correctly. I had Nancy Sinatra. You're eating lunch on your birthday, and suddenly Nancy Sinatra shows up. You don't get that on most gigs.

One day Emma was about to get on a plane and a big group of Scottish bagpipers showed up. And she wasn't even wrapping the fucking movie—just leaving for a month or two!

EMMA THOMPSON: You have to annotate the context, otherwise you'd just think Mike had lost his marbles. At the end of *Wit*, I was lying naked on a table and he made a speech to the crew, and he forgot to thank me. And I went back to my trailer and I thought, *Oh, that's odd.* When he realized what he'd done, first of all, he rang Diane, who just said, "Oh dear!" And then he came into my trailer and he said, "Do you know why I forgot? Because you're part of me, and so I don't separate you out anymore." It was such a beautiful thing to say, and meant so much more than anything he could have said publicly—that somehow we were one in some way, creatively.

So he made up for it on *Angels*. For my birthday, he organized a Scottish pipe band in kilts, a goofball choir, Audra McDonald, and a fucking huge ice angel! It was hilarious, absolutely hilarious.

MIKE HALEY: For Mike's birthday, we set up Diana Krall on a stage with a piano at lunchtime.

MERYL STREEP[6]**:** Mike seemed not to be daunted. Maybe he was, but I never saw that. You have a very important piece, and you feel the responsibility to everybody who ever had AIDS. But it's funny. And funny is where stuff goes into your heart. It's how the toughest stuff is able to be rendered. So even when the material was really hard, he was always buoyant. It just felt like, *Well, of course this is possible. It's not that big a deal.* But it was. It was an incredibly ambitious piece.

---

6. "Mike Nichols," *American Masters*, PBS.

JEFFREY WRIGHT: Occasionally he would ask me, "What did you guys do? What did George [Wolfe] do?" This is the Mount Everest of pieces. It takes a Sherpa to climb this thing. It was a monster of a project and he wanted everyone's pack to be fully stuffed as we went marching on. There weren't going to be a lot of pit stops.

PATRICK WILSON: I remember the chatter: *Wait a second—this play is so important to the gay community, and how many of these people are straight?* And the way he dealt with that with us is: It's about love. It's about who you love and your own demons that you're battling. So it became less about sexuality, and who was gay and who was straight. I think that freed us up to just go for it.

TONY KUSHNER[7]: He wasn't looking for some big idea that he was going to shove home with the audience. He never said, "I want to make this about AIDS," or "I want to make this about Reagan." The meaning of his work—and I think his work is spectacularly rich and generative of meaning—comes from a deep engagement with the particulars. There's no overreaching agenda. It lives in the discreet moments. When the film was finally completed, it felt to me a story of relationships. As a man of the theater, Mike knew that's where the drama lives. These are embodied, incarnated ideas, and they're only going to work to the extent that you care about the people, and believe the stakes are very high.

PATRICK WILSON: Once a week, sometimes twice a week, I would get these calls from Al's office: "Hey, can you come up to Nola Studios?" So I go up, just me and Al. And we just worked through the scene. Because that's how he had to work. He had to get it up on its feet and do it. There was never any ego. If I wanted to do a scene again, it was, "Sure, let's try it again." It was awesome. I loved every minute that I spent with him.

AL PACINO: My only problem I had with *Angels* is that I didn't do it

---

7. Ibid.

onstage, and it is a role that demands the appropriate rehearsal. In the theater, you find the richness, the voluptuousness in these kinds of roles that I would call actor-proof. Thank God for Mike Nichols's guidance, but I always thought if I had to do it over again I would have taken it off-off-Broadway or out of town for a four-week run just to get it in me. It was my first run-in with shortcut acting. You only do something like that with a great cast and Mike Nichols at the helm. It was surviving, not thriving. But yes, I enjoyed working with Patrick and the whole cast and especially the great Jeffrey Wright who literally donated his time to me, because he was so consummate and had done it a couple times on Broadway. Mike had given us an outline in terms of staging and we familiarized ourselves in terms of where things where and who we were together and that environment allowed me to at least bring in a salvageable performance, but I still wished I had played it somewhere first.

BEN SHENKMAN: When we did the scene where Prior reveals the KS lesion on his arm, that was a scene I was kind of dreading. I went to Mike's trailer beforehand and he said, "Look, here's how I wanna shoot it." Line by line, he had an idea of how I would put my head down and cry on Prior's shoulder. It was extremely choreographed, and I was grateful for the structure. Other scenes, the way he worked was as far from that as possible. It was like, *Let's see what happens,* or he'd come in with an adjustment, or you'd have a conversation seemingly about something else and then, lo and behold, you shoot the scene and it has some content in it that it didn't have before. I asked him to play me the scene a little later, and he said sure, and I was moved as an audience member, watching it all cut together. And he said, "See? Nothing to be ashamed of."

Those emotional scenes were often particularly fraught for me as an actor. I would think, "Will I have full access to my emotions in the way that I need to?" And Nichols, who was aware of this struggle in me, was constantly trying to take that pressure off. I'd say, "This is bad. I'm pushing." He'd say, "Push!" I'd say, "No, it feels fake." He'd say, "Fake it! It's the movies!"

He was trying to say, this is how the sausage is made. I've been with them all, all the legends. Don't fuck yourself over by thinking it has to be this pure thing; you're getting in your own way. I thought it was all about having to be real and absolutely authentic. He'd say, "No, you've got that backward. You've forgotten about editing."

JUSTIN KIRK: I had some stupid idea for a particular scene I was doing and he said, "It would be like putting a hat on a hat." I've used that one since.

BEN SHENKMAN: He would always say, "The thing that the audience is constantly asking you is: Why are you telling me this?"

JEFFREY WRIGHT: One of his favorite expressions—which I still wrestle with at times—was "Life isn't everything."

PATRICK WILSON: With me, it was just tiny suggestions: "At the end of the scene you have to say, 'I'm a homosexual.' Try *not* saying that."

The scene where I make that phone call, I get out of the show, and *Oklahoma!*'s not like a one-act, so I was getting to set at like eleven thirty at night. I get in a car, and I drive up to Central Park. And I see all of Central Park West lit up like a Christmas tree, for twenty blocks. I went up to Mike and said, "Wow, look at all this. What's going on over there?" And he says, "That's for you."

JEFFREY WRIGHT: I was doing *Topdog/Underdog* at night on Broadway. It was pretty insane. I was just grinding through it. My son was eighteen months, two years old at the time. But I was exactly where I wanted to be.

AL PACINO: Everything Mike said or did—the way he moved, the atmosphere he created on a set, anything he did—it was all direction. When he talked about what he had for breakfast in the morning, it was direction—what's in the news, *The Osbournes* . . . Mike Nichols—I cannot say enough—loved him, still do.

TONY KUSHNER[8]: Nobody had ever really solved what these enormously powerful angels should be wearing in heaven. Ann Roth brought all these magnificent costumes and furs and leathers, just planeloads full of gorgeous things, over to Rome. And like a day before we started filming, Mike suddenly announced to me, "I think we're going to try just filming it with them in their rehearsal clothes." I was horrified at first. I thought, *That's insane.* But then we started doing it, and suddenly we're seeing Meryl and Emma and all these people in their normal clothes. It pulls you into a very complicated and challenging place. It makes you wonder, *Why, at this moment, are they stripped of all frippery?* And of course the answer is because they're getting to know absolute horror; it's not more smoke and mirrors, it's just these people talking. I thought that was a stunning, very daring choice.

Again, this is somebody who understands that one of the most powerful things in theater is that it can't help playing with illusion and reality. The more it tends to create a reality onstage, the more it challenges you to see behind the reality to the trickery that's doing it, because it's right there in front of you. Failing at illusion is almost as important in theater as succeeding at it. It teaches you to look at things in a double way, and Mike understands that.

JOHN BLOOM (*film editor*): Mike, to say the least, had style. He had taken some offices just opposite Carnegie Hall. It was the most luxurious suite of cutting rooms I'd ever seen in my whole life, and no doubt would ever see again. He didn't tangle his Oscars and posters and so forth all around the place—just nice pieces of art, as I remember. If he had the money, my God, he spent it. He was the most generous man you could ever imagine. A Château Rothschild 1982 or something, which cost, I don't know, a couple of thousand dollars, would be a Christmas present. After *Angels,* however successful it had been, I think he started to get a bit nervous about the amount of money he was spending, and we had to give up those rooms.

---

8. "Mike Nichols," *American Masters*, PBS.

Some executive had seen a cut of the film and was thrilled, but had quite a few suggestions, which he aired most diplomatically, because Mike had final cut. There were some very good suggestions, and some very bad ones, but a lot of them were at least worth trying. Mike absolutely, point blank, refused to do any of them. He was not interested in other people's opinions, except his friends'.

BARRY DILLER: Mike once said to me, "Can you believe that person tried to give me *notes*? I don't take notes," though he didn't say it that way. It wasn't arrogant. He was bewildered that anyone would give him, quote, notes. Because he was clever and manipulative, he tended to always get his way.

COLIN CALLENDER: The best thing you can do for a Mike Nichols is give him the resources he needs to do his work and then get out of the way. We didn't give a single script note on *Angels*. He knew what he wanted, and what's on the screen is what he wanted.

BEN SHENKMAN: They arranged a screening of it in the Brill Building for whoever of the cast was available. I think Justin was in LA, but Patrick and Mary-Louise and Jeffrey and I went, and watched part one, and then had a little catered lunch and then went back and watched part two. I remember first seeing the title sequence and hearing the music and thinking, *Oh my God, it's almost too beautiful.* It was fully an hour before the adrenaline in my body would allow my legs to stop shaking.

MARY-LOUISE PARKER: I don't watch my own work, so it was a little hard for me, but I was so wowed by it. And I think Mike was really proud of it, though it's not like he took credit for it. He felt like it was a collaborative thing, but of course, it was his. It wouldn't have been that *Angels* with any single other director. He understood the humanity of it and the poetry of it equally.

JEFFREY WRIGHT: I thought to myself, *Wow, he did it.* And he did it beautifully. There were some others who might have been able to pull that off, but not many. And in this lifetime, it was him.

JOHN LAHR: His film is the definitive rendition of that play. It's a marvel of condensation.

JACK O'BRIEN: He called me to see a screening of *Angels in America*. And at the end of it I turned to him and I said, "Not only do I think this may be the best thing you've ever done, it may be the best thing anybody's ever done." And he burst into tears.

I do stand by that, by the way. I knew all those people very well, and they have rarely been better.

TOM STYRON: The premiere was at a big theater on the East Side—I think it was the Beekman. I was standing outside, and I saw Mike's car arrive and go down the side street. He got out and walked as unobtrusively as he could into the theater to take his seat, in contrast to the other high-wattage celebrities pulling up in their limousines in front of the paparazzi.

JOHN BLOOM: If somebody had dropped a bomb in the room, half of New York's intelligentsia and financial sector would have been destroyed. We had these amazing people coming to a screening, not realizing in fact that they were in for about six hours. It was a great thing for these extraordinary power people to spend six or seven hours at one screening. We ran part one, and then went around to a local Thai restaurant around the corner from the screening, and dinner was laid on, and then we trooped back again. So it wasn't actually six hours without a break, but it was still very long.

I sat next to Richard Avedon. When the curtain came down after part five, he got up to leave, and I had to lean over and say, "I'm afraid there's another hour still to go." He said, "Oh, okay," and sat down again.

COLIN CALLENDER: *Angels* broke the record previously held by *Roots* for most Emmys awarded to a program in a single year: eleven awards from twenty-one nominations.

JOHN BLOOM: I think it was a sort of rebirth of Mike's career. He started with two masterpieces. In between were some good films, and some bad films, of which he was more than aware. To rise like a phoenix once again, for him, was very important. To sock it to 'em: *This is what I'm capable of doing.* He never expressed it openly, but you could see it.

RICHARD PLEPLER: At the premiere, Diane came up to me and said, "Thank you for giving my husband 'more life,'" which, of course, was a reference to one of the key lines in the play. As Kushner explains in the notes to *Perestroika*, "more life" is Harold Bloom's translation of the Hebrew word for blessing.

BEN SHENKMAN: In 2010, I was at a screening of Philip Seymour Hoffman's movie *Jack Goes Boating*, and I saw Nichols outside. I asked him if he'd seen the revival of *Angels* at the Signature Theatre. And he said, "Yes. They're all brilliant. But it's ours now." I got a full-body chill. He was saying, *This is a great production, but we made the movie.* He did once say to me, "I think we've made something that will outlive us."

I think the play dramatizes characters struggling with being a good person, being fully human, being compassionate. Even Roy Cohn, in a strange way, is a meditation on what morality is or isn't. I think that resonated with Mike, who had to teach himself to be a better person.

RICHARD PLEPLER: We're living in a very, very trying moment. It's too mean. There's too much invective, vitriol, too much hatred. The best antidote to that are our artists. They're our last best hope, and I think that Mike understood that. I think he basically understood that in the end, the only thing that works is love, and art is our last best hope. I think Mike felt, *The best way for me to take on Roy Cohn is not in a public fight or in an election—it's through art.*

TONY KUSHNER[9]**:** He was basically his grandfather's grandson. He was, at heart, a kind of anarchist. I think he had a great mistrust of government and of politicians. He felt that most people who lead us are probably not entirely fit to do so. And he was very skeptical, in an enormously pleasant and entertaining and civilized way, but he was a

9. "Mike Nichols," *American Masters*, PBS.

skeptic. And I think his view of human beings in general was that we're all sinful and corruptible *and* completely delightful and wonderful, some of us more so than others. He didn't love everybody equally. But I think he saw human frailty and failure as being part of what makes people precious and dear, not as something to be despised or denied.

I think he was a liberal with a powerful social conscience. He paid great attention to what was going on. Injustice upset him. Oppression was an anathema to him. I think to the extent that he believed art could contribute to political struggle, he wanted his art to be on the side of history, the side of the good and the just and the righteous, and not to contribute to the problem. But Mike had a feeling, that I share to a large extent, that the power of art is an indirect power. That if you're making art, your job is to make the art as good as you can on its own terms, and not to pretend to be making art while you're really making a polemic or propaganda. At one point I wrote a scene with all these fantastical places that Prior should go through on his way to heaven: a hospital waiting room full of people with KS lesions in various stages and then people from Africa . . . Mike read it and said, "I'm really moved by this, but it's going to look like a public service announcement. It would be worthy as a PSA, but it's not drama." And we never spoke of it again.

COLIN CALLENDER: The story of *Angels in America* was Mike's own life story. In the opening scene, the rabbi talks about the grandmother coming from the shtetl, and says there are no more journeys like this anymore. But that was Mike Nichols's journey. I've often said that directors' greatest work tends to be about themselves, and in many ways, so many of the themes both in *Wit* and *Angels in America* were meditations on who Mike Nichols was as an individual and where was he in his life. *Wit* is the story of a woman who hides behind her fierce intellect and her learning and her wit and is reflecting on the price she's paid for certain choices she's made. I remember him talking about winning an Oscar and going back to the Polo Lounge at the Beverly Hills Hotel and sitting there alone, wondering, *What the fuck does this mean, really?*

And *Angels* delves into so many themes, from his own heritage to his relationship with so many people who died of AIDS. One of the last lines of the play is "We are not going away." When that was first performed, that was a sort of rallying cry. When the television version of it came out, the line was less a rallying cry and more a statement of fact: "We *are not* going away."

And in addition to all the other things that it was, it was equally his tribute to New York. New York was his city.

JEFFREY WRIGHT: The whole process for Mike seemed to me a kind of caretaking for the play as a body. There was just a meticulousness about his respect for the body that is this play, because it was representative of bodies that were meaningful for him in his life.

TONY KUSHNER[10]**:** We didn't have a lot of political discussions, which is hard for me, because everything that comes out of my mouth is fuming and ranting. And he would let me do that sometimes. But I know that in the course of his life, he showed up for some very important things. He was there for McGovern, he was there in Selma. He knew a lot of people who died of AIDS. He and Diane are amazing caretakers. When people who were really close to them got sick, the amount of time and attention that he devoted to people who really needed it was sort of astonishing. [The HIV/AIDS nonprofit] Friends in Deed was an extraordinary thing that he did.

There's a Yiddish term—a mensch is a stand-up person, somebody who's reliable and dependable. A luftmensch is somebody who's more than that: a sort of higher being. Not quite a saint—somebody who's human, but who has a kind of grace about them. Mike moved through his life with this kind of astonishing radiance and grace.

CYNTHIA O'NEAL: At the height of the AIDS epidemic, people you loved were dropping all around you. I became involved in various ways, spent a lot of time in hospitals. There was some lovely young man lying on the bed and nobody there. Their family back in Wisconsin just couldn't deal. And they got that double-barrel phone call:

---

10. "Mike Nichols," *American Masters*, PBS.

"I just want to tell you I'm gay, and I have AIDS, and I'm dying."
One phone call. I thought, there's got to be a place where we can
support these people without a lot of fear and hysteria—just be there
for them. Here were all these gorgeous young people who knew they
were dying, but where do they talk about it? It just became so clear to
me that something was desperately needed that didn't exist, because
in our wonderful culture, nobody wants to talk about death or dying.

So I thought, well, who could I talk to about this? And, of course,
the first person who came to my mind was Mike. I said, "Can we have
lunch? There's something I want to talk to you about." I told him what
I was seeing and feeling, and he listened. He really listened. When I
finished my spiel, he said, "I have been thinking that I needed to do
something, but I didn't know what to do, and you just told me. Thank
you." Those were his exact words.

Within forty-eight hours, we went to look at the space where we
could do this, and he was on the phone to friends. Harrison [Ford]
immediately responded with a most generous check. I couldn't have
put the startup money together by myself, but Mike sure did. He just
called everybody, and the money came in. And then he put together
our first fund-raiser [for Friends in Deed] at a small Broadway theater.
Simon & Garfunkel sang. That was an emotional night because they'd
really been at odds. The sense was that things were bad between
them. And then up on the stage it all got mended, you could see it. By
the end, everybody loved everybody again. God, that was wonderful.
Then Mike and Elaine performed. I think they did the rocket scientist
calling his mother. It was fantastic.

Afterward, I was walking down the long hall with Mike on our
way to dinner and I said to him, "It's not bad what we've done here,
pal." And he said, "It might be what I'm proudest of."

Mike in 2012, directing *Death of a Salesman*, two years before he died. He re-created the set from Elia Kazan's 1949 production, which Mike saw as a teenager, an experience that, together with the Kazan-directed *A Streetcar Named Desire*, changed the course of his life. *(© Brigitte Lacombe)*

CHAPTER 14

Making Friends with Death

JACK O'BRIEN: He called me the morning after the first preview of *The Country Girl*, and he said, "It's a disaster." I was stunned.

JON ROBIN BAITZ: He'd do an autopsy. He'd try and look at the tracks on the road before the crash happened, the skid marks, and deconstruct it. He would look for reasons in himself that the thing hadn't worked. In the case of *Country Girl*, he saw that it might have been as simple as a casting problem, but that didn't stop him from berating himself.

DOUGLAS McGRATH: He sat down and he wrote pages of notes about what he did wrong. The fact that he could be seventy-something and not think, *I have this many Tonys and an Oscar. They must be wrong.* But he didn't think that way. He never deceived himself into thinking that something that wasn't good was great just because he worked on it. He kept that clarity right through.

EMANUEL AZENBERG: *Country Girl* was a failure, really a disaster, and a disaster I suspect that Mike has something to do with.

I don't know who's responsible for *Salesman:* Is it Philip Seymour Hoffman? Is it the play? But it was good. It was better than good. If I'm petty envious in my life, I would have loved it if Mike called up and said, let's do *Death of a Salesman*.

PETER GALLAGHER: *Country Girl* is a difficult play to do now. And Mike was pretty preoccupied with his mortality. When you're struggling in the play, it can probably seem like a confirmation of your waning powers.

That's why I'm so happy for *Salesman*. That was *his*. And I was there closing night. I saw Phil too. It was like talking to a ghost. It was like *Long Day's Journey into Night* for real.

FRANK RICH: No one else would have found Dustin Hoffman for *The Graduate* and no one else, I think, would have felt that Phil Hoffman was ready for Willy Loman.

AUSTIN PENDLETON: Phil and I have a mutual friend, a playwright, and this guy said to me that once in a while they'd have breakfast while *Death of a Salesman* was playing, and Phil said, "I can't take this."

CANDICE BERGEN: Mike said that Phil really suffered during the rehearsal and the production and that it was sort of torturing him. And I know that Mike did everything he could to shore him up.

CHRISTINE BARANSKI: It haunted him, Phil's death. He felt that in asking him to play that part, that Phil had to call upon such a tremendous depth of darkness.

JACK O'BRIEN: Mike was fascinated by the fact that I had been part of Ellis Rabb's great production of *You Can't Take It with You*. I told Mike that Ellis had reproduced the ground plan that George S. Kaufman had used, and then he embroidered on that. He was fascinated that Ellis, at the top of his craft, chose to acquiesce to the original director. That's when he got the idea of using the original set.

GREGORY MOSHER: I said, "Don't do that. You have to get a new set, because as you're figuring out the set, you'll figure out a lot of things about the play," and he said, "No, I know what I'm doing here," and he was right. Whether he wanted to do it out of regard for the play, or as a kind of circling back to this thing that made him believe in the theater so much, I don't know.

HANNAH ROTH SORKIN: Opening night, I was the only person there who doesn't have a big Wikipedia entry.

TOM HANKS: I wept openly three times in the course of the play, and much of it was because of the younger version of Willy that Mike and Phil Hoffman brought to it. It was a devastating night in the theater. We went to Orso after and I said, "Mike, that was devastating. How did you do that?" "Oh, thank you, thank you. One of the lighting cues was off in the second act."

JOHN LAHR: As far as I'm concerned, it was absolutely the finest production of *Death of a Salesman*, and one of the high points of my theatergoing experience in New York. I've seen the play a dozen times, but I've never seen a better production, never will.

When you have a really good director with the kind of acute literary sensibility that Mike had—because Mike was a really good reader, a naturally voracious reader, he got elements in that play which are there, but it's a bit like a brass rubbing: never brought out. What you got at the end of the production was Willy's envy. The tragedy really was not only that he was not successful, his tragedy was that because of the envy, he was never even able to *be*, to inhabit his own life. He was either looking backwards or looking forwards.

JON ROBIN BAITZ: Mike went out with a triumphant *Death of a Salesman*, which I saw a bunch of times. *Salesman* was, in some way, really autobiography for him. He linked himself to it. What is a man like Mike under the surface if not deathly afraid of the Willy Loman within him? One schleps one's bag of tricks and tries to sell them, and in the background always is failure and catastrophe and starvation. I think the mythology around Willy Loman is one that Mike was very afraid of in his own life. *Am I a laughingstock? Am I over it?* I think that was kind of an act of alternate history for him, an alternate Mike Nichols in the form of Willy Loman.

TOM FONTANA: When he was directing Philip Seymour Hoffman in *Death of a Salesman*, he could not have been more deliriously happy. *Betrayal*, same thing. He was so pumped to be that young man, back in the game and really having a great time doing it. His memory was going, but my memory sucks too. He was bursting with ideas and truth about life.

RAFE SPALL (*actor*): Mike wanted *Betrayal* to be fast and sexy, because that's what he was like, and that's what Harold Pinter was like, so that's what we did, but Ben Brantley thought it was bawdy. We made it funny because Mike was so brilliantly funny and lightning quick. I just stayed quiet through most of the rehearsal period. I used to come away wishing I was 20 percent more intelligent.

I come from a theater landscape where you get a great review in the *Times*, a bad one in the *Telegraph*, and a medium one in the *London Evening Standard*, and it's even. There's not one guy who's putting a monopoly on whether something's good or not. Everyone made out like they didn't care about Brantley's review [in *The New York Times*], but after it came out, everyone was devastated, even though at the time *Betrayal* was the highest-grossing straight Broadway play in history.

TOM FONTANA: He was frustrated that he wasn't being allowed to do a feature. He very clearly said to me: "I cannot get a feature made." And I think Mike was the kind of person that—unlike Sidney Lumet, who, when he couldn't get a big studio picture was like, fine, I'll just make this indie thing—I don't think Mike was interested in the indie route.

EDWARD ST. AUBYN (*writer*): I think at one time, Mike was probably responsible for at least half my American sales. He seems to have sent my books to everyone he knew. I happened to be going to Martha's Vineyard just after we'd first met, and he and Diane gave a dinner party for me while I was there. I sat at the dinner between Diane and Caroline Kennedy, who said, "Everyone on this island is reading your book because of Mike, but I'm holding out!"—determined not to follow into the preposterous cult that Mike had started.

He wanted us to work together, and I was, of course, incredibly enthusiastic about the idea. But I'd been conceiving novels. Writing a screenplay is a whole other art to master. So we couldn't come up with an idea. There was just the desire to one day collaborate on something, which was very exciting. And then something very odd happened. Michael Jackson and Rachael Horovitz came over and pitched themselves as producers for the TV series of the Patrick Melrose novels. And I chose them, among other people who wanted to do it, and I'm delighted by the results. I'd sent them an email when they were flying back saying, "Okay, you've got it." And Mike rang while they were on the plane and said, "I realize that what I really want to do with you is make the Melroses." But my email was floating over JFK waiting to land on their devices when they switched them on. I'd already made them a promise. It was so strange and devastating, because I would have loved to work with Mike.

RICHARD PLEPLER: David Geffen called me and said, "I think I can get *Master Class*. Here's the talent: Mike and Meryl." I said, "Done." David had to get the rights from Faye Dunaway. It was his idea; he packaged it. I remember reading the play and thinking about the two of them, and thinking, *This is going to be quintessential HBO.*

DAVID HYDE PIERCE: I heard that Mike was going to be directing this HBO movie *Master Class*, based on the play by Terrence McNally, with Meryl Streep playing Maria Callas, and I told my agent, "Look, I'm way too old for this part, and he may not want me to do it, but I do play the piano." The pianist has no lines virtually, but I just thought the idea of being in that room with the two of them would be so incredible.

CYNTHIA O'NEAL: I remember thinking, there's no way Mike is going to die before doing *Master Class* with Meryl. Because that was like heaven. Meryl, he was just mad about her. "I am in her thrall," he once said. Well, if you're gonna be in someone's thrall, that's a good one to be in.

BARRY DILLER: He was prepping *Master Class* and he was also doing some play with Scott Rudin, but Mike said several times to me that he was thinking of quitting and not really working anymore, certainly as a director. It was just a period of steady weakening.

BUCK HENRY: Lincoln Center did a Nichols appreciation evening. You go up on the stage and try to be funny while you're raining endless compliments on this person. And at the end of our ass-kissing, Mike takes the microphone and says a paragraph about every one of his friends, each much more interesting than what we had to say about him. He shortstopped us.

NATHAN LANE: He was being honored at Lincoln Center, and when he got up, he said, "Where's Dustin Hoffman? Dustin Hoffman not showing up at this is like the monster not showing up at a dinner for Dr. Frankenstein."

DOUGLAS McGRATH: During one of our calls from the editing room on *Becoming Mike Nichols*, where we'd just sort of chat away, he said, "To tell you the truth, I think most directors do their best work early. I did. I think *The Graduate* is my best film." I nearly dropped the phone. I think it's his best film too, but I didn't think he would admit it. I said, "Do you think there are great filmmakers who end up doing good work later?" and he said, "It's really a young man's game in many ways, because of the energy that it takes." I said, "You know who I thought made a great film at the end of his career was John Huston with *The Dead*." He said, "You're right! You're right. *The Dead*. It's great." And I said, "And you know who else made a great film right at the end? William Wyler with—" and he goes, "*Funny Girl!* Oh my God, *Funny Girl*. Amazing." He had his theory, but he wasn't rigid about it.

ERIC FISCHL: Mike was relatively young when he was plugging into the young generation, and then he stayed true to what his experience showed him, which is something that has inspired me. As he's getting older, the characters are getting older, the relationships are getting more complex. There's such bravery in that because—I certainly know it's true in art, and I'm sure it's true in the movies—when you become known for something, they just want you to keep doing it. I think he was disappointed that his later work didn't achieve the same sort of acclaim. But it was still so skillful, so significant. This guy really believed in theater, in literature, in bringing quality to the masses.

STEVE MARTIN: As we get older we either become our worst selves or our best selves, and I think Mike became his best self and had learned so many lessons in life that he actually absorbed. I just remember being struck: *You were never kind to producers before . . .*

GREGORY MOSHER[1]**:** People who had traumatic childhoods build up walls around themselves through fame and through their dress, and all of those kinds of things. But Mike, while he may have those walls, has thousands of doors through the walls. And he marches in and out and invites people inside the walls constantly. So it's not that they aren't there, but they're porous, these walls. And he works hard to make them porous.

CHRISTINE BARANSKI: Mike told a story about his flying to his daughter's school in Switzerland to see her in a school play. She saw him and said, "Dad, it was last night." And he literally teared up—it was a pain he could never get over. To be creative at that level, to be a great artist, you must always be haunted by the fact that you're fundamentally selfish, for the world comes to you.

EMMA THOMPSON: Because he was intellectually so able, he could be very mean, and that's something I think is very important to acknowledge. We're not talking about some sort of saint here. We're talking about a person who was very, very aware of his own foibles and his own failings.

CANDICE BERGEN: He always knew when he misbehaved, and he regretted it. I don't remember which play he was directing, maybe

---

1. Courtesy of the John Lahr collection at the Howard Gotlieb Archival Research Center, Boston University.

it was *Hurlyburly*, but he had said something to one of the ushers, a sarcastic remark, and she said, "You always expect the worst from us, Mr. Nichols." He berated himself for the way he could diminish people and demean them.

JACK O'BRIEN: He fired people. He humiliated people when he could do it. He was not proud of his past.

DOUGLAS McGRATH: He said, "I've been reaching out to people and trying to make amends."

PAUL SIMON: Having experienced similar career arcs, I could say this: it's very hard when you're in your midthirties, with an extraordinary amount of fame and praise, to be nice. I wasn't very nice. I think if you asked him in his midthirties, *Do you think of yourself as a nice guy?*, he would've said, I do. It takes you a while, maybe decades, before you start to describe yourself in the way that he did. He became a very caring guy with a little bit of a sentimental streak, which was probably always there.

JEFFREY SWEET: Audiences tend to imagine that the values expressed in a director's films are, in fact, the values of the director. This was very much the case with Frank Capra. When his autobiography came out in 1971, I wrote to Capra care of his publisher. To my surprise, I got a short letter back (which, like an idiot, I misplaced). "Dear Mr. Sweet. I hope you will take your inspiration from my films and not from my life."

The Graduate, Catch-22, and *Carnal Knowledge* in particular overtly challenged a lot of received values of those who came of age in the wake of World War II. I think Mike was aware that people would expect to see a correlation between his perspective in these films— comedy fueled by moral outrage—and his behavior. And I think that as he became aware that some of his personal behavior was out of sync with the values his work expressed, he determined to become the person who was entitled to do that work.

MERYL STREEP[2]: Earlier in his career, I saw him sort of level people. I remember thinking, *Whew, thank God that isn't me.* Because he could do more with smiling disdain than anybody could with a Gatling gun. It would always be something that would make the entire crew laugh, except for the person it was aimed at. After Diane—AD—he was happy and he was grateful, and much kinder.

JON ROBIN BAITZ: During lunch at Marea, he said to me, "I've hurt so many people. I'm at this point now in my life where I'm just taking stock." He was talking about promises that he never lived up to, things he said he would do that he didn't, people whose dreams had been probably raised and then broken by Mike in some way. I said, "I think life goes on, Mike. It's just you sitting there with this toxicity about it." But he said, "I just can't let it go." David Geffen, who happened to be in the restaurant, came over and said, "Look at what *I've* done to people. You're a saint!"

DAVID GEFFEN: Mike used to worry that he hadn't behaved as well as he could have. I used to say to him, "Give yourself a break, for Chrissake. You have this in common with humanity. They have forgotten it, or they have forgiven you, I promise you—none of these things matter that much." But they did to Mike, because he knew when he was not behaving at his highest level. I said to him once that there was a line in a Jackson Browne song he ought to hear which says, "Please don't confront me with my failures, I have not forgotten them." After he married Diane, he was the happiest that he'd ever been. He always said that and meant it. He said, "I finally got it right."

EDWARD ST. AUBYN: Mike would tell this, to me, unbelievable story that he'd once been a difficult person but Diane's love had transformed him. There would be tears in his eyes when he talked about her. I'm very unused to seeing couples who are in stable, deep love

---

2. "Mike Nichols," *American Masters*, directed by Elaine May, produced by Julian Schlossberg, season 30, episode 1, aired January 29, 2016, on PBS.

with each other. I found that really touching as a possibility that really hadn't crossed my mind, not being very good at secure attachment.

To someone who had a rather troubled relationship with his father, Mike was like an antidote to this snakebite that was suddenly administered rather late in the day—and I felt completely cured. It was possible to love an older man and not be paranoid, or denigrating, or anxious.

ROSE STYRON: We didn't see much of them the last couple years. I hadn't realized how sick he was. I think the last time that I was with him for more than a day might have been on the Vineyard, in late August or September before he died. It was a big anniversary for *The Graduate* and they asked Mike to come and talk all about the making of the movie. If there was a name he couldn't remember, he would say, "Diane, who was it that I said that to?" Diane was in the front row and she'd give him a cue and then he'd go on. It was very funny.

ROBERT NICHOLS: Did you see how fragile he was accepting the last Tony he got on television? He wasn't himself, and I was worried. I called or emailed Diane that he didn't look right. He was so fragile. She gave me an interesting explanation. Mike had been on the outs with Mandy Patinkin for years—I think most of the out was on Patinkin's side, because Mike had dropped him from a movie—and they had just made up. Patinkin came up to him at the Tony Awards ceremony and congratulated him and hugged him and tears were shed. Mike was very moved, and right then and there he had to go up and get the award and speak. Diane put it down to that: he was emotionally fragile because years of hostility had resolved itself into an emotional reunion. But he wasn't himself when he spoke. Diane was kind of excusing away his obvious physical frailty from his terminal illness. He was not well at all the last couple of years.

JAMIE BERNSTEIN: "Love me, love my cough," he'd say.

SUSAN FORRISTAL: Greg Mosher, his girlfriend, and Mike and I went to a Brecht play in the bowels of the East Village. And Mike started to cough. Oh my God, that *cough*—it was so frightening. You could tell it was really serious. Finally the intermission came and Greg says, "I think we should leave," and Mike goes, "I can't leave, they're expecting me to come backstage and that would mean I didn't like the play." Then he wanted to go to dinner. We kept saying, "Go home! You've got to go home! Let's skip dinner." And he kept saying, "No, because then Diane would know, and I won't be let out again."

LIZ SMITH: He wanted to go out every night, and she never wanted to go out. Then, maybe in the last year, he knew he was sick, and Diane began appearing with him in public.

RAFE SPALL: Mike had a really bad chest when we were doing *Betrayal*. He would have these coughing fits that would go on for ages. Mike came to every single preview, but when the show opened, he didn't come for a long time. He'd gotten very ill. Gravely ill, I thought, but it didn't turn out to be so at that time. He came back again near the end.

CANDICE BERGEN: We saw him diminish physically. I mean, as brilliant as he was, he was not going to think his way out of it.

ANJELICA HUSTON: He sat beside me at a dinner and he just seemed in a really good place. I told him that I was seeing somebody, but that I hadn't been out with anyone since my husband died and I was feeling a bit fragile. He just looked at me and said, "Go for it." That was Mike. He wanted everyone to be as happy as he was.

CHRISTINE BARANSKI: I can't tell you how many times in those last years I'd get together with him, and his eyes would fill with tears and he'd say, "I just can't believe how lucky I am." His life really did come to this graceful denouement.

JAMES GRISSOM: Mike said, "I think I belong in the game, but if we start talking about the biggest jewel in my crown, it's luck."

WALLACE SHAWN: He wasn't just lucky. He was someone who had the capacity to see his own luck and enjoy it. An awful lot of people who are lucky don't recognize it and make everybody else sick by complaining about their lot when everyone else knows they've had such great luck. Mike was very, very well aware of being a lucky person. He was passionately grateful for his having found Diane. I think he was aware every minute that Hitler might have cut off his life before he was ten years old.

PEGGY NOONAN: I walked into his and Diane's apartment once, and I was just standing in the living room looking at everything, and I noticed a chair, and on the chair was a pillow, and embroidered on the pillow were the words *Nothing is written*. And Mike pointed excitedly and said, "Do you know what that is?" And I said "Lawrence of Arabia." And he said, "Yes!"

ROBERT NICHOLS: I had read something in a review of a Gore Vidal novel: "The happiest of lives are only splendid wrecks of what used to be a future." It wasn't true for Mike. He didn't regard his life as a splendid wreck of what used to be a future. It was the culmination of one.

CANDICE BERGEN: I knew that when he was in the last three or four years he was feeling, you just don't want it to end.

CHRISTINE BARANSKI: We were talking about how you face the end, how you face frailty, and how you face physical decline. Mike talked about how in one of those Nordic countries people, literally, they get together with their family members, they have a wonderful meal, and they go to bed surrounded by their loved ones and say, "Okay, that's a wrap. Cut." He said, "That's what I want."

JOHN LAHR: I asked him how he was and he said that he was "making friends with death." Typical Mike to turn a phrase and make a startling psychological statement.

CANDICE BERGEN: He would joke about it when it was far enough off. He said, "Buck and I have agreed that we should edit each other's memorial clip reels," but then as it got closer, he said, "I don't want anything."

ERIC FISCHL: The last time I saw Mike was particularly sad. There was a show of degenerate art up at the Neue Galerie, so I said, "Hey, do you want to go and check it out?" As I'm walking across the park to meet him I get a call from Diane, who says, "Don't say that I called you, but could you please come and pick him up?" It was closed that day, but we arranged to get a tour from the curator, so it was incredibly quiet—it was just us. And we start going through and the curator's talking, and pretty soon Mike is moving ahead. He's moving into the next room and the next, and I'm thinking he's probably looking for a place to sit down, but he wasn't. When he came back, you could see he was devastated. But then he started to talk to me about how he was in Berlin at the time and his father had left for America. The mother stayed behind—she wasn't strong enough to travel. He was left with a kindergarten teacher who took care of him while his mom was in the hospital, and she watched out for him and hid him as the stuff was beginning to really unfold. And then when he and his mother finally left, the schoolteacher was arrested. That was the end of her. All these memories were flooding back to him. I was apologizing profusely—the last thing I wanted was to bring him back to that place—and he was like, "No, no, no. It's good to remember."

NATALIE PORTMAN: The last time I saw him was when I showed him my movie [*A Tale of Love and Darkness*] in our editing room. The movie's in Hebrew, and takes place during the creation of the State of Israel. This was about three weeks before he passed away. He was crying at the end, and then he started laughing or smiling while he was crying, and he said, "I've been such a bad Jew."

PETER GALLAGHER: A couple weeks before he died, we all met—Mike, Tom, Christine, a bunch of us—at the revival of *The Real Thing*, which was opening at the Roundabout Theatre. I could tell that there was a part of him that was a bit relieved that maybe his production might not be obliterated entirely from people's memories. He was in the fifth or sixth row, next to Stoppard, and we were a couple rows behind. And then just after the curtain went up on the second act came this deep, heavy cough. I remember thinking, *This is the last time I'm going to see you alive, Mike.*

CHRISTINE BARANSKI: I emailed him and I said, "I have a few days off from *The Good Wife*. What about lunch?" And he said, "Well, it just so happens that Thursday is my birthday." I said, "Great. Should we get some folks together?" I had gotten in touch with Cynthia Nixon, who was playing Charlotte in the revival of *The Real Thing*. I said, "Cynthia, are you around? It's Mike's birthday." She said, "What about Glenn?" Suddenly, Glenn was onboard. Then Cynthia said, "What about Whoopi?" Whoopi, by some miracle, was also free.

So there he was at his favorite restaurant, Marea, thinking it was me and his old friend Jamie Niven. He walks in and there are four actresses from the year 1984. He held court. It must have been a three- or four-hour lunch. It could have gone on for six. Two weeks to the day, he passed away.

DAVID GEFFEN: We would always go to breakfast at the Gramercy Park Hotel, or lunch, at either Marea or someplace he read about which we would only go to once. The next time we'd go back to Marea. He always sat in the corner table when you walk in. Anyway, he picked me up. This was days before he died. I got into the backseat of his car, and we kissed—we always kissed—and I said, "You look terrific." He said, "I feel like I'm on borrowed time."

CANDICE BERGEN: We all saw it coming. Diane kept him alive for longer than he should have been, and sorted out the mess of doctors. I saw him the day before he died. We had lunch together with a friend and he gave me a lift home and he said, "I'm just going to have a routine procedure. I'll be home tomorrow afternoon." And I said, "Okay, I'll talk to you then." There are no routine procedures.

WALLACE SHAWN: It's a fortunate thing to die in a good mood. He had all sorts of plans.

SUSAN FORRISTAL: He died with a full dance card. Everyone you talked to had just seen him.

MARLO THOMAS: It's like that wonderful Auden poem "Funeral Blues": "Stop all the clocks, cut off the telephone . . . Let the traffic policemen wear black cotton gloves." Everything is less. Of course, life goes on, but when somebody makes an impression on your heart, you think the lights should dim a little bit. It's a way of saying something is lacking.

CANDICE BERGEN: Since the loss of my husband, he was the biggest loss by far.

PETER GALLAGHER: I never cried when my father died. My dad, he wasn't much of a talker. But I cried when Mike died. The feeling I had was, there's nobody left to impress.

MIKE HALEY: I never could figure out why I got along with him, why he selected me to be with him. He always was the kind of guy who liked people with pedigree and class and here I am, just a blue-collar kid. Here was a man who was almost from another planet, and yet we had this very strange connection. The last time I saw him was at lunch. I don't want to use the word "ethereal," but it was as if I knew and he knew that this was going to be it. I opened up to him about my feelings, what he meant to me, and he opened up too.

He's the only man even beyond my father who I may have to say I love. He actually asked me once, when we were driving, he said, "What do you think happens when we die?" I told him I had my philosophies about what happens, and I said, "What do you think?" He said, "We wake up in our dreams." We still work on movies in my dreams. Sometimes it's fun, sometimes it's insane, but he's there and I'm always happy to see him. He's with me constantly.

TOM STOPPARD: It was the most wrenching bereavement I can ever remember experiencing. I'm not reconciled to it yet. You just want to carry on thinking he's up there high on the East Side, going into the Met, and going downtown to see a play.

ART GARFUNKEL: I can't stand that New York doesn't have Mike. To me, the entire New York, the whole culture that I live in—which is pathetic in this age anyway, but it had some lovely stars, and the loveliest of us all is no longer there.

JULIA ROBERTS: It's his voice that I miss and I can hear it so clearly in my mind, and it's really comforting sometimes to be able to hear it so clearly, like he's right next to me.

ERIC IDLE: I miss him so much because—well, just to be able to pick up the phone—sometimes I'll think of a funny line, and I'll go, "Oh, I have to tell Mike!" He was a great appreciator.

BOB BALABAN: What was he, eighty-three when he died? He didn't seem any older to me than he did when he was thirty-five. But he did seem wiser, he did seem happier. I think Diane Sawyer had a lot to do with that. His own evolution never stopped.

ROSE STYRON: I remember Diane coming over a year after Mike died. She still hadn't had a service for Mike. I'd call Mike's assistant Colleen and say, "I'm going to be in Timbuktu on such-and-such a date; if this is when the celebration is could you let me know so I could get back?" I really did that three or four times. Diane said, "I just couldn't get it together to have a memorial service. What if I had a birthday party for him and invited his close friends?" And I said I thought that was a terrific idea.

TONY WALTON: At this sort of memorial party for Mike in their apartment, we were all stumbling up toward each other. I remember stumbling up toward Meryl, who said, "What are we going to *do*?" I had thought—as I'm sure many thought—that I was pretty much the only person who tried to speak to him on the phone almost every day to unravel whatever particular challenge I was going through.

SIGOURNEY WEAVER: I feel he's still with us, reminding us not to take it too seriously.

PETER LAWRENCE: When Tom Stoppard spoke at the big memorial, he said, "Welcome to the last ratfuck."

ROSE STYRON: There were one hundred people there at least. Diane von Furstenberg had very carefully done all of the seating, and I was sitting with all Leonard Bernstein's children and grandchildren. There were huge pictures of Mike on the wall in every stage of his life, which was really fun because I'd never seen the really young ones.

ROBERT GREENHUT: Elaine said, "The food tonight is going to be Mike's favorite meal of all time: Thanksgiving dinner. There's no fish."

J.J. ABRAMS: The room was filled with people who all felt, I think, the same thing, which is utter gratitude for having known the man at all.

CYNTHIA NIXON: Tom said, I will tell you a secret, which is that every play I write, I'm writing for Mike Nichols, whether he directs it or not. Because, Tom said, he's the only person who's going to get every inch of it—the thoughts, the references, the feelings, everything. He said, I feel not only bereft to have lost my friend, but I've lost my audience. I've lost the single person who is my best audience. He said, I sort of feel like, *Who am I writing for now?*

TOM STOPPARD: I did used to think of Mike as my spiritual first reader and wanting to be good for him.

RENATA ADLER: I thought, *Gosh, the same is true for me.* When I write, I often wonder, *What would Mike think of this?*

ROBERT NICHOLS: In my speech at Mike's memorial, I said, "The most important thing about Mike's life and my life by far is that we had lives that stretched beyond eighty years of age instead of dying miserably as children in Europe." I don't think Mike ever lost sight of that. It's never far from our thoughts: that very easily we could have died as children, and that's that.

Larry Pine, Mike, Kevin Kline, Stephen Spinella, Debra Monk, Philip Seymour Hoffman, John Goodman, Meryl Streep, Natalie Portman, and Christopher Walken in a photo taken for *The Seagull* in 2001. *(© Brigitte Lacombe)*

CODA

That Guru Thing

EMANUEL AZENBERG: When Kazan's autobiography came out, Mike asked me, "Did you read it?" And I said, "Yes, but it should be titled *And Then I Fucked . . .* , because it's all about who he slept with. But Mike said, "No, no, no, that's what we directors do: we seduce. Literally and figuratively."

JULES FEIFFER: One of his heroes as a director was Kazan, but Kazan was just the opposite of Mike. Kazan deliberately conspired to create fights and acrimonious relationships because he thought that's the way he'd get the best out of his performers. Mike did it as a love story.

SUSAN SONTAG[1]: I've seen lots of directors work. Jonathan Miller, Peter Brook—the list is very long. I've never seen anyone work exactly the way Mike does. It's so delicate. It's so not pushy. Mike just has a way of calming people down in a wonderful way.

JUDE LAW: His reputation for being gorgeous company preceded him. People would always say, you're going to have so much fun. It was very happy and intimate, and I don't want to say easy, because when people talk about things being easy, they think lazy. You're working

1. Courtesy of the John Lahr collection at the Howard Gotlieb Archival Research Center, Boston University.

hard, but it had ease in that everyone was happy to be working hard and happy to be in each other's company. There wasn't friction.

TONY WALTON: I called him when I first tried directing, and said, "How come you never told me how much fun this was?" And he said, "Shh! Too many people want to do it already!"

SWOOSIE KURTZ: His stationery had "Mike Nichols" at the top and his business address and everything, and then at the bottom there was a drawing of these two trained seals with a big ball, and underneath it says, "Of course, what I'd really like to do is direct."

HANNAH ROTH SORKIN: His business card said, "Mike Nichols: Films, Plays, Snotty Remarks." It didn't have an address.

NATHAN LANE: He understood all of the things a director needs to be. He's a father figure and therapist. He wouldn't say a lot in terms of direction, unless you wanted it—God knows, he could talk, and he always had a reason for everything—but he would create this wonderful atmosphere where you felt free and comfortable and extremely loved. I mean, he *loved* his actors. It was like entering into a romance with him.

LORNE MICHAELS: I remember once he was talking about how this actor in *Hurlyburly* was upset because this other actor had the dressing room closer to the stage. He said, "It's what I didn't like about myself when I was an actor," because a year or two earlier he was in a play and he said all of it came back, just like that. And so to be the one who looked after the others—which was what he was, as a director and as a producer—the benign parent, a sort of dream version of the parent, everything you always hoped for: understanding, patience, a lot of smiles and hugs, and a lot of really good food.

HANNAH ROTH SORKIN: What he did, aside from the art, was build families. The actors came back again and again, and so did the crew members. He loved that family feeling.

ROSE STYRON: Everybody had such a good time on Mike's sets, and everybody was so depressed when they were over. And so was Mike. He always said, "It's like they're taking my family away again."

MERYL STREEP[2]**:** The Mike Nichols set was a place that he himself never wanted to leave. He would just weep when it was time to go into the editing room: "No one's there, except Sam." He made it a place where everybody felt smart, welcome, safe, appreciated. He was a great appreciator. And he was delighted to be a director. So many directors are so unhappy with their lot in life. Everything is a trial. When Mike came to work, he was happy to be there.

CHRISTOPHER WALKEN: When we did *The Seagull*, we rehearsed down at the Public Theater on Lafayette Street. There was a section of the room with tape on the floor indicating the doorways and so on, and Mike had a desk in front of that. Off to the side were these long tables and chairs so that when he was rehearsing a scene with other actors, you didn't go off and leave the building or go home. We sat there, so we all listened to each other rehearse, which is something that usually doesn't happen. We always had our ears open to what was happening in the scenes that we weren't in. Afterward I thought, that's very smart, because then you're aware of what's going on in the whole play. You see yourself in the context of everything else that's happening. I've been in movies with actors whom I've never met. You work on different days, sometimes different weeks and months, and you see the movie and you're kind of surprised. Rehearsing a play with Mike, that wouldn't happen. You were always involved in the entire thing, you were always there. I think he did that on purpose, and it was very wise.

MIKE HALEY: It wasn't like Sidney Lumet, who blocks it all out and gets you up and has everything taped out. Mike's way was to sit

2. "Mike Nichols," *American Masters*, directed by Elaine May, produced by Julian Schlossberg, season 30, episode 1, aired January 29, 2016, on PBS.

around the table and talk because he got to know the people and the people got to know him.

TONY WALTON: This seemingly casual chat, just before the first read-through, would usually—to some degree, or to a very large degree—hint at why this particular project was particularly relevant for him at this particular moment. At the end of one of these chats on *Waiting for Godot*, Steve Martin looked up and said, "Can we dash home and write in our journals?"

MERYL STREEP[3]**:** They were part of the thing that pulled you in. That said, *We're in this together. I know what this is about. Isn't this just like life?*

PETER LAWRENCE: He would often tell humiliating, embarrassing stories about himself—about the way he behaved with family members or colleagues—as a way of letting actors know in a rehearsal situation that there was nothing they could do that was worse than what Mike had done, and it would free them up.

JON ROBIN BAITZ: Mike directed through anecdotes, usually self-deprecating stories, and if you were the right kind of actor, the anecdotes triggered something within you, allegorically or indirectly or unconsciously. They were always relevant, and you either went with it or you didn't. There was one actor in *Country Girl* who despised it, because this particular actor lived in literalism. They just didn't get it. But for everyone else, it's magic. It's hypnosis. I watched the other actors build a performance simply by being hip to Mike's energy. He uses himself as a kind of living specimen jar: of history, of moral tales, of debasement.

JULIA ROBERTS: He taught me the value of rehearsal and spending that time. On *Closer*, the five of us would just sit and talk, and it all seemed so random. And yet I think it informed ultimately so much

---

3. "Mike Nichols," *American Masters*, PBS.

about our relationships with one another. You realize he has a master plan going at all times in this very loving, uncontrived way.

TOM HANKS: Our rehearsals for *Charlie Wilson's War* were no different from long dinners or being on vacation with him. If we had a four-hour rehearsal schedule, we'd spend three hours and forty-five minutes talking about everything under the sun, and for fifteen minutes we'd read a little bit. And then we would be having dinner in Morocco, same thing: we'd have a five-and-a-half-hour conversation around the table, and without even knowing it we were somehow commenting on the film and the work that we had done that day and the work that we were going to do the next day.

NATALIE PORTMAN: During the rehearsals of *Seagull*, we'd all sit around and talk about experiences that we had that were similar to things that happen in the play, as a way of getting to know each other. Then we would get up and try the scenes on our feet, and he kind of just let it happen. He seemed to think that his main job was reminding us always that we were telling the same story. He was always saying, "Name it." Name the moment. This is the moment they fall in love. This is the moment she sees him as a fool for the first time. This is the moment she feels her lowest. Naming those moments throughout helps you map out the trajectory, so we're all on the same page about what we're creating together.

MERYL STREEP[4]**:** *The Seagull* was the first play I'd ever done with him, and I was surprised at how little he had to say to everybody. I think we had three and a half weeks of rehearsal, and he really let the first two and a half weeks go by without saying much of anything. I thought, *Is something wrong with him? Is he on drugs?* But he was watching, I think, in a way that you can't with a movie. He was watching the whole thing evolve. And then, after it had taken shape, he came in and put his hands on it more.

---

4. "Mike Nichols," *American Masters*, PBS.

JUDE LAW: While it was incredibly entertaining, there was also a part of me thinking, *Gosh, when are we going to look at the text?* Of course, I realized that what he was doing was building an environment of confession and trust. We were then safe to bare everything.

NATALIE PORTMAN: It gives you a real confidence when Mike Nichols trusts you. It gives you a lot of courage to try things.

CHRISTOPHER WALKEN: There is something about actors together, the way they communicate, the process of how you get to a performance. Mike understood all of that, and the actors who worked with him knew it. There was that quality with him, an apparent ease, a kind of effortlessness, a grace to it that happens when you watch a great dancer, a great actor, a great musician. It looks easy, when of course, it isn't.

He never did line readings, but he was able to convey, to point you in the right direction. When I'm in rehearsal, particularly the early days, I flounder around, throwing things at the wall, going this way, going that way. He would let you do that for a while, and then one day he'd say, "Why don't you try this?" and you'd think, *Yeah, that's it.*

PETER LAWRENCE: Basically he worked by suggestion and indirection. He would tell stories about himself, and then he'd say, "Okay, let's go back and try the scene again," and the actors would always somehow incorporate the spirit of what Mike was talking about.

JACK O'BRIEN: A lot of people, even smart people, even people in the business, don't understand what directors do. I think the longer we do it, the less we do. In other words, when we start out, we're very directing-oriented, but by the time you get to be Mike, you're just in the room and it starts to go right. Now that's not true—he's operative all the time—but he's not touching you, he's not showing you. He's allowing you, he's encouraging you.

EMANUEL AZENBERG: Mike was able to get actors to be probably better than they were. It's that guru thing that he had.

BOB BALABAN: I got the feeling that when I was with him I could do anything. And I'm not an actor who particularly feels they can do anything.

DAVID HYDE PIERCE: The underlying message of all his direction is: *You are enough. I don't need more than you. I don't need less than you. You're enough.* It quietly grounds the actor and gives you confidence.

PEGGY NOONAN: He said to me, "I don't direct movies, I cast them."

ALEC BALDWIN: Nichols was the same as other great directors, where casting was a skill they had, and they wanted to solve as many problems in the casting as they could—they didn't have to worry *too* much—but he had a lot to say about what you were going to do on the day and why.

HARRISON FORD: I was always intimidated, for want of a better word, by Mike's more academic approach to acting—or what I assumed to be an academic approach, because I knew he was doing his master classes, which were taken very seriously by other people. Yet somehow our relationship made it extremely easy to forget about the acting part and just talk about the story. We loved to talk about the story, the potentials for different behaviors. It was always easy. It was always in the moment. I felt a freedom that I didn't always feel with a director, and an improvisational opportunity. Whatever ideas came, he was very confident about making choices at the last minute without asking the company assembled necessarily—just going for it.

PETER LAWRENCE: He would say to me, "It's the job of the director to give an actor back their first impulses." He always wanted to put that instinct onstage and see how it panned out.

HANNAH ROTH SORKIN: The grips would be going insane, because they haven't figured out the shot yet, because it's going to come from the actors. Mike made it about the actors every single time, and that's why they loved him.

ROBERT GREENHUT: He wasn't going to be rushed through anything, so when we laid out the schedule for "the money," we just made sure that there wasn't anything too aggressive or overly ambitious. It had to be eleven weeks instead of ten weeks to make sure that we didn't paint ourselves into a corner on some particular day. But you have to have a cast that plays ball with you.

SIGOURNEY WEAVER: He once said he liked to produce because it was a lot less work. And I said, "I'm surprised to hear you say that because producing is a lot of responsibility, you have to put the whole thing together." And he said, "No, a producer just goes in, sees the show, says, 'Change the shoes,' and walks out."

JULIAN SCHLOSSBERG: There was a Germanic side to him. He knew what he wanted, and he went and got it. While he could be wildly charming, he had steel inside, as any director would have to.

EMANUEL AZENBERG: Was he dictatorial? In his own way, yeah. You had to know how to deal with it. If an ambulance went by, he'd say go out and make it quiet on the street. You'd say, "Mike!" You had to know not to take it seriously. But he was very good with the crew and with people who worked. He was a benevolent dictator.

PETER LAWRENCE: Mike taught me how to fire people. He said, "The thing about firing people, Pete"—he's the only person who's ever called me Pete—"is you have to give people their dignity back. You have to fire people face-to-face and preferably over a meal. Make them know that it's really about the situation and not about them." He said, "Everybody serves the play—the producer, the director, the actors—and if you can't serve the play, you have to get out of the way."

NATALIE PORTMAN: Mike told me that he tries, on a movie, to cast the same person in every role. All these different behaviors could be the same person, because as the moviegoer, we need to be all of them.

SIGOURNEY WEAVER: It's almost like he could feel being Martha, he could feel being George—same with *Working Girl*, same with *Hurlyburly*. He made you feel like he was in your corner, and it was your show, and it was your story, and he made everyone feel that way.

PETER LAWRENCE: He said of auditions, "the actors will show you who the characters are."

JULIET TAYLOR: He would cry in auditions sometimes. He almost directed this musical, *Sparkle*—eventually it was made into a movie. Irene Cara from *Fame*—she was still a teenager then—she came in wearing a little dress, white socks, and Mary Jane shoes, and she sang "Over the Rainbow" and Mike started to weep. I'll never forget it. He would do that in readings with actors—laugh or cry—he was so emotional.

A lot of directors who were performers don't really like the casting process. It makes them really uncomfortable, because they've been there. Sydney Pollack didn't like it. Clint Eastwood does everything on tape. Paul Newman once told me, "I overidentify, I get so anxious for them." And Woody isn't social enough. But Mike just loved it.

He definitely does fall in love with actors a little bit, though. Sometimes the person wouldn't really be right, but he would have been just so swept away by them. He could be very impressed and a little suggestible, to be honest. But mostly he had a great radar for talent. I remember during *Streamers*, I had seen Peter Evans in a lunchtime play at a church on the Upper East Side, and thought, *That guy's really good.* So I asked him if he would come in and be a reader. He ended up getting the lead. Mike was so open to stuff like that.

EMANUEL AZENBERG: I asked Michael Kidd, the choreographer, once about how he picks people, and he said part of the equation was the "F.F." I said, "What's the F.F.?" And he said, "It's

304 | LIFE ISN'T EVERYTHING

the Fuckability Factor." Men or women, it didn't make any difference. You see it and you know it. Mike knew about that. There was a sensuality in his casting, and I'm being polite—there's a sexuality.

FRANK RICH: There's nothing a Broadway producer likes better than to have the insurance of stars with a straight play, and after the first two Neil Simon shows, Mike did pretty much everything with stars. And you couldn't blame him—usually, they're good actors.

Actors trusted him. He could lure them into doing theater, which is a crapshoot for a Hollywood star, not so much because of selling tickets, which one assumes they would do, but because they might embarrass themselves. I think they trusted him to make sure that didn't happen, and I think it generally didn't happen. I can't think of a show of his where a big name fell flat on his or her face.

MERYL STREEP[5]**:** People ask me, "How did he direct you?" And honestly, I can't remember any piece of direction he ever gave me, except he would often say, "Surprise me." He'd also say, "Do everything you just did, but faster."

MATTHEW BRODERICK: He was very actory and all that—great notes. Other times he would just make a face and tell you to make that face. If things were going well, he let actors do their thing. But if things weren't going right, he would pick up this megaphone and say, "Must I do *everything* myself?" One of the really mean things he would say fairly often to all of us was, "Let's do it again, but let's pretend it's a real movie."

JACK O'BRIEN: Being funny gets a director out of a lot of shit. If you have no sense of humor, I don't know how you get through a rehearsal. And Mike was hilarious.

TONY WALTON: That was, of course, his secret weapon, even when things got tense, which of course, they inevitably could, Mur-

---

5. "Mike Nichols," *American Masters*, PBS.

phy's Law being what it is. He could always defuse it with humor, so nothing ever festered.

PETER GALLAGHER: Mike talked about the obligation one has in storytelling, right at the beginning beat, to reassure the audience that they're in good hands.

HANK AZARIA: Another Mike-ism was, *When in doubt, go back to what's real.* Forget about what's funny, forget about what needs to work. What would you really do if you were in this situation?

MARLO THOMAS: One time during the rehearsal for *Social Security*, Olympia Dukakis said to Mike, "I just can't make this transition," and he said, "Well, then don't." We were all startled. "In life, we don't make transitions. Something happens, and then you do something else."

DAVID HYDE PIERCE: He was a big fan of real life. I remember him saying to us, "If you're running lines, and someone comes up and interrupts you and says, 'Oh, I'm sorry, I didn't realize you were running lines'—that's the greatest compliment you can ever get as an actor." Because they thought you were just talking.

DAVID RABE: When I started directing, his influence was complete. I was following the rules that I felt I'd learned from him; not about text, not about what to cut, but about how to stage something. I remember him talking about when he'd seen a Kazan-directed play, *Streetcar* or *Salesman*, he said he saw then that your goal was to make the action appear so it looked like life. The actors in *Streamers*, he drove them a little nuts until they got used to it. They were always shining their shoes or putting on talcum powder, they were reading notes, or they were writing letters. There was rarely a moment where they were just acting. They had to act *through* these activities, which was brilliant, I think.

JAMES GRISSOM: He hated it when people would go, "I loved it. It was so like real life." Mike said, "Nothing at the Circle in the

Square is like real life." There was nothing real life about *Streetcar*. The emotions were real, there was something really big at stake, but it was highly theatrical. The actress Marian Seldes liked to quote this line from Joseph Conrad: "To snatch, in a moment of courage, from the remorseless rush of time a passing phrase of life." Those are the moments that brought Mike Nichols up, and that he reached for as a director.

PETER LAWRENCE: There were so many laughs in *Social Security*, and sometimes the laughs would go on for a minute. Ron Silver said, "Mike, what are we supposed to do when the audience is laughing that long? Just stand there?" and Mike said, "Ron, they're not there. There are three times when you're not there: when you're sneezing, when you're coming, or when you're laughing. The audience isn't even aware of you, they're just laughing. Whenever they're done laughing, go on."

CHRISTINE BARANSKI: Mike always said it was the mark of a really great comedian to do as little as possible to get a laugh, not as much as possible. Keeping an audience on a short leash where they literally have to sit up slightly in their chair to get what you're going to say next because it's rather like an act of seduction with an audience. You make them come to you. That expression, the audience was eating out of the palm of your hand, well, your hand shouldn't be there; your hand should be *here*.

In a performance, I would often think, *If Mike were in the audience, how would I calibrate this?* And often, he was in the audience.

JOHN LAHR: He's fascinating on silence—and how silence works for an actor. He's thought about these things—how it makes an audience lean in.

SIGOURNEY WEAVER: There are a lot of directors who haven't come through theater and don't know how to speak to actors, so they just don't. And nowadays, they don't give you rehearsal because directors don't know enough to ask for it.

ALEC BALDWIN: I was always heartbroken, truly, that I couldn't get back into that world of his again and work with him, because he's everything in terms of the text. He's everything in terms of the material. The directors you work with now, they don't have anything to offer. They know next to nothing about acting and how to interpret the material. It's not a criticism of them, because we live in an age now of the fully self-directing actor. You're just expected to do everything yourself. They're hiring you because they've determined in advance that you know exactly what to do. They're looking for risk-free, director-proof casting.

When they say that a director gets a performance out of somebody nowadays, that's complete and utter bullshit. No directors get a performance out of anybody except Woody and Mike, and probably Marty. There may be a handful of others, but I'd say for 99.9 percent of them, it's out of the question. Nichols was the greatest at that. Nichols was somebody who really could lead you to where he wanted you to go.

TOM HANKS: I don't think he ever went into anything with a show-business perspective, thinking, *This is a sure thing.* It was like, there is only one way this thing can be, and we have to find out what that thing is.

AARON SORKIN (*screenwriter*): We'd meet at his place in New York every day for a few weeks, going through the script [for *Charlie Wilson's War*] scene by scene. After about ten days, Mike looked up from the script and said, "What's this movie about?" Then the two of us were silent for another three days. Neither of us could articulate what the movie was about. That's embarrassing for the writer and frightening for the director. Then one day, out of nowhere, Mike told me a story about a village and a Zen master. A boy gets a horse for his birthday and everyone in the village says, "Isn't that great?!" And the Zen master says, "We'll see." The boy falls off his horse, and everyone in the village says, "Isn't that terrible?" And the Zen master says, "We'll see." Then there's a war and all the young men in the village have to go fight, but the boy can't because of his broken leg, and everyone says, "Isn't that great?!" And the Zen master says, "We'll see." We both decided that that was what the movie was about, and I ended up writing the story as a speech for Phil Hoffman.

PETER LAWRENCE: Mike's mother was still alive when he optioned *Social Security*. It was a play about a rich Upper East Side couple whose mother comes to live with them, and the jokes are on the schlepper mother. He saw it as a kind of sendup of his own mother. Before the show went into rehearsal, Mike's mother died, and he flipped the idea of that play to being about this phony Upper East Side couple who were helped by and educated by their mother. He made it a comment on himself, about how he basically had—"disrespected" is too strong a word, but judged his mother incorrectly sometimes in his life. He corrected his own attitude as he directed the play. The words on the page didn't change. It was Mike's adjustment in his attitude toward it.

When *Elliot Loves*, a Jules Feiffer play I did with Mike that ran off-Broadway, went into rehearsal, Mike fell in love with Diane. So he made a play that was essentially about misogyny into a play about a character who was trying to leave the world of men and cross over into the world of women. And that's because of what was happening in Mike's life.

LORNE MICHAELS: He loved to laugh. Comedy is too important to be left to professionals because professionals tend to go, "That's funny," and nod.

JOHN LAHR: He was the undisputed champion laugher of all time. His laugh was a volcanic eruption. He would explode, and then he would turn various colors of pink, then his eyes would water, then out would come the handkerchief, and then there would be an aftershock of laughter at the laughter that he was having.

You worked for that. Not that I ever a got a laugh from him that big, but it was a great event, and so I can understand how actors would want to go for that touchdown.

MARLO THOMAS: To have your director laugh like that was pretty great. It's so encouraging if you're working in a comedy and trying things out. The whole idea of rehearsal is to be able to make a fool of yourself and be as bad as possible until you get good.

PETER DAVIS: Mike saw that comedy and tragedy were different sides of the same coin. Even Aristotle didn't see that, because he had totally different definitions for tragedy and comedy. I'm not saying Aristotle was wrong, far from it. I just think Mike saw them as two sides of the human coin. He once said, "If it's human, it's at least funny."

JOHN LAHR: Comedy is refusal to suffer. Mike knew all there was to know about suffering, and to be able to lighten your load, to be able to have the gift of managing gravity is a big deal, and what was rare about him—and it's rare in the culture; tragedy is easy, joy is hard—he could make joy, and so fuck the rest. Basically, he had that ability, but you could only have that ability if you know the other. The thing that gives juice to the compulsion to make joy is a sense of the tragic. It makes it valuable. Mike had that understanding.

GREGORY MOSHER: There's a famous Beckett line, "There's nothing funnier than unhappiness." Mike could be true to the unhappiness and find the funniness in it.

JON KORKES: Mike spoke in adult terms and put himself forward with all his neuroses. He used to say the director has to get naked before his cast does. He was a whole person operating there in front of you. It was embodied in his "What's it really like?" comment, meaning to me that there are no rules for human behavior. That the things you feel about yourself, about others, about life, that you are ashamed to say to anyone, except perhaps to a shrink behind closed doors, all make up the motherlode for us as artists. Yes, we are all ridiculous, foolish, pathetic, even awful, but isn't it fascinating? Isn't it fun?

CAROL SILLS (*director*): There was a moment when Paul [Sills] said to Mike, "I need to stay in New York, but I'm not sure quite how to pull it off," and before you could say Jack Robinson, Mike said, "Why don't we start a theater school?" And then he said, "You couldn't run a school, Paul. I couldn't run a school. But George"—George Morrison, another University of Chicago friend—"could run the school." George Morrison taught Method acting, Paul improvisation, and Mike did what he loved to do best, which was scene study.

LAURA PIERCE: I saw a small ad in the paper that they were auditioning. I went to George's apartment, did a monologue for him and Paul, got in, and started a couple of weeks later. I think of it as the greatest school that nobody ever knew about. Later, I realized they were re-creating what their experience was at the University of Chicago.

DIANE PAULUS (*theater director*): The original location of the New Actors Workshop was on Eighty-Ninth Street between West End and Riverside. It was on the second story of a Greek Orthodox church. I joined the first year the school was founded, in the fall of 1988. We were the guinea pigs for the whole experiment. The next year we moved to West Thirtieth Street, right below Penn Station.

LAURA PIERCE: It had no facilities, nothing fancy. It was one big room in a beautiful old church and three great theatrical minds. Even though they were all famous, there wasn't a lot of that *we'll get you out there working* sort of talk. They kind of made it clear in the beginning that Mike wasn't going to hire people from the classes, because they didn't want that vibe.

Everybody I ever spoke to—casting directors and other students—has said the same thing to me: "Oh, but Mike never really showed up." I'm like, "He showed up all the time!" In fact, in the first year, George got very ill—he had Legionnaire's disease, and he was quite sick—so Mike was there even more so. I don't know why nobody believed it.

JEFFREY SWEET: You got a strong sense that some of those very long scene study nights that he did were some of the happiest hours he spent.

DIANE PAULUS: Mike's master class was Wednesday nights from six to ten. What was amazing is you could bring anything, and literally people were picking Shakespeare or Neil Simon or Jules Feiffer or Chekhov or Jean Genet or Wendy Wasserstein. It was across the gamut. There were thirty of us. You got a partner and you picked a scene. Once a month, or every five weeks, you got your turn. You would prepare the scene on your own. You had to figure out, okay, where should the scene start? Where should it end? How should we block it? I've become a director, and I really credit a core part of my directing muscle to those two years I sat in scene-study class with Mike Nichols.

His driver would drop him off. Everybody would be nervously pacing, and then someone would come running up the stairs saying, "He's here! Mike's here!" We would run into the room and get organized. He'd walk in and sit down in a chair in the front row. The lights would go down, and you'd start. He didn't know in advance what scene you were doing. He didn't have the text. He would just watch and listen. Then you'd turn the room lights back on and pull up a chair and he would start to talk, and all his directorial tools would come out. Every now and then he'd say, "Let's get up and do it again," but more often than not you didn't get out of your chair.

Occasionally, he couldn't make it, so he would send guests to teach for him. In walks Meryl Streep, or David Mamet, or Gregory Mosher.

LAURA PIERCE: Neither Mike nor Paul ever gave real feedback like they do at a lot of acting schools where somebody does a scene, and then the teacher gives their opinion, and then the actors go and change it to suit the opinion of the teacher. That's the normal mode, and it definitely wasn't like that there. People didn't always do it a second time, so there was no sense of grading or anything like that.

Mike would try to illuminate what he felt the scene was about through stories. He would tell a story about something, a real-life story of something that had happened to him that wasn't exactly parallel, but was connected in some way, and it was kind of your job to figure out what he was trying to say, and people didn't always manage to do that.

DIANE PAULUS: He would always start by saying, "What's the event of the scene?" Sometimes you wouldn't know. He'd say, "Okay, what's the first thing that happens? And then what happens?" He'd make you analyze it. He would say every scene has a dead whale in it—a giant dead whale on the floor, stinking up the whole room. But you and your scene partner are not dealing with it. At some point, the stench of the dead whale becomes so intense, it comes to the fore.

LAURA PIERCE: He told a story about sitting at a party in Chicago. Somebody was talking about was so-and-so sleeping with so-and-so. Mike was sleeping with one of the people who was being talked about. Finding out about a betrayal in a group of people—you might think if you're just an actor reading a script, *I would stand up and throw a beer bottle.* But what would you really do? If you've had a parallel experience, what *did* you do? Not what would a theatrical idea be, but what was it really like? To bring it into you as much as possible. He talked about how Elaine didn't go toward the role, she pulled the role in toward her.

DIANE PAULUS: He'd say that all the time, "It's like when . . ." It was never like, "Okay, what's the Method acting moment?" He never talked like that. He would talk about Bergman's "secret cause." You have to peel all the layers of the onion, and then deep down in the middle of the onion is the secret cause. Or, an actor would do a scene, and then he would say, "Well, as André Gide said, 'Please don't understand me too quickly.' We can't understand our characters too quickly." Every class I had my little marble composition book, and it was filled with these things.

LAURA PIERCE: He was talking about various guys who used to go on late-night TV and push a domino and a whole big thing of dominoes would all fall. He said that that's what a good play or movie that is alive should be like, and that the placement of each domino is very important. "You need to know where to place the dominoes so that they will fall in the correct way. If one domino is off, the rest of them aren't going to fall. The random is our enemy."

DIANE PAULUS: He said, "We lie all the time. Every five minutes we're lying. 'How are you?' 'I'm fine. How are you?' 'Fine.' Lying, lying, lying. See if you can live your life one day where you don't tell one lie." That's what that master class was like. No acting-class shenanigans. The focus was the scene, and how are you communicating the story? He just sat there and talked to you. It was like you were at dinner with Mike Nichols every Wednesday night.

LAURA PIERCE: There might be a main event in a scene, but often, he said, the most important things were in the little moments between people onstage, so there was always more to discover. Every time I'm looking at that person, I may be discovering something new about them. He wasn't advocating improvising exactly, but that mentality. You can approach a scene as if it's an improv, and that keeps it alive, really being in it with the other person.

Aside from all the genius things that he said about the plays and acting and everything like that, he was so generous and kind with us, and I know that he could be other than that. He admitted that he could be other than that. He was always sharing and patient, even when sometimes I thought students were doing things that he should have given them crap about. He never did, and I thought, *He's worked at this. He's worked at and is still working at being a good person.*

DIANE PAULUS: When I look now at what I do in the room as a director, I know I am channeling my experience of him as a teacher. The best actors I work with are actors who come into a rehearsal and they're contributing. They're not just, *Tell me what to do, where to go.* They're contributing their idea of how to interpret the role, the story, the event. They're bringing things. Mike's class wasn't just acting technique. He was telling us how to be thinking actors.

CHRISTINE BARANSKI: People have always asked, "Why was he such a great director?" Nobody can actually answer that question. Somehow by osmosis, some truth was communicated through his ability to articulate human experience, which was laserlike in its acuity and its humor.

JULIAN SCHLOSSBERG: There have only been two great directors of theater and film, and that's Kazan and Nichols. That's it. Orson certainly did some wonderful theater, but you would never say that he was great. Theater and film are wildly different. You look over the credits of big film directors, you see a lot of them have tried and failed miserably. And conversely, theater directors have tried to go to film, and they can't do it.

EMANUEL AZENBERG: You can show all the mistakes and the foibles, and they're there, but if he walked into this place and said, "Let's do this play," we'd all say yes.

CHRISTOPHER WALKEN: He could have picked anything he wanted to do and all the best actors available would have been willing to go with him.

DOUGLAS McGRATH: He had no signature visual style. You can look at a Woody Allen movie or a Scorsese movie or a Hitchcock movie, and the visual style alone tells you who it is. Mike didn't have that, nor did he have a kind of obsessive subject he returned to over and over the way Woody and Marty and certain people do. He worked across genres. He did all kinds of different things. I think what distinguishes Mike's movies is that they are always acutely alert to the human idiosyncrasies that make one character different from another, and I think partially that comes from being young and needing to figure out what *in* is, which I think got further refined when he went into improv.

TONY KUSHNER[6]: Working with Mike and then Steven [Spielberg] is like working with Mozart and Beethoven. Mike really is, in his marrow, a classicist. Steven's more of a romantic. Spielberg pulls you very deep inside the event. In Mike's body of work, even in the close-ups, there's a coolness, a very elegant, very composed, very considered—"detatchment" is the wrong word, because that makes it sound like it's not emotionally full, and Mike's movies are immensely powerful and emotional. "Disinterest" is not quite it either. It's an observing eye. He always had an outsider's perspective on American culture. I'm sure that was part of being a German refugee. I think part of it comes with him being Jewish. There's a slight sense, a slight tension of, *Do I belong? Do I not belong?*

MERYL STREEP[7]: I don't think you can make a general rule that every director should study acting. But I do know that he understood the process more than any other director I've ever worked with, without question. That's why he trusted that if he saw the spark of something in you, he knew he just had to entertain it out of you.

But I think that more profoundly, he was acting all the time. Right from the beginning, he was acting being an American. He was acting being a blond. He was acting being confident. He was acting being the smartest person in the room. That is actually a definition of acting: You have all these things that you want desperately to be real. And you live in them and they become you. Whatever that process is, I really don't understand. But I know that he understood it.

6. "Mike Nichols," *American Masters*, PBS.

7. Ibid.

ACKNOWLEDGMENTS

To quote our subject, the biggest jewel in our crown is luck.

We are grateful to Gillian Blake and Steve Rubin at Henry Holt for bringing us into their storied publishing house, as well as David Kuhn and his crack team at Aevitas, specifically Kate Mack, Becky Sweren, and William LoTurco, for their peerless representation. This book took long enough that we must also thank Ben Schrank, Steve Rubin's successor, for taking such an active interest from day one. Thanks also to Richard Pracher for overseeing the art direction and to the incomparable Chip Kidd for this elegant jacket. A special thank-you must go to our editor, Libby Burton, for not giving up on us, despite a few missed deadlines, and for being such a dogged ally.

As this book sprang from a feature in *Vanity Fair* magazine in 2015, we wish to thank Graydon Carter, who ran the piece at twice its originally assigned length, and our editor, Doug Stumpf, for his unerring editorial judgment.

When we recommenced our work in early 2016, picking up where we left off with the *VF* piece, we found ourselves confronted with a major obstacle: Mike had outlived many of his best friends and closest collaborators, and a few of his contemporaries were no longer spry enough to sit for an interview. Happily for us—and for the reader—we were able to supplement the testimony of the living thanks to the kindness of others who came earlier to our subject. We would like to express our profoundest gratitude to Julian Schlóssberg—a true luftmensch, to borrow a phrase from Tony Kushner—the producer of both *Nichols and May: Take Two* and *American Masters: Mike Nichols*, who gave us unfettered access to a boxful of his interview transcripts. (The only trick was figuring out which box.) We are only marginally less indebted to

John Lahr, who wrote the definitive profile of Mike for the *New Yorker* and encouraged us to rifle through his papers up at Boston University's Howard Gotlieb Archival Research Center. We must also thank Janet Coleman, the author of *The Compass: The Improvisational Theatre that Revolutionized American Comedy,* and Jeffrey Sweet, the author of *Something Wonderful Right Away: An Oral History of the Second City and the Compass Players*—two books that were invaluable in our research—for allowing us to include a handful of key quotations. We strongly encourage any reader who finishes this book wanting to know more about Mike, Nichols and May, or the history of improv to dig into the above-mentioned documentaries and texts, not to mention Bobbie O'Steen's *Cut to the Chase: Forty-Five Years of Editing America's Favorite Movies.*

An oral history starts out as hours and hours of recorded speech, some taking place in restaurants amid clinking glasses and chattering diners, some over crackling transatlantic phone calls. For doing the hard work of getting those often difficult-to-decipher words on paper, we would like to thank Carole Ludwig, David Murrell, Elizabeth Cantrell, and especially Phyllis Greenhill. Thank you also to Ann Schneider for her photo research, which added so much to this book, and to Gahouray Dukaray for her research assistance. For their help in arranging all of the aforementioned interviews, we owe a small army of publicists, agents, managers, attorneys, and other representatives, too numerous to list here, but we must single out Mike's longtime publicist, Leslee Dart, who arranged Sam's initial conversations with Mike and provided our original entrée to many of his intimates.

For their assistance and encouragement, we would also like to thank Robert Nichols, Laura Bickford, Juliet Taylor, Andre Bishop, Jack O'Brien, Jay Fielden, and for her unwavering support, Tate Delloye.

Several people read early versions of this manuscript. We would like to thank Nancy Schoenberger, Michael Hainey, Bruce Handy, and Alex Belth for their many thoughtful suggestions.

Mark Harris, who is hard at work on a traditional biography of Mike Nichols, might have regarded us as the competition; instead, he chose to extend an olive branch. For his uncommon magnanimity, we would like to express our sincerest admiration.

Diane Sawyer could have turned this book into a pamphlet with a word, but didn't. We hope she is pleased and knows that our hearts are full.

And finally, we would like to thank Mike himself, who allowed Sam to interview him on three occasions for *Vanity Fair*—for a story on the making of *The Graduate*, a conversation with Mike and Julia Roberts, and the first joint interview with Elaine May in fifty years— and who was good enough to give Ash his first paid employment as a P.A. on *Charlie Wilson's War*. What can we say? Like so many in this book, we were seduced.

INDEX

Page numbers in *italics* refer to photographs.